Conversations with Ayckbourn

plays by Alan Ayckbourn published by Faber

A CHORUS OF DISAPPROVAL

WOMAN IN MIND

A SMALL FAMILY BUSINESS

HENCEFORWARD . . .

Conversations with Ayckbourn

Ian Watson

faber and faber
LONDON · BOSTON

First published in 1981
by Macdonald Futura Publishers London
This new edition first published in 1988
by Faber and Faber Limited
3 Queen Square London WCIN 3AU

Photoset by Wilmaset Birkenhead Wirral
Printed in Great Britain by
Richard Clay Bungay Suffolk
All rights reserved

British Library Cataloguing in Publication Data

Ayckbourn, Alan, 1939–
Conversations with Ayckbourn.
1. Drama in English. Ayckbourn, Alan, 1939–
Interviews
I. Title II. Watson, Ian, 1942–
822'.914

ISBN 0–571–15192–2

Contents

Introduction

The only time I ever met Tom Stoppard was one Saturday afternoon when we found ourselves playing for the same cricket team. The closest I came to Harold Pinter was at a private supper party, when I played first slip to an intense discussion of cricket between him and Gawn Grainger.

Tracing a finger over Alan Ayckbourn's wall-chart planner, to find moments in the year when the conversations in this book could take place, I tripped over small, red, cricket ball symbols. 'Scarborough Cricket Festival,' he explained, in a tone that strongly suggested that these dates were to be regarded as sacred. It would seem, *prima facie*, that there is somewhere a thesis to be written on the correlation between the obsessive game of cricket and modern British dramaturgy. This is not it. Nevertheless, it is that same Scarborough Cricket Festival that is responsible for this book, for it was there that I annually spent my youthful summer holidays, watching the lighter moments of Trueman, Hutton, Wardle, Benaud, Lindwall and Miller by day, and the early stirrings of James Saunders, David Campton and Alan Ayckbourn by night.

Scarborough is a solidly middle-class town standing on the coast of north-east Yorkshire high above two very beautiful bays, separated by a crumbled, but still picturesque, castle. Everything there combines to make it an ideal place not to have a permanent company theatre. Its population of less than 50,000 is roughly half that which administrators reckon is required to sustain such a theatre. Its economy, based firmly in tourism, is seasonal and inevitably fluctuates with the climate. Its hinterland, the north Yorkshire moors and the Vale of York, is highly attractive and visitable; but the resident population is more likely to fetch up slaughtered and roasted on the dinner table than alive and responsive in a theatre auditorium. Schools there are, and a college, but the nearest university is more than forty miles away in the City of York, which has its own repertory theatre.

It was in Scarborough, nevertheless, that Stephen Joseph found the right mix of circumstances and individuals to base a revolution in British theatre that was precisely contemporaneous with the revolution George Devine was fostering with his stable of writers in Sloane Square. While Joseph, like Devine, was running a writers' theatre, it was on theatre form rather than the subject-matter of plays that his revolution was based.

In retrospect, the cause of theatre in the round might appear a limited one on which to base a revolution. Indeed, at the time, the journal of the young theatre turks who regarded the Royal Court as their Mecca – the much lamented *Encore* (incidentally edited by a man who worked with Stephen Joseph's company, the late Clive Goodwin) – while broadly acknowledging Joseph's work as bringing much-needed new perspectives into a dangerously moribund theatre, tended to regard his obsession with theatre form as, at best, a little irrelevant. For them, social content was all. The theatre Establishment was more virulent: to a man, it embraced the new-found phobias of that prophet of Devine's revolution, Kenneth Tynan, concerning the rear view of actors and the uncomfortable proximity of their perspiration. Even when the Establishment succumbed to Joseph's unfailingly charming rationalism and enthusiasm, it dismissed his passion for opening out the proscenium arch as sheer battiness. With the benefit of hindsight, it is impossible not to note that he was personally responsible for founding two of Britain's most exciting theatres – those in Scarborough and Stoke-on-Trent – and that, without his influence, many other theatres, including the National Theatre on London's South Bank, would, at best, have been far less stimulating structures.

About Stephen Joseph's influence on playwrights it is inevitably more difficult to give chapter and verse. He helped, fostered, tutored and gave opportunity to a great many. After the initial failure of *The Birthday Party*, he picked up and encouraged Harold Pinter. He guided and worked with David Campton, James Saunders, Mike Stott and the American playwright Michael

Weller. And, of course, he drew out the mammoth writing talent of a teenage actor in his Scarborough company, Alan Ayckbourn.

Stephen Joseph's theatre in Scarborough was not the first theatre I had ever seen, but it was the first to give me ambition. Stephen, ever available to his audience, recognized and encouraged that ambition, and I became a student of his in the Drama Department at Manchester University. I first worked for him at Stoke-on-Trent in the traumatic period when, during his final illness, he was warring with another of his protégés whom he had appointed Director there, the excellent Peter Cheeseman.

From Stoke, I moved to Scarborough, in the closing months of Stephen's life, and it was there that I worked with Alan Ayckbourn. *Relatively Speaking* was already a big West End hit (despite my own review for BBC North Region radio, which pooh-poohed it in terms that, I thought, would endear me to *Encore* and place me in line for Tynan's job on the *Observer*). *The Silver Collection* was to be Ayckbourn's great follow-up hit, and I was pleased to be its stage director. At the read-through, *The Silver Collection* (already advertised throughout the town) turned up as *The Sparrow*, and was denied an Arts Council New Play guarantee on the grounds that it would undoubtedly be very successful and make its author a lot of money. (Then, as now, the Arts Council was never so endearing as when it was hopelessly wrong.)

The Sparrow called for a setting of unbelievable grottiness. With my stage management team, I offered token disarray. 'Watson's a bloody useless stage manager!' shouted Ayckbourn. (Dame Edith Evans gave me a similar accolade some years later in Accrington, when, already well into her eighties, she undertook a tour of one-night stands for me in north-east Lancashire towns, and I, noting her to be in real danger of collapse from exhaustion, brought the curtain down before her encore.) Working on *The Sparrow*, I got my first inkling of what Ayckbourn means when he talks of 'playing the truth'. He had written filth, and filth he wanted.

Alan Ayckbourn has never been the writer that others have wanted him to be. He is temperamentally incapable of standing still long enough for critics to pigeonhole him: perhaps this is why, almost uniquely among modern playwrights, he has still not been the subject of extended critical evaluation in a book. London critics have awarded him gongs for plays that audiences have steered clear of, and audiences have at times flocked to see plays about which the critics have been, at best, lukewarm, even grudging. The fact remains that, translated into twenty-four languages and constantly played throughout the world, he is our most successful living playwright; a paradox in itself, when it is recalled that he rarely spends more than two weeks a year writing. In Scarborough, audiences wait excitedly to see what he is going to offer them next: they respond to his unpredictability, and, after more than twenty years, they know that, whatever it is that he puts before them, it will challenge and probably delight them. No wonder he wants to stay there.

Preface to the second edition

Since *Conversations with Ayckbourn* was first published in 1981, Alan Ayckbourn has written a further eleven full-length theatre shows, three of which have gone into the National Theatre (one – *Way Upstream* – threatening to sink it without trace) and another three into the commercial West End. He has also written ten shorter pieces, predominantly intended as lunchtime or late-night entertainments with music. On top of such a prolific writing output, which has served to re-emphasize his position as the most successful living playwright in the world, Ayckbourn confirmed, in the course of a two-year sabbatical from Scarborough spent as a Company Director at the National Theatre, that he is also one of the United Kingdom's major directors.

For his services to the theatre, Alan Ayckbourn has, since 1981, been dubbed a Commander of the Order of the British Empire (CBE), been granted the Freedom of the Borough of Scarborough and been awarded three honorary doctorates by British universities.

A simple reissue of the book as published in 1981 would have been pointless. In addition to several necessary corrections to that text and to updating the appendix of play synopses, we have replaced the chapter entitled *Frenetic '80* from the first edition with two entirely new conversations, which took place in the latter half of 1987. These cover his plays from *Way Upstream* through to *Henceforward . . .* and the whole period of his relationship with Sir Peter Hall's regime at the National Theatre.

[x]

It is unlikely that there will be any further updating of these *Conversations*. In a recent note to me, Ayckbourn wrote: 'I rather enjoy being the least documented playwright of the twentieth century.'

IW
Scarborough, 1988

Alan Ayckbourn:
A Chronology

1939 Born, Hampstead, 12 April

1951 School at Haileybury

1956 Left school. First professional theatre job with Donald Wolfit at the Edinburgh Festival

1957 Joined Stephen Joseph's Theatre in the Round company at Scarborough

1959 First and second plays, *The Square Cat* and *Love After All*, performed at Scarborough

1960 *Dad's Tale* performed at Scarborough. National Service at RAF Cardington, Bedfordshire (2 days)

1961 *Standing Room Only* performed at Scarborough

1962 Founder member (and Associate Director) of the company at the Victoria Theatre, Stoke-on-Trent. *Xmas v. Mastermind* performed at Stoke-on-Trent

1963 *Mr Whatnot* performed at Stoke-on-Trent (London Production, 1964)

1964 Left the Stoke company. Last appearance as an actor in William Gibson's *Two for the Seesaw* with Heather Stoney in Rotherham. Joined the BBC in Leeds as a radio drama producer

1965 *Meet My Father* performed at Scarborough (London production, under the new title *Relatively Speaking*, 1967; television production by BBC, 1969)

1967 *The Sparrow* performed at Scarborough

1969 *How the Other Half Loves* performed at Scarborough (London production, 1970). *Ernie's Incredible Illucinations* published and performed in London. *Countdown* performed (as part of *Mixed Doubles*) in London

1970 Left the BBC and became Director of Productions at the

Library Theatre in the Round, Scarborough. *The Story So Far* performed at Scarborough (subsequently revised, 1972, as *Me Times Me Times Me*; London production, under the new title *Family Circles*, 1978)

1971 *Time and Time Again* performed at Scarborough (London production, 1972; television production by ATV, 1976)

1972 *Absurd Person Singular* performed at Scarborough (London production, 1973; television production by BBC, 1985)

1973 *The Norman Conquests* performed at Scarborough (London production, 1974; television production by Thames TV, 1977). *Evening Standard* Best Comedy Award for *Absurd Person Singular*

1974 *Absent Friends* performed at Scarborough (London production, 1975; television production by BBC, 1985). *Evening Standard* Best Play Award and *Plays and Players* Best Play Award for *The Norman Conquests*. Variety Club of Great Britain Playwright of the Year for *Absurd Person Singular* and *The Norman Conquests*. *Confusions* performed at Scarborough (London production, 1976). *Service Not Included* (television play) transmitted on BBC2

1975 *Jeeves* (with music by Andrew Lloyd Webber) performed in London. *Bedroom Farce* performed at Scarborough (London production, 1977; television production by Granada TV, 1980)

1976 *Just Between Ourselves* performed at Scarborough (London production, 1977; television production by Yorkshire TV, 1978). The Scarborough company moved from its seasonal fit-up in the Library to its own year-round permanent theatre (subsequently named the Stephen Joseph Theatre in the Round) in a converted school

1977 *Ten Times Table* performed at Scarborough (London production, 1978). *Evening Standard* Best Play Award for *Just Between Ourselves*

1978 *Joking Apart* performed at Scarborough (London production, 1979). *Men on Women on Men* (late night revue with music by Paul Todd) performed at Scarborough

1979 *Sisterly Feelings* performed at Scarborough (London production, 1980). *Taking Steps* performed at Scarborough (London production, 1980)

1980   *Suburban Strains* (with music by Paul Todd) performed at Scarborough (revived for London season, 1981). *First Course* (lunchtime revue with music by Paul Todd) performed at Scarborough. *Second Helping* (lunchtime revue with music by Paul Todd) performed at Scarborough. *Season's Greetings* performed at Scarborough (London production, 1982; television production by BBC, 1987)

1981   *Way Upstream* performed at Scarborough (and toured to Houston, Texas; London production, 1982; television film for BBC TV, 1987). *Making Tracks* (with music by Paul Todd) performed at Scarborough (revived 1982, and for Greenwich Theatre, 1983). *Me, Myself and I* (lunchtime shows with music by Paul Todd) performed at Scarborough (as late night entertainment, National Theatre, 1986)

1982   *Intimate Exchanges* performed at Scarborough (subsequently transferred to Greenwich Theatre and Ambassador's Theatre, London, 1984). *A Trip to Scarborough* (variation on the play by R. B. Sheridan) performed at Scarborough

1983   *It Could Be Any One of Us* performed at Scarborough. *Backnumbers* (lunchtime revue with music by Paul Todd) performed at Scarborough. *Incidental Music* (late-night revue with music by Paul Todd) performed at Scarborough

1984   *The Seven Deadly Virtues* (with music by Paul Todd) performed in Scarborough. *A Chorus of Disapproval* performed in Scarborough (London production, 1985; film by Michael Winner, 1988). *The Westwoods* (lunchtime shows) performed at Scarborough

1985   *Woman in Mind* performed at Scarborough (London production, 1986). *Boy Meets Girl/Girl Meets Boy* (lunchtime revues with music by Paul Todd) performed at Scarborough

1986   Started two-year sabbatical from Stephen Joseph Theatre, Scarborough. Went to the National Theatre as Company Director. *Mere Soup Songs* (lunchtime show with music by Paul Todd; London production, 1986) performed at Scarborough (as late night entertainment, National Theatre, 1987). Granted the Freedom of the Borough of Scarborough. *Evening Standard* Best Comedy Award, *Olivier* Best Comedy Award and *Drama* Best Comedy Award for *A Chorus of Disapproval*

1987 *A Small Family Business* performed at the National Theatre, London. *Henceforward* . . . performed at Scarborough (UK and overseas tour, 1988; London production, 1988). Received CBE in New Year Honours List

1988 Returned to Artistic Directorship of the Stephen Joseph Theatre in the Round, Scarborough. *Evening Standard* Best Play Award for *A Small Family Business*. Plays and Players Award for Best Director for *A View from the Bridge*. *Man of the Moment* performed at Scarborough

Conversations: 1981

Early Days

IAN WATSON: Your father was leader of the London Symphony Orchestra; your mother was a journalist; and you had a stepfather, from the age of seven or eight, who was a bank manager. Which of those three exerted most influence on you?

ALAN AYCKBOURN: It must be my mother, simply because I was with her much more than with anyone else. My real father had a sort of romantic influence on me, in that, because he wasn't around, I tended to idolize him rather.

IW: So you didn't get taken to concerts?

AA: Not a lot. My mother took me a bit. She took me, for instance, to Brighton to meet Herbert Menges, the conductor there; and I saw a rehearsal, I remember that very clearly. And she took me to the odd concert. But even if my father had been there, I doubt if he'd have taken me to concerts. Like a lot of professional musicians, he loathed music. He liked certain artists – he would listen to Kreisler, and thought he was wonderful – but he'd lunge across the room to turn off Beethoven's Fifth. 'Bloody old bore!' he'd cry. And I suppose, if you're sitting sawing it out day after day under Beecham and such people, that's not what you want to hear when you get home. But he liked light music: I know he always loved Al Bowlly and all those people. And I do remember him listening to certain pianists – Rubinstein and people – and enjoying them.

I listened to radio a lot and then later I had a gramophone and I spent a lot of my early money on records – all classical stuff. That was my first influence, not pop at all. I never bought pop.

IW: Your father wasn't around after you were about five?

AA: Not really. He married again and went to live in Norfolk. He gave up music. To all intents and purposes, I don't remember him being at home. We moved to Staines, Middlesex, I remember – that was where I had my first schooling, when I was about the age of four – and he wasn't there then. He used to pop home occasionally.

IW: Your mother was a journalist. What sort of journalist?

AA: Well, I think 'journalist' is the wrong description. She wrote. She started as a novelist. She wrote several novels which were published by Michael Joseph. He encouraged her and she knew him well. When she got married, I suspect, her career dissipated a lot, and it was only when my father went off, and times got hard again, that she had to start to support us. What she did become was queen of the short story world. She wrote – while I was between the ages of about four and fourteen, for ten years certainly – a phenomenal number of stories for magazines such as *Woman's Own*, *Home Notes*, *Woman*, which were syndicated; she was, of her type, a star. She worked in a very peculiar way; they used to send her illustrations and she used to write stories for them. And she used to tell of the peculiar code of each magazine: I can't remember exactly what, but in *Woman's Own*, at that time (for example), your girl heroine could fall in love, but not with a married man; then in another magazine, you could have a married man, but they must have an unhappy ending. There were various codes. And she wove in and out of these codes, and somehow managed to write original stories.

IW: You sound as if you read them all.

AA: No, I didn't read them. I watched her write them, because she used to thump them out in the kitchen. And it sounds a corny anecdote, but she really did – I suppose if Mummy had been washing up all day, I'd probably have become a very good washer-up – she gave me a little typewriter and I started to thunder out my own awful tales. I wrote stories and *I* wanted to be a journalist: later things changed! When she married my stepfather, she continued to remain quite independent. Having married the local bank manager, she decided she didn't want to stop writing; in fact she was in the supertax bracket for quite a long time. She earned more than he did. The marriage was quite a surprise to me. I was away at boarding school and she said, 'I'm getting married . . .'

[4]

IW: And you wrote her a letter: 'Dear Mummy, I hope you'll have a very happy marriage. Love, Alan.' Which is really a terribly desperate, sad little letter. Were you just not happy about the idea?

AA: It was supposed to be good wishes! I wasn't *very* happy.

IW: You had no brothers or sisters?

AA: I had a stepbrother.

IW: So the bank manager had a son; was he at school with you?

AA: No, he never went to school with me. He was much, much younger. My stepfather tended to take care of his education and my mother took care of mine. And they each said, 'Leave my kid alone.' That was the feeling. So my ma paid for all my education.

IW: She sent you away at what age?

AA: Seven. I went to the local boarding school. Actually, I came home every weekend. We were living in Billingshurst; and then they got married, and he was having a bungalow built in Wisborough Green, so we moved in there. And we used to go for school walks past the bungalow and raise our caps to my mother.

IW: Were you happy about being away at school?

AA: I didn't mind going to school. I was very unhappy when I first went, but then I quite liked it, and I think as time went on I got on very well at school. I had very many mates, because a lot of local kids were there. I didn't get on *very* well with my stepfather. I got on better with him when I was older than when I was younger.

IW: The evidence of the plays you've written in your adulthood seems to suggest that the home that was provided by your stepfather might have been a major formative influence, in terms of subject-matter. Is that fair?

AA: Well, yes. My mother had a very tempestuous relationship. They had a lot of rows. But you know, kids are marvellously adaptable: I mean, we weren't really upset, or marked.

IW: Is there any element of exorcism involved in using this background in your plays? Are you trying to work it out of the system at all?

AA: No, I don't think so. I remember at the time wondering why my mother had got married again. The horrible bit came much later — what happened to her. I cruised on, and what happens to you if you're a boarding-school child is that you get a tremendous detachment from your home, which, if the home is at all rocky, is not a bad idea. You come home and look at it, and you get angry about things occasionally, and you get upset, but you're not really touched, because it's not any more your base. What worried me was that I did see the relationship — from being away from it — deteriorating, which was a bit worrying. And later on, one day I came home and my mother looked awful. Then came one of the few positive acts I've ever taken: I'd left school just . . .

IW: So you were just seventeen at this time.

AA: Yes, and she was still at home. I was just going to Edinburgh for the Festival, and I was in London rehearsing. I found her a flat, and a job as an assistant to some writer. He was some madman who threw books at her, but nevertheless he got her back working. She'd stopped writing, dried up; she'd got very unhappy. She took this job, and I said, 'I'm off to Edinburgh for three weeks.' When I came back she met me at the station. And she'd got jeans on! She was about twenty years younger. It was absolutely amazing — the best thing I ever did. I'm sure she'd be dead now if I hadn't done that.

IW: Some time before that, you went off to Haileybury. Presumably about eleven, was it?

AA: Twelve, actually. I was a bit young to go. I won a bank scholarship. Barclays Bank gave away quite a few — three or four — scholarships, mainly based upon scholastic achievement at one's prep school, but also based, I think, eventually on interview in Lombard Street — whither I went, in my grey suit.

IW: You said earlier that you were tapping away on your toy typewriter while your mother was writing her bits for *Woman's Own* and so on. Were you consciously developing writing at this age or not? For school magazines, for example.

AA: I was very ill at my prep school, for a term. I don't think they ever found out what it was, but anyway I got better, so it can't have been that serious. But I adapted a Jennings book as a play, and it was done at the end of term. I'd got the acting bug while I was there: I'd played a Sea Scout in something, I remember – with glasses on, which I thought showed good character acting. And I then wrote this play, which they performed, though I never saw it. Anthony Buckeridge can now sue! I'd written myself in as Darbyshire, the character man, the part which got all the laughs. But I never even got to see it. That's my only writing memory. Oh, I'd written a story, one of those during-the-war spy stories – which I'd been told was rubbish, so I got a bit depressed. I was writing a bit of poetry. But I certainly wasn't playwriting – playwriting was third on the list until I got to public school.

IW: It was while you were at Haileybury, then, that you decided that the theatre was for you. How early did that come, and what did you see yourself doing in the theatre?

AA: Well, right up until the bloody last minute, I was still tinkering with a journalism career. But there was a master at school called Edgar Matthews, who had been a friend of Donald Wolfit's and indeed whose daughter had been Wolfit's secretary. He was getting near to retirement age and was teaching French at the school, and once a year he organized a Shakespeare tour during the school holidays, taking a party of boys off to the Continent; to France and Germany and all over the place.

IW: In English, to the Continent?

AA: Yes, schoolkids. He was a wizard of organization. He also directed the plays and his wife and daughters acted in them. You weren't allowed to go in for them the first year or two, but I auditioned when I was fifteen, I think, and I got into the first one I could. I got a small part, as Peter, in *Romeo and Juliet*. And off we went to Holland and we toured around there. And that was magic. That was the first real 'theatre' theatre I'd experienced, which was just terrific – you know, all that spirit gum and greasepaint.

IW: Who did you play to?

AA: Oh, quite a lot of people. I suppose they were the same audiences as Scarborough plays to now. A lot of people speak English in Holland. The English Speaking Union drummed up people. We played very odd places: some were quite good theatres, other places were quite primitive. I don't think our Shakespeare was earth-shattering, but it was fairly good.

IW: So you went in on this purely as an actor? You weren't in on technics at all; you weren't doing sound, lights, anything else?

AA: No, I was just acting. This was tremendous. And I think Edgar must have thought I had a bit of talent. The following year I came back, and he'd marked me down as a comedy actor. They were doing *Macbeth*, and I didn't want to play that boring old porter, so I plunged in hoping to play Macbeth. He really didn't think I was up to that – I didn't really have the weight, I was a six-stone weakling – but he did cast me as Macduff. And this year he decided to really go to town. He was going to take us round America. We went over on the *Queen Mary* and we came back on the *Queen Elizabeth* – the first, not the second – and that in itself was worth all the money in the world: a group of public schoolboys, fifteen, sixteen, seventeen, getting themselves absolutely slewed all the way over – it was wonderful. And this was touring gone mad, because we had all the joy of touring with none of the professional responsibility. We didn't actually care if the show never went on. We arrived and we went up the East Coast: we played in Maine, at the university there, and then we went up into Canada and played in Ottawa. And we played in Quebec, then we went down to Niagara and we played there; then we came through to Pittsburgh – and along the way we also took in Boston, Montreal, Peterborough and Washington DC. It was a very strange tour, but we did see a hell of a lot of America by Greyhound coach. I don't think the whole thing was more than about four weeks.

IW: The whole of Haileybury cannot have been theatre, though. Presumably, like most British public schools, it was fairly rugby-orientated, and sporty, and a whole lot of other, rather less salubrious, things. Did you take to it all right?

AA: It was tough to start with. My prep school had been an extraordinary place, because it had actually run down while I was there. The headmaster and mistress had decided they'd had enough of running this place for so long. So by the time I was leaving, there

were only five of us left. It was idyllic, my las...
our exams. So we stayed with this smashing coup...
and we looked after the place – they'd turned it int...
the pigs and all that: terrific! So, going to Haileybu...
from that, where we were lords of the manor, we be...
right down there somewhere: it was a huge shock. And it ...
tail end of an era. You know, I read about it now, and ... e
introduced girls into the place: there seems to be some sort of
semblance of equality. But it was still run, as most of those schools
were, on the most extraordinary lines, where everything was done
to make you feel unwelcome. It was a very tough school.

IW: How did you react to the public-school system?

AA: Well, I think there's a way to do it and that's to play the
system and create your own niche. And it sounds madly preten-
tious, but we formed a sort of bohemian section.

IW: We?

AA: Well, there were about three or four of us. This was two or
three years in: it took that much time. Before that, you just hoped
nobody noticed you. We behaved as we thought artists and writers
did – you know, we didn't clean our studies much, and we were
always a bit longer-haired than the others. We tended not to join in
any of the functions, we were a bit anti-Establishment, and we
were thought of as a bit Left. And people sort of gave us a wide
quarter, including the masters. They used to rail at us a bit; we
were bypassed for any sort of promotion – none of us ever became
a prefect or was given any responsibility whatever. And, in fact, we
joined in organized games. I wasn't too bad at cricket and I was an
average rugby player, so we were in that side of it: we were out of
the social and the more regimented side. And the school was big
enough and flexible enough to allow that.

IW: Neither then nor, apparently, now – because both your sons
went to public school – did you object to the system in principle. Is
that right?

AA: It did give me a bloody good education. I don't say I took
advantage of it. Everybody should be offered that: that's the
answer to that.

IW: Just before we leave your public-school education: you've done all this acting. Any writing?

AA: I used to write the house play at the end of every term. That was in the way of revue sketches, really. And I also edited the house magazine. Which, because I was such an inefficient editor and could never get any contributions, I used to finish up writing myself as well, under various assumed names. I used to type through the night on old stencils, and the housemaster used to stand over me, furious because his house magazine was always later than everybody else's. It was obviously a thing of great import in the staff room. But no, I hadn't really started writing anything serious until after I left.

IW: Before we leave your schooldays, it's worth just recording that whatever Haileybury did to you, you clearly didn't inflict any lasting wounds on Haileybury, because early in 1988, the school opened its new theatre, the Ayckbourn Theatre. You left at seventeen. There was never any suggestion of any form of further education, was there?

AA: They tried to persuade me, because I got the A levels I was asked to take – English and History – I was in the English Sixth. And they said, 'Well, you must go on for S level.' But honestly, by that time, I thought I didn't want to. Actually one was leaving because one didn't want to stay, rather than because one wanted to do anything. But, as I was leaving, I went to Edgar Matthews, the man who'd sent me off on tour, and said, 'I want to go into the theatre. Can you help me?' And he said, 'I have two contacts. One is Donald Wolfit; the other is an old boy of the school, Robert Flemyng. I'll give you letters of introduction to both. I don't know: I can do no more.' As it happened, Donald Wolfit was on the very point – I think the following Monday (I was leaving on a Friday) – of starting a revival of *The Strong Are Lonely*, a play he'd successfully had in London, I think, with Ernest Milton. He was reviving it with a slightly less starry cast – Robert Speaight was in it – and was looking for someone to play a sentry, an acting ASM, really. Edgar had assured him, I think, on the phone, that I had been in the school cadet force and could stand at attention without fainting for forty-five minutes. So, in the most extraordinary way – and at that point Equity, as far as I knew, didn't exist – I joined his company and was rehearsing at the YMCA in Tottenham Court Road, with one or two lads straight out of drama school saying, 'Where did you train?' I said, 'Train?' I was tremendously green. I sat around the rehearsal room and did what I was told and gawped at all these – it was an all-male cast – these wonderful old actors.

IW: Yes, Wolfit has been terribly maligned since he died. There's the awful story which compares his Lear with Gielgud's Lear: Gielgud's was a *tour de force* and Wolfit's was forced to tour. Was he really awful?

AA: I had nothing to compare him with. He was awfully big! I'd never been that close to an actor of that size. I hadn't been close to any actor. And standing on quite a small stage and seeing this man towering through things, I mean on a scale that would be unheard of today –

IW: He was tall as well as broad, was he?

AA: He seemed very big. I don't think he could have been that tall, but he seemed enormous to me, in all directions. He used to wear cloaks and big black hats, and his hair was always brushed back, and there were his wonderful saturnine eyebrows, and this make-up line that was always in his hair, because it had been there since 1910. And everyone stood back and stood up when he came in, and he swept through. And his performances were majestic and huge, and they were all about acting, they weren't about anything to do with the character. By modern standards, it'd be quite a shock, I'm sure.

I watched him very closely, because I was on stage. He'd fling himself on his knees at the end of the second act, after being excommunicated by the Pope's emissary. He began to kneel and say the Lord's Prayer, with tears rolling down his face – and he did genuinely move the audience. But as the curtain sank, he used to slowly turn his head upstage and just continue the prayer, but it became a vicious attack on the audience. 'Coughing bastards!' he'd say. And I was so shocked. I wasn't shocked by the blasphemy, I was shocked by the fact that a man could come out of such a moving moment with such apparent ease. And he could do that all the time. He'd fling lines upstage at you: 'Stand up!' he'd say, and carry on performing.

We were playing in the Lauriston Hall, which is a Jesuit Hall, in Edinburgh. It was one of those exciting plays where you could start with the curtain open: it was an electric curtain. And, as I used to call the half, Donald would say, 'You know, there's no harm in a little drink before a show. Can you get me some drinks in here?' And he gave me some money. He said, 'I want a bottle of gin and six bottles of Guinness.' So I said, 'Yes.' He said, 'Don't let them be seen coming in, because you know what I'm dressing in, don't you? You know what this room is?' I said, 'No.' He said, 'It's the confessional.' I said, 'Ah, is it?' And he said, 'And the priests are outside, so can you bring them in quietly?' So I whipped out to the off-licence and I smuggled in these bottles, past these long-garbed, eagle-eyed gentlemen who were standing on the front step, smiling at the audience as they came in. And I took them to Donald Wolfit – and this is a true story that no one ever believes. He poured himself a gin, then he said, 'Some water.' There was no water, obviously, in his dressing room. And I said; 'Well, the only water is at the other side of the stage, Mr Wolfit, sir. And the curtain's up, so I can't get across.' He said, 'Use your initiative! There must be some water in the building!' And he strode away, with me in tow, crashed down this passage, opened the door, and we were in the chapel. And there was this barrel – I swear – that had 'Holy Water' on it. And he topped up his glass with holy water and said, 'You see what I mean?' I'd never seen a man drink gin and holy water before. Wonderful!

IW: He has a reputation for having surrounded himself with lousy actors.

AA: I don't think they were all lousy, but they were actors who were not going to give him much trouble.

IW: Did he take any trouble to try and make them any better, or did he enjoy the fact that they were considerably less good than he was?

AA: Well, he tended to bully a lot. I think he was a kind man: he certainly has a record of being very kindly. But on the stage, there was no doubt about it, he shunted people around. And when he did meet opposition – as, I believe, he did in the original production, when Ernest Milton was in it, who was a force to be reckoned with – the blood was endless. They fought and fought. I remember, Wolfit decided to wear black, and there was a scene with the papal emissary, which Ernest originally played. Ernest decided, quite shrewdly, to wear white. And all through Wolfit's big scene, all Ernest did was sit at the middle upstage in his white robes, and not a light could be seen on Wolfit. So every night – the electrician told me this, in the wings – every night, Wolfit would come off and he'd say, 'I think there's a little bit too much light on Mr Milton, you know.' And the lights went down and down and down, until it was absolutely black, and Ernest was still glowing, like life after death!

They used to have this wonderful battle at the curtain call too, because Wolfit loved to take his solo at the end. And so he used to give his sub-stars a little solo bow: on would come all the principals, bow, bow, bow, and get off as quick as they could, so there was plenty of applause left. And then the second principals, and off. And then Ernest would come on, and Ernest would stand there for hours, till they were all weakening. And Wolfit could be heard shouting from the wings, 'Ernest! Ernest! Get off, Ernest! Ernest!' Wonderful stuff! I was privileged to hit the end of an era. Admittedly he was, as it were, the last of the dinosaurs; but it was marvellous to see all that, and to see him bouncing up and down in the wings, and then, at the moment of entry, to hang on to the curtain, and come round the curtain, as if exhausted from the performance, and to get the audience going: 'Oh, look, he's on his knees, poor old bugger.' 'Thank you, public!' – he'd do all that bit, then bound off again for his drink. It was all tricks of the trade, but you don't see them these days.

IW: Did you learn anything useful from him?

AA: Yes, I think so. I think I learned that theatre is show business. Some of the stuff he portrayed I didn't admire. But, eventually, it's what the audience wants. He played for them. I think some would say he played to them to the exclusion of everybody else. The fact is that he hated them at the same time – a lot of artists have a love-hate relationship with their audience. But there was no doubt you'd been to the theatre when you went to see Wolfit.

IW: Did you do any technical work with his company, or are we still not there yet?

AA: No, I learned only basic stage management, really.

IW: How long were you with Wolfit?

AA: Oh, very, very short. I was three weeks at the Edinburgh Festival. But it was like three years simply because it was a holiday job and it did give me three weeks at the Festival. And I saw so much else, because all these wonderful old actors that he employed were also past masters at getting into every show in the business without paying. So I saw all the operas and the ballets and the Piccolo Theatre of Milan – it was a very rich festival that year – not to mention all the orchestral stuff and the tattoo.

But when I got back to London, that was the whole burned-out end, because I'd said to Wolfit that I'd go to drama school – in fact, he'd put in a word for me – and then I thought about it and thought, 'No, I don't think I can, I can't afford to.' So I didn't take that up, and obviously I couldn't go back to him. So I then took up my other loose end, my other letter of introduction, which was Robert Flemyng, who was living in Hove, I think, at the time. And I went to see him one afternoon. He was very nice, and he said, 'Well, I don't know that I can do much for you. I don't run companies like Donald Wolfit, I'm just an actor.' But he added, 'I do know Melville Gillam at Worthing and I might be able to get you a job there.' And he did get me a job of sorts. In fact, I took a salary cut from £3 a week to nothing. I went as a student ASM, and my mother sold her caravan, I remember, to pay for me. I was there for about six months. Weekly rep at Worthing had Dan Massey, Michael Bryant, Roland Curram, Ian Holm, Elizabeth Spriggs – an extraordinary collection of young actors – not to mention Peter Byrne and people like that who were there at that time. There was a welter of experienced names there that I could learn off.

I learned all departments there. I worked for some weeks in the scenic department, didn't see the stage at all. I did a little bit of acting, two or three tiny parts. I got to be a lime operator, and I worked in the scene dock; I worked all around. I didn't do electrics but I learned a lot more about stage management, and I was, by the time the money ran out and the season finished, fairly proficient.

I then met another person who helped me. I went to see Carey

Ellison of *Spotlight*, who's helped a lot of people, and he introduced me in turn to Hazel Vincent Wallace, who was looking for
an ASM at her old Leatherhead Theatre. She was a very particular,
idiosyncratic woman, who liked me very much – well, liked the
look of me anyway – and engaged me as the ASM. So I went to
Leatherhead. At that point, I started to do a lot more acting. She
sort of took a shine to me, and if Hazel took a shine to you, you
tended to get the parts.

IW: Had you been working towards this? Had you been yearning
for the acting?

AA: I was looking for the acting, yes. I was a stage manager and
waiting, biding my time. And I played out the rest of that year.
I did quite a lot of acting: Percy in *Flare Path*, that boy in *The
Rainmaker*, Jimmy Curry, and the coloured servant, Sanyamo, in
South Sea Bubble. It was weekly rep again, but I worked with a lot
of good people there. Actors are quite generous people, really: they
do tend to help. Sometimes it's terribly misguided help, but they're
always there to say, 'If you take my tip, kid, don't enter that way, it
doesn't look so good.' So I was learning. I was still a long way from
the technical side, but the stage manager there was a man called
Rodney Wood. At the end of that season, Rodney Wood, who
thought for some reason that I wasn't bad at my ASM job, asked
me and a part-time carpenter who was there if we'd like to come to
Scarborough and form the stage team there, with me as stage
manager and him as ASM. And that was the moment that I got to
hear of Stephen Joseph and the Theatre in the Round. And one
Sunday, we went up to town and we had a look at some of this
man's work, although I wasn't to meet the man himself for quite a
long time. We went to the Mahatma Gandhi Hall and saw a
production of *Huis Clos*, which sticks out still in my mind as one of
the most exciting things I've ever seen in the theatre.

IW: Was this the first time you'd encountered theatre in the
round?

AA: Yes. It was an absolute knockout. It was a pretty racy play,
for its time, you know. And I thought, 'This is terrific.' I also liked
it because it had no scenery, and that meant less work. So we
rehearsed in London that first season: again I was acting because it

[15]

was a small enough company. The late Clive Goodwin was directing, and there were two actors, two actresses – Clive also acted later, and Rodney then directed. Stephen had very little to do with that season; he didn't direct. And I stage-managed with John, and there was a girl ASM called Anne Taylor. We did our two weeks, or whatever it was in London, we went up to Scarborough and we started playing, and there was still no sign of this Stephen Joseph man. That was a great summer. I did the lights, John did the sound – that's how it started.

And eventually, Stephen turned up, this amazing bloke. He introduced himself, and he was obviously a man much more interested anyway in the technical side of the theatre than in the acting side. So we hit it off immediately: he liked our end much better. We spent a lot of time chatting about sound and how to improve it. It was all rather new, we were in the pioneering days of tape-recorders. It all seemed as though it was going to be a rather brief, one-season affair. Anyway, at the end of that season a certain director from Oxford, a man called Milos Volanakis, had been up to see a couple of the shows and had liked my performances – at least, I put it down modestly to the idea that that's what he'd liked. He wanted me to audition for Oxford Playhouse, which he ran with Frank Hauser. I was always to be fated like this, to be drifting from one job to another. I never, in all my years of acting, was ever unemployed. Once I started at Worthing, I didn't stop: Worthing, Leatherhead, Scarborough, Oxford, Scarborough . . .

IW: So at what stage did you start choosing your jobs?

AA: Well, I never chose anything. Things just happened. It's this divine inertia. I went to Oxford, and again fell right into a very, very nice situation. I was very lucky there, because once again there was a big, talented company, a marvellous man running it – Frank Hauser, who was again a man genuinely interested in young talent who went out of his way to help – and it was a theatre that was on the up at the time. I suppose if I'd auditioned for it, I'd never have got in. I did *Under Milk Wood* there, and I played the romantic juve with Mai Zetterling. In fact we did a lot of exciting things that were good for a boy at that age.

Frank Hauser was quite interested in my staying on and wanted to offer me more parts; but Stephen rang up and said, 'Do you want to come back to Scarborough and do another season?' I told Frank I was leaving, and he was very upset and said, 'Oh, why? We're offering you this and that.' And I said, 'Well, no, I think I want to go back to Scarborough. I don't know why.' So I went back and I was again acting. But I was still lumbered with this stage management which I couldn't shake off. You can get any amount of bloody actors, but stage managers are terribly rare, and people who were actually able to understand all this machinery were like gold dust. I was beginning to get quite good at it because I'd been doing it at Oxford: they'd got a tape machine there, and none of them knew how to work it.

Stephen was beginning to introduce these winter tours, so my work pattern began to get established for the next couple of years in that I worked for thirteen weeks in the summer and then was unemployed again until about November. And then I worked through till February/March.

IW: The writing of *Square Cat*, which you wrote that winter, 1958–9, was a reaction against something. Was it a reaction against the fact that you weren't getting enough acting?

AA: Well, I didn't like the play we were in. I was doing Nicky in *Bell, Book and Candle*.

The Joseph Years

IAN WATSON: Everything one wants to say about Stephen Joseph seems to be in extremes. To those who knew him, he was a great man who inspired much love, although he never married. You've been quoted as describing him as 'half genius, half madman', which falls into the same category of extremes. Let's see if we can get any closer to pinning him down. I guess one's got to start with the objective things: Stephen, who died of cancer in 1967, was the son of Hermione Gingold and the publisher Michael Joseph.

ALAN AYCKBOURN: Note the link!

IW: Yes, indeed, your mother's friend; though that coincidence played no part in either your meeting or your work with Stephen. I suppose, objectively, now, one can see a lot of theatres that he was very much responsible for. He founded, obviously, the Theatre in the Round in Scarborough, though he never saw the one that you're now in. He founded the Victoria Theatre at Stoke-on-Trent (now replaced by the purpose-built North Staffordshire New Victoria), under Peter Cheeseman's direction; in fact, he converted it with his own hands to a large extent. Those are the two theatres he actually founded. But his hand obviously can be seen very much, too, in Manchester University Theatre, on which he worked as consultant; in the Nuffield Studio at Lancaster University; and I would think there's very little doubt that neither the Bolton Octagon nor the Royal Exchange Theatre in Manchester, neither the Cottesloe nor the Warehouse, nor perhaps The Other Place of the RSC, could have come into being, had Stephen Joseph not done what he did.

AA: Yes, I would think that's true. I have the very clear impression that, when I started in the theatre, there weren't any other sorts of theatres than proscenium arches. Stephen was a lone voice in the wilderness, and certainly in my experience – and I did go to a lot of theatre at that time – seeing theatre in the round at the Mahatma Gandhi Hall was the first time I had seen any sort of theatre other than a conventional proscenium arch. I believe there must have been end-stages around, but there certainly weren't in-the-rounds; I'm sure there weren't even thrust stages. And he certainly opened up, in many people's minds, the alternatives. He was an extremist for the round, but then he was, as you said, an extremist about everything. But I think being a pioneer makes you extreme: you have to take an extreme point of view in order to get your point across. He said, 'Theatre in the round is the only sort of theatre', and you know he didn't actually believe it.

Though he intensely disliked the pros. He really did. And I think he didn't like – as I don't actually like – the compromises that came up: the thrust stages. He believed that you should go the full round or not at all. He marched down St James's, you know, when Olivier and Vivien Leigh were marching, saying, 'Save the St James's Theatre.' He marched the other way, saying, 'Pull down the St James's (and build a more sensible theatre in the basement of an office block that'll pay the rates).' Which didn't make him very popular. But he very much believed that all new theatres should self-destruct in seven years, which was his other great maxim. I think he meant the personnel as much as anything.

IW: One of Stephen's claimed reasons for getting so deeply into theatre in the round was economy, of course. At the time that he was starting the theatre company neither he nor his friends had enough money to do anything else. Is that believable?

AA: I think it is. He was Jewish as well and he was very clever with his pennies. He was well aware of the economics of theatre in the round. We've blessed him ever since for it, because, although our budgets are certainly horrific when compared with the ones he used to work with, I still suspect that a larger part is spent upon the most important element, which is the human element, than in any other sort of theatre. We have less need for the material trappings. If you've got a great big stage to fill, you've got to fill it. The audience will get very annoyed if you don't have a few scenic flats around occasionally. And I think he was very clever in that sense, that he was able to produce theatre that didn't lose quality by cheese-paring.

IW: But his love for the round was not based upon economics.

AA: It wasn't based on that, I don't think. I think it was based upon the immediacy of it. His great concept – and this is something he did say a thousand times – was that the only thing that mattered about theatre, when it came to it, was the actor and the audience. This was the most important concept and the round, more than any other medium, emphasizes this most strongly. The actor is in the middle and the audience surrounds him, and there's nothing else there, really.

IW: There's something of a paradox there, isn't there, that the man who believed that theatre was – in the expression he used in an article – 'a passionate affair between the actor and his audience', should in fact get into the position of founding a writers' theatre. The writer, the director, were both relegated to secondary positions as far as he was concerned, and yet here he was: the man who gave Pinter the chance to get *The Birthday Party* going after its first flop; the man who gave Ayckbourn his first chance. And David Campton was, I suppose, the house dramatist when you went in?

AA: Yes, he was. And an occasional was James Saunders who was very new then: I think we did his very first play, *Alas, Poor Fred*. Yes, Stephen was full of paradoxes like that. But then he wasn't a great one for improvisation – you know, where actor and audience say, 'Well, stuff the dramatist, let's get on and create our own stuff.' He held one or two rather half-hearted improvisation classes when I was there, but they were mainly to improve the art of the actor, not to replace the dramatist; although he would always emphasize that the dramatist, in the last analysis, was serving the actor, which I think is right – eventually the audience, whether they like it or not, are watching the actor and not the dramatist. They're watching the dramatist through the actor, and if you don't get your actor right, there's very few dramatists who can actually survive.

IW: Would it be fair to say that he wasn't a man particularly interested in the ideas of plays? It's hard to imagine him, for example, doing a George Devine, who, at roughly the same time, was running a very different sort of writers' theatre at the Royal Court.

AA: He had rather strange tastes in plays. One of his favourite plays was Housman's *Victoria Regina* which he thought was a wonderful play and was an unashamedly romantic piece: the old queen dying, waving. I once found I was playing Prince Albert in that and I described it as a load of rubbish, I remember, at some heated rehearsal. He got very white and said, 'This is my favourite play and I won't have that.' I said, 'I'm frightfully sorry.'

But, at the other end, he was a great supporter of the new drama, and John Whiting, I know, he was mad about. He was very excited by all the new stuff coming along: the Osbornes and so on.

IW: You described first getting to know Stephen more or less over the sound console, because you were both in the nuts and bolts of the theatre. In his book, *Theatre in the Round*, he's writing about the appointment of Joan Macalpine as Manager, who wanted to come into the company because she wanted to write plays. He said, 'Would-be playwrights are two a penny, but Joan could drive the green lorry.' One suspects that this side of theatre was actually more exciting to him than anything that happened on the stage.

AA: Joan tells the story of her interview with him. He was such a shy man when you first met him, he always stared at his blotter, and she, being a sort of early liberationist, was J. Macalpine, so she signed herself 'J. Macalpine'. And there really wasn't any indication as to her sex. And she sat there nodding and not getting a word out while he outlined the job: 'Well, I expect you to do this, and I expect you to do that, and I expect you'll want to do that, and I see you've got a licence, and so on. Can I offer you the job?' And she said, 'Oh, thank you.' And he looked up in total amazement and saw a woman. I don't know how true it is, but it is quite possible for Stephen to have done that. I know he auditioned one actor, and he engaged him purely on the strength of his walking in when his gramophone was playing. Stephen said, 'What is this music?' And the actor frowned and said, 'Bach.' He said, 'Right, yes, well, you start on Tuesday.'

IW: Yes, he claimed that he never auditioned an actor: he always interviewed them. He also made a claim that he never directed plays: he only trained actors.

AA: That's right. I've been in several of his productions and can vouch for that. His claim – and it was quite a legitimate one in many senses – was that in theatre in the round, particularly when two or three alone were gathered together on stage, it was quite possible, if the set was reasonably well laid out, to allow the scene to take its course. Which is fine, except that this did rely on the fact that they were all experienced actors, all tremendously equal in terms of generosity, and so on – and of course, as one knows, you do need something a little stronger. Which is why I suspect – although there were moments in his productions when they worked very well – I would say he wasn't the strongest of directors.

He knew more than any person I've known about playwriting, when it came to talking about it, and he knew more about directing than any living person, and I suspect he knew an awful lot about acting. He certainly managed to talk about it very lucidly and entertainingly and interestingly, although he must have been the world's worst actor. So he was a teacher and not a doer. He was a doer in other senses, but it was always to do with the fringe things: putting the noticeboards up in the foyer, and designing the new theatre. I always felt that Stephen's mind was on higher things than the performances. They were rather small beer in Stephen's game. He was on another plane.

IW: He said of your *Mr Whatnot*, 'The play made a pointing gesture in the direction of anarchy.' Which is an interesting reflection, because he always called himself an anarchist. He was a sort of benevolent anarchist and profoundly distrustful of authority, which is why he didn't actually believe in the business of directing, but rather in the business of encouraging actors to act (which didn't always work). I wonder whether there was at that stage any sort of meeting of minds between you on this?

AA: Yes, I suppose so. I always think of the *Whatnot* theme as being the Id figure who bounds along, the one inside me that would like to up-end and destroy – not destroy gratuitously, just to up-end, really, and confuse a little, upset *status quo*s. And I suppose Stephen was much of a oneness with that anyway. I always liked the way he would leave many a meeting in uproar. He did awful things: he used to insult the press regularly, which any theatre manager will tell you is not a very good idea. When it comes to your next meeting, there's a lot of very injured men dipping their pens into something rather violent! The other thing he used to do was to invite them all to tea, which was also not a very good idea. They'd all arrive, ready for a nice stiffening bracer and find themselves faced with biscuits and cups, because he was teetotal completely. Well, he got drunk with me once. Somebody gave him a bottle of whisky as a 'thank you very much' present, and he said, 'Here's a bottle of whisky. Would you like to share it with me?' And he really did drink like a non-drinker: he poured himself half a tumbler and swilled away. I had some water with mine, but he drank three-quarters of a bottle, and he suddenly fell off his chair. 'Do you know, Ayckers, I'm completely pissed.'

We spent a lot of time together. When he was ill – and he was quite a lot with various things – I used to cart round my portable gramophone and play him all my corny old records. He used to say, 'Oh dear, oh dear, have you got any chamber music?' But I used to play him all my Tchaikovskys. Always when he was in bed he used to decide to make a new cardboard theatre – the ultimate theatre in the round. He was into the sort of things we're still talking about – walk-around grids and so on. But he was also into two-storey theatre, and I'm still looking at the idea. In *Taking Steps* I came near to it, but I decided to set it on one floor. His idea was to have two floors, so the play could take place on two levels. And he worked out that it could be done in the theatre structurally, with perfect sightlines in the round. Hell of a difficult thing to build, though.

Then he got into fish-and-chip theatre, and that was really beyond me. My instincts as an actor were such that I couldn't bear the thought of people eating fish and chips all around me when I was trying to give my performance. But he did promise that they'd be behind glass. And they'd have you amplified – in which case, to me it seemed you were better off on television.

IW: He felt the natural theatre critics – the real theatre critics – were the holidaymakers at Cayton Bay, who talked through the bits they found boring and sat absolutely rapt through the bits which made them absolutely rapt. It doesn't seem to me to hold a great deal of future for the playwright at all.

AA: Well, no, it's rather like children's theatre, in the sense that you've got to keep the action going. I think theatre is actually a very thinking art: you have to go with your brain fairly clear and be prepared to give it quite a lot of attention. Half the joys in theatre are often in being stimulated sufficiently by the dramatist, either because of the ideas he puts out or simply, for example in the case of *Taking Steps*, because of the fact that you have got to grasp the concept of three floors and, having grasped it, enjoying that in much the same way you might enjoy an executive toy. None the less, you can't really afford to be knackered from a day digging trenches, when all you actually want is to put your feet up, have a pint of beer and be sung to by a lady with big boobs. I remember Tony Church saying, 'King Lear takes an enormous amount of work and effort, and of course there will always be people who do a hard day's work who will want to go to the theatre and see it, and who will very much enjoy it. But not the majority of people.' And I know when I've done a bloody hard day, the last thing I want to do is go and see *King Lear*. I want to watch something really vulgar on telly. And by very vulgar, I mean something very simple and very colourful and great fun, preferably American, with a lot of cars going round corners on two wheels.

IW: But the fact is that most of those who do go to the theatre have got to go after a day's work, because there's no way we can take a day off work just to prepare ourselves for the business of going to the theatre.

AA: Yes. That's why when we put the word 'comedy' after the title, many more people go than to a 'drama'. But the other side of the coin is that I think the theatre has a great responsibility. It is not sufficient for plays to sit there and say, 'Come and get me.' You've got to go out and get the audience, and I think there is an entertainment quotient which plays ought to contain. The best ones, I think, do. Shakespeare's plays are highly entertaining if they're produced half well. Usually the story's quite sufficient to keep you going on the best ones, and if you happen also to be a freak for language and metaphor and all sorts of other things, you can get into that as well. But there's a dramatist who actually knew that he'd got down in his pit a lot of guys who'd done a hard day's work, and needed to be entertained on a fairly basic level. That's not to insult them, merely to acknowledge when they say, 'God, mate, I can hardly hear one word in three: make the plot simple tonight.' And that was very important.

IW: If you extend that a little bit further, you get into circus, don't you?

AA: Yes, but then you throw away the other bit. Yes, you do get into circus – but I think that's what Stephen used to preach. He had a very strong feeling towards fish-and-chip theatre on the one hand, and yet he did grasp quite difficult plays.

IW: How did Stephen come to be in Scarborough?

AA: The story goes that he was in search of premises in which to establish a theatre in the round for longer than one night – which is what he was doing at the Mahatma Gandhi. He obviously was looking outside London. I think he got as far as Leeds for some reason, and he met John Wood, who was the Education Officer, who tipped him off that the Library in Scarborough had a rather good, although shortly-to-out-go, Chief Librarian called Smettem, who was quite sympathetic.

IW: Yes, William Smettem. He was a man who did a lot for Scarborough. His widow tells very proudly of the day when he saw this dejected young man sitting in the library, and stopped to talk to him. 'I've never been so miserable in my life,' said Stephen. He had just spent a fruitless week looking round Scarborough for premises, and he was filling in time waiting for a train back to London. Smettem listened to his story, persuaded him to wait another day and put him up overnight in the family home, while in the meantime talking to the Chairman of Scarborough Libraries Committee. Next morning, it was all arranged, and he took Stephen down to the Library, showed him the Concert Room and Lecture Room on the first floor, and said, 'They're yours if you can use them.'

AA: Stephen outlined what he wanted to do – which was six or eight weeks of new plays, in the summer. And Smettem, who was obviously a man of some vision and imagination, but who was also on the verge of retirement, so probably had less to lose than a man who was coming into the job, said, 'Fine!' And Stephen moved in there.

IW: Mrs Smettem also tells the story of the first night at the Library Theatre, when who should turn up but Hermione Gingold, who in all honesty hadn't had much of a hand in Stephen's upbringing . . .

AA: No, and when they flew Stephen and his brother out to the States for Hermione's *This Is Your Life*, which was of course a live show, she swore blind that she'd never seen them before. 'My sons are much younger than that,' said she.

IW: Anyway, at the party after Stephen's big first night in Scarborough, Hermione swept over to William Smettem, proffered her hand and intoned, 'Accept a mother's thanks!' I imagine the bellow of Stephen's laughter was heard in Whitby! But at all events, the theatre was launched, and Stephen had pulled together a company to work with.

AA: PB's story (she was his housekeeper) is that the company all came up and stayed in one house. He advertised for her, actually, in the paper, and she came along.

IW: She was living on a houseboat at the time, wasn't she?

AA: That's right. She'd never cooked before for anyone.

IW: I think it's worth just establishing her. She was Veronica Pemberton-Billing.

AA: She was another person he took completely on trust. She was a wonderful woman, the widow of Pemberton-Billing the MP. Her past is slightly shadowy, in that she never said much about it, just little anecdotes. But she had a very colourful marriage with a very colourful man. She was a slim, very beautiful girl, obviously a flapper of some quality, who got involved with gun-running and everything else that Pemberton-Billing got into – all his court cases and all the scandals – and adored him, absolutely. And she said she was an absolutely silly: you know, she couldn't open a door unless somebody did it for her. She'd certainly never cooked, since she used to sit around on sofas, eating bonbons and being patted by the big man. Then he died quite suddenly, and she, knowing her terrible irresponsibility with money, put it all into a trust which gave her, at the time, an adequate but quite restrictive income which forced her to go out to work.

She answered Stephen's advertisement. I don't know if she'd done anything before that; I think not. He took her on because he liked her – she grew rather large rather quickly after her husband's death – took her up to Scarborough, gave her the house that he'd taken for the summer, in which all the actors were living, and said, 'Cook us a meal by one o'clock.' And they all went off to rehearse and she ran around in absolute panic. Two of the actresses had children, so she had those there as well – she had someone to help her with them. All she knew was that if you got a joint, and put some fat with it and stuffed it in a tin and put it in the oven, it would cook in time – how long, she didn't know. The company all came home at lunchtime and it was all right. And over that summer, she said, she learned how to cook, she learned how to housekeep and she also was absolutely captivated by Stephen, and remained so.

IW: She was sort of Mother Superior for the whole company, wasn't she? She called herself the Mother Hen.

AA: She was. The only thing you could really do to upset PB was ever to criticize Stephen in her presence. She was just like a dog with its master. And he used to treat her appallingly. He would think nothing of breezing in about eleven, saying, 'Hello, PB. I've brought eight people in for supper.' 'Yes, Stephen,' she'd say. She'd chase around and, in a way, she loved it. She would sit there, nodding in on his conversations, and he treated her in an affectionate, but fairly patronizing way: pat her on the head and say, 'Yes, well done, PB: off to bed.' She'd do anything for the man, and indeed nursed him in his last days. She was wonderful.

IW: The work pattern when you joined Stephen was twelve weeks in Scarborough in the summer.

AA: Yes it was, by the time I joined: it was their third year. There was a two-weekly pattern, and we put on an awful lot of plays. No – the first year I was there, it was three weeks, because it was only four plays we did, but he did step it up after that. We did do six or eight: it was quite heavy, and it was quite hard work. You didn't get a lot of time off in Stephen's day.

IW: What was the work? I'm never clear. He didn't rehearse you.

AA: Well, we did rehearse, but he wasn't particularly involved. He'd sit there jogging one leg and making notes about something else – except when he was doing other things. I remember dress rehearsals where he was actually drilling in the auditorium, putting up new banister rails. And we were screaming about the bloody din and saying, 'Could you keep it down please, Stephen, we're trying to dress-rehearse!' 'Well, you won't get anybody in tonight, people, unless these banister rails are secure.' So you'd carry on desperately against odds like that. One got the sense that in general he found rehearsals extremely boring. I had occasion to sit next to him in rehearsals when he was doing my play. He said, 'Oh, for a team of trained acrobats, or something! Oh, that these people could get on with it!' I said, 'Well, you know, they're doing their best. They've only just dropped their books.' I don't think he had time for all that, really. He liked the first bit of rehearsal and the last bit. It was the middle bit which was the one which caused the black hole where everything disappears.

IW: There's an impression one has that he was almost running a constant seminar with you in the earlier days – not you personally, but with the company. Is that right?

AA: Yes. He believed that all of us shouldn't be purely concerned with our own little role in theatre, that theatre people should be total theatre people. That, in fact, if you were an actor, that didn't mean that you didn't know about the box office. In fact, on the contrary, you *should* know how ticket stubs were dealt with. I found it invaluable that he would not think it peculiar that an actor should work the sound. In fact, if an actor was interested in the sound, then it seemed a very good reason for him to work it and, if necessary, one would rewrite the play in order that he could work it – give him an early exit so he could play the music. He was very flexible to that extent.

IW: And to that extent, if you hadn't had that sort of training, most of your plays you couldn't have written, because most of them are based in stage management of one sort or another.

AA: I adore lighting and I love sound, and he encouraged both aspects. He found that admirable that somebody should have those interests. And one regrets – I do, and I'm sure he would – the demarcations which have happened in the theatre, by necessity. Very few actors ever go up into the control box nowadays, whereas it would then have been a natural thing for half the cast to be up there at any one time, because they were probably doing something of importance up there.

IW: Did you drive the green lorry?

AA: No, I was not a driver at that time. I used to 'mate' with Joan Macalpine, if you'll pardon the expression. She drove, and the only thing she wasn't able to do was to put the handbrake on. She wasn't strong enough for that, and so I used to stand up, and she'd say, 'Brake!' suddenly – and, two-handed, I'd hoick the thing up, which was actually beyond her, and let it off again.

IW: Because, after your summer season in Scarborough, you went out on the road, right?

AA: Yes.

IW: How much of this did you do? How many years of this?

AA: Two or three. I did the Leicester–Birmingham–Hemel Hempstead–Harlow run quite a lot.

IW: Did you go to Wellingborough?

AA: I directed the three plays for Wellingborough, yes.

IW: What were they? Camptons, were they?

AA: Yes. Oscar Quitak and Pat England were in them, and I was in them, and there was a total disaster area of a stage manager called Kenneth Colley, who went on to become an extremely good actor, but he was a man who claimed to know all there was to know about tape-recorders.

IW: Seen as Jesus Christ, incidentally, in *The Life of Brian*.

AA: Yes. A wonderful actor. Out of work, came along, got the job because he was the only one who applied for it – Stephen, I think, advertised it in a window in Soho, or something. Anyway, this guy turned up. I said, 'Can you operate a Brenell tape deck?' 'Oh yes, yes.' Right. You could tell as soon as he stared at it that he'd absolutely never seen a tape deck in his life before. So, technically, in Wellingborough the show was a disaster. I could hear him winding to and fro, looking for cues, as we vamped our way through a play Campton had written which had, I suppose, almost as many sound effects as *Mr Whatnot*. It was riddled with them: a play called *Out of the Flying Pan*.

But my great moment of touring with Stephen was Hemel Hempstead. We were playing in the Adeyfield Hall, and there was one Wednesday when the place was needed for a dance. Anyway, Stephen, not to be done out of this performance, had booked us into the Standard Telephone and Cables Company, or some such, for a performance of a different play, for that evening. This entailed us taking down the entire auditorium – all those touring rostra, all the set – loading the lorries, driving over to this telephone place, setting it up to do *Dial M for Murder* for one night, taking it down again, driving it back and dumping it that night. The crew to put it up was Stephen, Rodney Wood (the manager), John Smith and I, who were the stage management, and one rather limp girl, who didn't do very much really, except stand there and wave her arms. We guessed four of us could put it up in two hours. But there were only two of us, because Stephen's van had broken down in London and Rodney had broken down somewhere else. So John and I had to put the whole auditorium together on our own. We'd arrived at ten and we finished at two. We hadn't lit the show. The matinee was at two thirty, the actors had turned up and we said, 'What are the bookings?' And the bookings were two people – who were parents of one of the cast, so we couldn't cancel the show. So I remember I went in to the dressing room and said, 'I'm terribly sorry, I think we're going to go mad, so we're going home. Can you do the show with no stage management? We'll just put all the lights on.' 'Certainly,' said the actors, realizing we were very near a crisis. So we went home and had a bath, and they did the show. They welcomed the audience individually as they came in, sat them down and did the show to them. And that, I think, was my low spot of Stephen Joseph touring! He turned up at three saying, 'Sorry, people! Got it up, have you? Well done!'

IW: Did you ever count the number of rostrums that there were?

AA: Oh God, there were hundreds!

IW: They were heavy, I know.

AA: Yes. And there were a lot of them. He also had – which we didn't put up this day – a portable grid; a sort of thing like a flying bedstead, which was built out of scaffolding poles, locked together with Allen keys, and which stood in a rigid structure on which you hung your lamps in a square round the acting area. I remember at one place the grid arrived, and he said, 'This is going to be exciting: we're going to erect it now.' And we erected this thing, or we tried to, with everyone holding on to one foot of it, and it didn't stand up. It was unstable. For once, Stephen's mathematics and engineering brain had totally left him. This thing swayed and it hurtled: to let the public in would have been fatal, without even hanging a lamp on it. He was undeterred: he sat down in the middle of the room. We were holding on to these poles, saying, 'Come on, Stephen, for Christ's sake, it's falling down!' He said, 'Just a minute, people!' And he redesigned the existing structure, like a kid with a Meccano set. We then rushed around and built eight separate towers. And that, with modifications, became the basis of the touring kit.

IW: You were touring what – weekly? Or fortnightly?

AA: We were doing a show a week. We used to take about four plays out. There was a distinguished time when, I remember, we opened with a Campton, then we played one of mine, then we played another Campton, then we played another of mine: it really was like ducks and drakes. Sometimes we had even more in the repertoire. We did seem to have an awful lot of plays going around at that time. It was a very small company, certainly the first tour we did: two girls and three men, plus me as an acting ASM and an acting girl ASM.

IW: And you did all the plays in each place?

AA: Yes. We did four weeks. But then in Leicester we went to two or three venues, because we were only there for one week in each.

IW: And dismantling all this kit all the time?

AA: Yes, we totally dismantled it all. Stoke was one of the nicest places: we played in the Municipal Hall at Newcastle-under-Lyme, which was lovely, except it was upstairs. But once up there, it was this big, big, big room, and I think some of the happiest memories of touring were there. There was a lovely big kitchen, and PB was a great house mother. She used to make huge bowls of soup. There was always food after the show.

IW: She was cooking not only for the company, but for the audiences as well. She used to make the most amazing cakes for every performance, didn't she?

AA: That's right. But to the hungry ones of us, of which I was one of the most, she would always tip the wink and say, 'There's some sausage rolls in there if you want them.' And it was very much a family thing. We used to strike Scarborough Saturday night and drive through the night then to Leicester, and arrive there some time on Sunday, snatch some sleep and then start setting up for a performance on Monday. There was no messing around. I remember arriving in Leicester, and sleeping on David Campton's floor. We crept into the house, and we ran out of rooms. Somebody had nipped in and shut the door, and Stephen and I were left in the sitting room. We split the cushions, and lay end to end in the sitting room. And he said, 'Would you like my feet or my boots?' I said, 'I think I'll have your boots tonight.' I went to sleep with these great big, size 12 boots near my face.

IW: You were telling me how you came to write *Square Cat*. You said you were getting sick of playing Nicky in *Bell, Book and Candle* by John van Druten. Now what was Stephen's role in getting you to write?

AA: He said to me, 'If you want a better part, you'd better write one for yourself. Write a play, I'll do it. If it's any good.' And I said, 'Fine.' And he said, 'Write yourself a main part' – which was actually a very shrewd remark, because presumably, if the play had not worked at all, there was no way I as an actor was going to risk my neck in it. So at least I had to have reasonable confidence in it. It was during that first tour, and it was in the digs on the tour that I wrote *Square Cat*. It was untypical of me in that, firstly, it was written over quite a long period and, secondly, it was written with a great deal of help from Christine – structurally, not dialogue-wise. She was very helpful. We talked out: 'What if. . . ? What if. . . ? What if. . . ? How about trying it this way round?' And it was very much an exercise, in the sense that we were trying to get effects.

IW: Christine's your wife, and she was an actress in the company.

AA: Yes.

IW: Did you go back to Stephen with it a lot as well?

AA: Only when it was finished, I went to him then. He did very Stephenesque things: he scribbled huge examples of the dialogue he thought ought to have taken place in the margin, which were awful. And then he got very upset. He said, 'You didn't use any of my dialogue,' and I said, 'Well, it didn't quite fit my style, Stephen, but it was very good.'

I was aware that he'd had a very strange effect on David Campton. Stephen had very strong ideas, although he couldn't actually put them into practice, about plays. He didn't necessarily give David the plots, but he certainly encouraged and channelled his writing towards what was then the comedy-of-menace school, and threw in his thoughts on nuclear disasters. Campton was for some years one of the front runners of comedy of menace. But he also had another strand to his writing, which was a much more romantic and, I think, a much more human strand, which he suppressed – plays like *Cactus Garden*. I'm never quite sure how David's talent would have developed, had he been allowed not to be quite so strongly dominated by Stephen saying, 'This is what I want, David; can you write it?'

The only time Stephen tried that with me was on *Dad's Tale*, when I learned quite an object lesson. He wanted me to collaborate with David, and David wrote a synopsis for *Dad's Tale*, based on *The Borrowers*. By the time I got it, I found I was unable actually to work to other people's ideas. I was maybe too undisciplined, I don't know. So I totally went my own way.

Then again Stephen tried to stick his oar in with *Standing Room Only*. By this time he was getting into overpopulation. He decided if the human race didn't destroy itself, it was going to overbreed. He said – and this is typical of Stephen's suggestions – would I like to write about that? I hadn't really thought about it. He outlined his plot, which was set on Venus, where the population was now expanding because Earth had overpopulated. And I wrestled around trying to get up a Venus setting, but realized that by the time you'd established (a) what life was like on Venus, and (b) what life was like being overpopulated, there wasn't anything left for the play to do, except just tie it up rather neatly: somebody could possibly drop dead in the last five minutes. So I reset it in Shaftesbury Avenue in a bus – which actually turned out to be the best bit of the idea. Everything else got rather tedious, although the play worked quite well. I think. All the technical details of the overpopulation got a bit swamped in the more interesting things, which were the human relationships, as they always are. I saw a warning light then that Stephen's ideas, although exciting, were not for me, because they actually didn't lead me anywhere. I was having to rethink them quite radically. And by the time I'd got to *Mr Whatnot*, which was written totally independently of him, I had nothing directly whatever to do with him, in terms of writing, except the residue of his ideas – obviously that was still there.

IW: Let's go back to *The Square Cat*. You delivered the script to him. How did he react to it initially?

AA: He read it very quickly. My impression always was that he flipped the script through with his thumb, in some mysterious way, and was able to tell you immediately what was wrong with it – a little bit cavalier to a writer who's spent hours on it. He was usually right. In the case of *Square Cat* he had quite good suggestions to make – he always did. I got to learn later that suggestions he made about the structure were invariably right, about the content or 'a nice joke to go in here' invariably wrong, because he wasn't actually good at penning *bons mots*: they used to fall very flat, and if he put them in at rehearsal, you were always well advised to take them out again for performance. But, in this case, he structured the play for me again, although he didn't do anything radical. He cut it – he always cut everything quite ruthlessly – and left it then to production.

IW: What was the play about?

AA: It was about a family – it sounds terribly banal – about a husband, his wife, his son and his daughter. The mother has got an obsession with a pop singer. She's fallen in love with him from a distance, thinks he's wonderful and swoony. She therefore rents a

house in the country – (a little Anouilh coming out there: there
were a lot of definite influences in this play. In fact it's *Dinner with
the Family*, I now realize!) – in order to invite the pop singer down
for a marvellous weekend with her. And she was going to pretend
to be someone totally different; have no family, and be a rich
woman – she'd arranged it all. The family, having got wise to this,
followed her down.

I don't quite know why he comes, but anyway he agrees to come,
we find out later. The family has followed her down and is not
going to let mother get away as easily as that. They say, 'All right,
let him come.' She's very cross and says, 'No, you've spoiled the
whole thing.' He turns up – that's me – and of course he's not at all
the glittering figure of the silver screen, but shy and bespectacled
and wanting a quiet time – and this he thought was it. And he's
horrified to see that mother is a sort of elderly groupie. The family
roars with merriment saying, 'Look, you see, look at your hero.
He's really nothing very much.' At which point he bounds out and
comes back again in glitter costume, twanging his guitar, saying,
'OK, this is war' – or words to that effect (I can't remember much
of the plot). He gets together with the daughter eventually, and
romance blossoms there. Mother finds the error of her ways and
goes back to her husband. Jerry Ross finds true love with the simple
girl, and all fades into the sunset. I don't think it was very good as a
play, looking back on it, but it was OK for a first one. It's not one
that one would ever want to see done again.

IW: You managed all that with nary a twang of the guitar, and not
a sung word?

AA: It was so silly. I did actually set myself as an actor an
impossible task, yes. I did originally play a guitar, and sing a song,
and dance – none of which I do at all well. A bloke called Donny
taught me about five chords, in order that I could sing 'I gave my
love a cherry', which seemed a nice, extremely boring, morose song
which goes on for ages. But even that I used to have very great
difficulty with. I used to sing it on some nights – whenever PB was
in, she would insist I sang it – but on other nights, I would nod
vaguely in the direction of the lighting box and they'd take the
lights out rather swiftly; so I would just play one open chord –
sploing – and the lights would go. And other nights I would sing,

excruciatingly, 'I gave my love a cherry' to a rather flat guitar, because I hadn't actually learned to tune it.

IW: Was this a light comedy?

AA: It was farce. I think it comes under the term farce, because there was a lot of leaping about and mistaken identities in it. It was certainly as broad as I got for quite some time. It was curious, because I didn't sit down to write anything particularly, except a play. I'd been writing before that, but they'd never had the test of production, and most of them, with a couple of exceptions which had been rather morose pieces, had been comic in tone.

IW: Had Stephen seen those?

AA: He'd seen some of them. He'd seen my Pirandello play, which was the one that everyone writes, about the group of actors with a director, and they all take on the characters – and he said, 'Yes, that's a Pirandello play!' I said, 'Yes, it is.' And I think I'd probably got a Ionesco play as well. I was very influenced by Ionesco.

IW: So you'd done all this before *Square Cat*?

AA: Yes.

IW: And what was the reaction to *Square Cat* once it got on the stage? Did the audiences come, in the first place?

AA: Yes, they came a lot. I don't know what it did in terms of percentage: it made me forty-seven quid, I remember, more than I earned in several weeks. It proved very popular because it was what it was – a farce, with no pretensions to anything else – and it did give people quite a laugh. And I think Stephen did recognize, if nothing else, that he'd found a writer who, nurtured a little, could possibly keep his box office afloat, allowing David, who was running in parallel with me, a chance to develop his less commercial style – because he had distinctly two. Stephen was much more keen for David to get on with his *Four Minute Warnings* and his *View from the Brinks*, continuing with *Lunatic Views*, than his commercial stuff. I was left rather in the position of being encouraged to carry on writing, in the hope of bringing in an audience. Which I did, for the next two or three plays.

IW: And *Love After All* was asked for, was it?

AA: Yes. Stephen directed *Square Cat*; *Love After All* was done by Clifford Williams. But at some period when it was touring, I went off to do National Service, and I left the company.

IW: Right, come on, we'd better have that out!

AA: I'd been pursued by these awful men to do National Service for years. They started when I was seventeen, I was now about nineteen.

IW: Nineteen, with a wife and two kids?

AA: Right – one kid, anyway, yes. There were rumours that National Service was finishing. In fact, it *was* finishing. But they're remorseless, these chaps, and they eventually cornered me in Scarborough. They had a sort of interview/exam and a medical. It was a pretty idiot exam, saying things like: 'You stop the car with: a Horn, a Rear Bumper or a Brake. Please tick the box you think is the correct one.' I was desperately trying to avoid this, so I thought, 'Well, if I can get qualified as an absolute moron, I might not get in.' So I ticked 'Rear Bumper'. It was rather sweet, because there was a guy next to me – a wonderful, big, thick fellow – who was desperate to get in. His ambition was to be a serving officer in some army – that would be his ideal. He'd spotted me as the genius around the place, and was cribbing off me. And I thought, 'Oh God, he's copying down my answers.' I was shaking my head and pointing to the correct answer, and he was laughing and was actually copying down half my answers, and then trying to correct me when he'd obviously spotted something – he obviously knew it was 'Brake'. So we had this embarrassing exchange, in which I'm sure I failed him. I got two right by mistake, actually.

IW: But they passed you because they thought you had a sense of humour?

AA: They passed me. I went in and this chap said, 'Well, ah, Mr Ayckbourn, you've scored an absolute total of two in the intelligence test, which is something of a record.' I said, 'Oh yes?' He said, 'Oh, but you do appear to have two A levels and so I think we can dispense with the intelligence test. Why do you want to join the RAF?' I said, 'Well, the real reason is that they don't wear boots, they wear shoes.' He said, 'Well, that is a reason for joining. It's not a very strong one.' I said, 'I hear you do less bull.' He said, 'Yes, we do.' Then he did their wonderful old trick. 'Look, here are your options as a National Serviceman joining the RAF,' he said, pulling down a screen. 'You can be one of the following: a clerk, or a male nurse. I think that's it. If you wanted to sign for three years – I mean, just for the extra year – you could be a fighter pilot! You see, the options do get somewhat wider.' And I said, 'Oh yes, yes they do. I think I'll stick with the National Service options.' He said, 'Well, male nurse?' And I said, 'Well, I do faint at the sight of blood.' He said, 'Well, it's down to clerk, then, isn't it?' I said, 'Yes, that'll be fine. I don't mind being a clerk at all. I'd quite like being a clerk, really.'

So, some months later, I got notice to join up. I did contemplate trying to break my foot in the lift, to get out of going. I actually lost my nerve, so I just got very, very drunk that night, said, 'Farewell for two years, dear wife, dear baby', and she went home to her parents, because I certainly wasn't going to see them for my eight weeks basic training. I caught the train and we got to Cardington. We roared into the camp in a lorry, and were marshalled into a hut with these other lads, most of whom were slightly younger than I was – I was getting on. This bloke was sitting there and he said, 'Well, first of all, chaps, let's just establish how long you are all signing for? Dawkins?' 'Five years, sir.' 'Nine years, sir.' 'Ten years, sir.' 'Seven years, sir.' I thought, 'Christ, what is this?' He said, 'I don't seem to have your name.' I said, 'Ayckbourn, sir.' 'No, it's not on here. How long are you signing on for?' I said, 'As short as possible.' He said, 'Are you a Regular?' I said, 'National Service.' He said, 'Well, you shouldn't be in here, this is a Regular intake. You can't sleep in a hut with Regulars.' So I was segregated, as if I had some awful, man-eating disease, and I was put in a hut on my own, a 48-bed hut. He said, 'Light the fire if you want to: here is some wood.' It was bloody freezing: it was January. So I took the blankets off about eight other beds and piled them over me, and lay in bed. I'd read the notice: *Reveille is at six o'clock. All men will be standing outside their huts in full uniform.* I hadn't got any uniform. I thought, 'Christ, how am I going to get up at six?' So I put my watch by my bed and I went to sleep.

When I woke up, I looked at my watch: it said half past eight! I'd actually missed Reveille! I'd seen films, you know, where everyone marched up and down with heavy packs for punishment, being shot at! So I got out of bed and I thought I'd better put things right. I looked at the notice, and it said: *Kit inspection is at nine, and all beds will be folded, with their blankets eight centimetres from the edge and –* you know *– three folds from the middle and the seam down the left-hand side . . .* I was reading this, and I suddenly realized that I'd stripped eight or ten beds, so I was going to have to make up ten beds in this extraordinary way. I started on this, and in came a corporal. He said, 'Morning!' I said, 'Look, I'm extremely sorry. I just overslept, and I genuinely didn't hear the bugle or anything.' He said, 'Well, I looked in on you at six, and you looked very peaceful, so I left you.' I said, 'Oh! Well, that was very nice of you. Is there anything I should be doing?' He said, 'Well, no, you can go to the NAAFI. Report back here at eleven. Should be some other lads arriving. Then you can be part of that.' I said, 'Oh, thank you very much, Corporal.' So I went across to the NAAFI and had breakfast. And I came back at eleven and I sat in my hut, and about a quarter to twelve another corporal came in. He said, 'What are you doing here?' I said, 'I'm waiting for the other corporal, who's probably gone out to meet these other men, you see.' He said, 'Well, don't hang around in here. Look, go to the NAAFI. Come back here at one.' So I said to him, 'Yes, right, thank you very much, Corporal.' I went back in the NAAFI. This went on most of the day. Every time I came back, he said, 'Don't sit around in your hut, go over to the NAAFI.' I was bloated with awful NAAFI food.

The next thing that happened was that he said, 'You're all right, now. There's some lads arriving. They're Glaswegians, and there's forty-seven of them.' I said, 'Oh. Oh, goodness!' And he said, 'No, I don't think that's a very good idea. No. I'll tell you what. No, not the Glaswegians. There's another lot. You're responsible, you look an educated sort of bloke. I want you to look after a feller. He's, you know, he's a bit . . .' I said, 'Ah, is he? Yes, right.' He said, 'He's a Maltese.' And I said, 'Ah yes, yes.' He said, 'He was a pilot officer in the Maltese Air Force, and he's got this thing about starting again in the Royal Air Force as an ordinary aircraftsman. He feels he should. And there's no way, because Maltese is rubbish, you know. And he's got a gripe, and he's had a go at the Commanding Officer with a knife. But we let it go.' I said, 'Oh? Really! Oh, good. Oh, super.' So I sat next to this brooding guy and

I started chatting to him, saying, 'I hear you've had a bit of bad luck.' It turned out that the real agony was that his girlfriend had left him. He showed me a picture of an awful old stripper from some club, who'd obviously slept with half the bloody army. Anyway, I soothed him down and was doing very well.

But then the mates I'd made in the NAAFI came rolling round and said, 'Come and have a drink in our hut.' So I was suddenly plucked away from all these blokes in my own billet, and I was sitting up in the Regulars' hut, getting pissed out of my mind with them, and hearing the most amazing stories about one of the sergeants' wives that they'd all been laying while he was off on active service. I staggered back to my hut and was promptly the following morning put in charge of it. The bloke said, 'You look a responsible man. You are responsible for the hut and the cleanliness of the hut, and you see these lads get on with their work. And you will be responsible for checking in the coal quota – and, by the way, some of the coal quota comes to me. You do that, and I'll see you're all right.' So I said, 'Oh. Yes.' I was into a whole racket, immediately! I was beginning to quite enjoy it. We were marched across to the medical orderly. Fortunately, I chose Door 3. Door 2 was a cantankerous old bugger: any man who could crawl in there was immediately sent in – very good for them. Door 3 was a National Service Officer, a medic, who was actually writing a book about his experiences as a National Service Medical Officer, brief as they were. So we got on to literature, and he found I was a writer, which I played up a little when I discovered that was his leaning, too. I also claimed to have an agent, which I did have at that time, just, and said I could probably see him right for his book. To which he said, 'Do you want to do this?' To which I said, 'Not a bit.' He said, 'No, I didn't think you looked too keen.' He said, 'But how do we get you out? You seem to be perfectly fit. Ah! Ah! A knee, a knee. What's this knee?' And I said, 'Well, it's cricket knee; I twisted it when I was young. I tried it on when I went for my medical in Leicester; they weren't prepared to buy it, but they did put it down as suspect.' He said, 'Well, it's graded "quite safe" at the moment, but, having had another look at it,' he said, 'I don't like the look of that at all. How far could you walk on that knee, if you were asked?' I said, 'Well, probably about as far as from here to the NAAFI *safely*, but not a lot further.' He said, 'Could it give?'

I said, 'It would probably give.' He said, 'And if it did give, do you realize what you'd be doing?' I said, 'No.' He said, 'You'd be invalided out of the RAF and we'd have to pay you a very large pension for the rest of your life. At nineteen years old, I don't think that is a responsible thing for me to do. So, all I can say is: get out, you're the sort of man we don't want!' So I staggered out of the hut with my pink chit, while the guy next door, who'd got a perforated eardrum, was hurled out by this nasty old bloke who'd said, 'You're perfectly fit!'

It's very hard to get out of the RAF, or any service. It's easy enough to get in: you see one man. To get you out you have to see fifteen, all of whom countersign your chit, any of whom at any moment, you feel, is going to say, 'Just a minute!' I got to the very last man at five o'clock that day, and he said, 'Closed!' I said, 'It's just to sign . . .' He said, 'Tomorrow morning! My office is open at nine. Not until then. Goodnight!' I thought, 'Hell! Another night: anything can happen.' I went to the pictures, and had an extreme amount to drink with my Regular friends again. I was actually getting delirious. They liked the fact that I was in show business, but they weren't too sure about just being in theatre. So I invented: I was a great friend of Cliff Michelmore, I remember. They said, 'Do you actually know him?' I said, 'Oh yes, yes indeed. Cliff and I have drinks together. And I write for television'. The following morning I rushed through the gates of the camp, past two suspicious armed guards, waving my exit visa – my promise that, if the war broke out, I would not be recalled, except as a sort of strategic, non-active combatant. 'Wait for the bus,' they said. 'No.' I said. 'I'm walking', and I ran to the station, phoned my wife and was home that day.

Oddly enough, I then phoned Stephen, because he'd tried to get me out. He'd written a long letter saying, 'The whole future of the English theatre depends on this man.' It hadn't had much effect with the army. 'Ah!' he said, 'I'm glad you phoned, because our electrician has just walked out. If you come to Newcastle, I'm lighting the show tomorrow afternoon. You know what I'm like with ladders. If you're there, I really will appreciate it.' I said, 'Stephen, there's no problem. I'll be there in the afternoon. Don't worry.' So, saying a brief farewell, I got on the train and went to Newcastle-on-Tyne. Getting back to Newcastle-under-Lyme took a long time! I arrived at seven, and ran up the Municipal Hall steps, and saw him at the top. I said, 'Stephen, I'm sorry. Did you manage to light it?' He'd got his whole arm in plaster, and he said, 'No, I didn't. I fell off the ladder.' I said, 'Oh Christ! I'm so sorry, I mean, it was the train, and I . . .' He said, 'I not only fell off the ladder, I fell on to the office.' From the description later, how he hadn't killed himself, I don't know. He'd fallen off a high ladder, off one of his own gantry things. He'd landed on top of the table which was, in fact, the office. He'd completely crushed the portable typewriter to death – it was just flat. And all the money and everything had gone flying. Anyway, I was back in theatre!

IW: And *Love After All* was in the repertoire at the time. That was a costume farce.

AA: Yes. I didn't write it in any particular period, because I wasn't that clever, but it was obviously going to be a period thing, because it was based on *The Barber of Seville*. I remember seeing the play at school. The suitor keeps coming back and disguising himself, getting in as a music teacher. I tinkered around with it a lot. And in the first version, with Clifford Williams directing, it was a very good production – it was very tight and quite fun, and we did it Edwardian. It was later revived, the following summer I think, with me playing the lead, and it was directed by Julian Herrington, who decided there were certain bits of it he didn't like very much, like its Edwardianness, and its rather jokey names. He brought it up to date, and I don't think the play actually gained from what we did to it. And the third play followed very hotly on that.

IW: Which was *Dad's Tale*.

AA: Which again Clifford came back to direct. And it was not a success. It was not a success (a) because I think we were into a winter season in Scarborough, which never established itself; and (b) because it was a children's play. It was certainly more successful than my second children's play, but we were actually doing it at a time when there weren't any children around! Instead of doing it in school time, when you could con a few of them in there, we were doing it just before Christmas. And it had a disastrous first night.

It had an extraordinary brief. It was written for two companies, us and the British Dance Drama Theatre, who weren't going to meet until very late on in rehearsals. Clifford was directing our company; Gerard Bagley was directing the dance company. And what I had to do was write the play overall, then write separately the story that the ballet should take. They were to rehearse this entirely separately, and then we fused them together when the two companies got together in Scarborough. In fact, once or twice the actors got involved in the ballets, but they were always pushed around or shoved into places. It was quite an adventurous show, really.

IW: Was it funny?

AA: It was meant to be. I think it was. It never actually got an audience to prove it.

IW: Your second children's play was *Christmas v. Mastermind* — that was the real disaster.

AA: That was the most disastrous play I've ever done. It was the only one of mine that Peter Cheeseman directed and I think we had very different views on what children's theatre should be about. Peter and I have actually grown together a lot more in recent years. At that time, I think we were diametrically opposed about many things.

We had some quite good arguments, and I was his associate director, so it was quite a merry time. But I suppose if you're living together for eighteen months, in those conditions, it's natural you're going to have big rows. Certainly, that play was one that he shouldn't have done. I probably shouldn't have written it either, but it had pieces of whimsy in it which we might just have brought off. It was the first winter in Stoke, so there was again no audience. It's lovely to see now that the theatre is pre-sold ten weeks, or something, but at that time we got no audiences at all. It was a play about Father Christmas, who was actually a very unpleasant old man. He was faced with industrial trouble. His chief gnome had called the men out. The gnome was inspired by an evil character called the Crimson Golliwog, who was not that at all, but who had a special gang whose object was to take over Father Christmas anyway. They incited the gnome to this revolutionary action just before Christmas and also abducted his fairy helper. It was quite a broad, jolly farce, with lots of fights in telephone boxes. And there were two policemen, who tracked everything down, disguised as hedges and letterboxes. But it was received in dreadful silence. None of it seemed to succeed and we died the death with it.

IW: All these plays we've been talking about are plays which you would rather forget in many ways, wouldn't you?

AA: I think you've got to be allowed a certain amount of learning time – you know, learning what you can do as well as learning what you can't do, really, and I think in *Christmas v. Mastermind* I was learning what I can't do. I can't write successfully for kids, because I don't have the interest. And all the best children's writers I've met have been totally devoted to what they're doing.

IW: But you later came up with *Ernie's Incredible Illucinations*, which got published and which is rather sweet.

AA: Yes, it does a tremendous number of performances. That is the exception. And I've had endless letters to write a sequel, which I've always resisted, because I think I could not actually do it very well. I said, 'The whole point of the script is that you write your own sequel. The thing is a starting point for imaginative games. And if you want to do *Ernie Goes to the Moon*, you do it.'

IW: But the first plays, the ones right from the beginning: you never allow them to be done?

AA: No. With all the best will in the world, however keen one was on my work, I don't think anyone would want to revive them.

To the West End – and Broadway

IAN WATSON: You talked about *Standing Room Only* to the extent of saying that its provenance was one of Stephen's current fads, which was the population problem. He wanted to set it on Venus and you couldn't quite get it together with Venus! *Standing Room Only* is set in the ultimate traffic jam, in a bus on Shaftesbury Avenue. And, as you said before, the play is actually about a whole lot of personal relationships rather than about the traffic jam. Peter Bridge bought an option on this for town, didn't he?

ALAN AYCKBOURN: Yes, it was the first play I sold to him.

IW: It looked very much as if it was going to get into town at one stage. I believe he even bought a bus to set it in, didn't he?

AA: Yes, he did, I think. It was the most rewritten play ever.

IW: Now why was that? In its Scarborough version it was very simple, a very small cast play. I've read three different versions of it, with God knows how many people in the cast. Was this all Peter Bridge's influence, that it had to be rewritten?

AA: Yes. It was written in Scarborough originally, and it was a nice, simple little piece. The reason it ever attracted attention – which may be the whole source of my being a successful dramatist – was that the *Stage* critic at Scarborough was unable to attend the show; and the *Stage* at that time was not averse to asking someone in a management to write their own notice. Joan Macalpine actually wrote the review, and she was the acting manager of the theatre. And she wrote a corker, because, well, who wouldn't? And she wrote, in an inspired burst, 'Will no management drive this bus into Shaftesbury Avenue?' This appeared dutifully in the *Stage*, on the rep page. At which point Peter Bridge, in his office, swivelled in his chair, thought, 'Good Lord, this is a must!' and rushed to Scarborough, introduced himself and took out an option. He was very impressive, promised – as Peter was wont to do – that this would be the biggy, but explained to me quite carefully that the West End was necessarily a star system. And Peter Bridge was particularly noted, of course, for mounting shows which were very, very star-studded. Most of his productions were revivals.

Then began the bizarre history of this play, when he offered it to one star and then another. And I suppose it was typical of my plays in that it didn't really have star parts: it had quite a good part for the father and a couple of reasonable parts for the girls, but none of the parts was particularly *per se* what you would call a star part. So what happened was he sent it round: Richard Wattis had it, Hattie Jacques had it, Sidney James had it and Ron Moody had it – all sorts. I think about fifteen or twenty stars had it eventually, all of whom were up for different parts. So, on each occasion, Peter would give me a quick ring and say, 'Look, I'm sending this to X. I've put him up for John. I think the part doesn't look so good: could you build it up a little? And he's six foot two, with glasses and thinning hair and a wart on his chin: I wonder if you could just build that description into the character?' So I'd write, '*Enter* JOHN, *a bespectacled man of six foot two, thinning hair, with a wart on his chin*', you see. And so this would go off for a start. He could hardly have been fooled by this artifice into presuming it was a coincidence. Anyway, they would then add their four penn'orth. I remember meeting the late Sid James, who said, 'It's a very good script. Very nice script, son.' He said, 'I'll tell you what's wrong with it.' I said, 'Oh yes?' He said, 'It wants a few more rudes in it.' I said, 'I beg your pardon?' He said, 'Rudes. It's a very clean script. You know, I mean, a few bloodies and things, just to liven it up.' I said, 'Oh. Thank you very much.' I didn't say I thought I'd achieved something monumentally clever by actually avoiding this! So off I went.

I got a bit angry eventually. And indeed, the script began to get more and more misshapen, as every single part was built up. In fact, at one point, when Sid James was in contention as the bus driver – he was at that time doing a television series with Sydney Tafler – I was encouraged to write a second bus driver in, called Bert or something, in order to cater for Sydney Tafler, who I don't think actually got to read the script anyway. I would have finished up writing in the entire *Carry On* crew eventually! So the play, from its slender Scarborough beginnings, became really very complex and unmanageable and unwieldy. And I suppose, over two years, I must have rewritten it again and again and again, till I had helicopters flying in.

IW: Yes, the ending changed quite remarkably. I seem to remember at Scarborough it ended up with the joyous cry of, 'We're moving! We're moving!' Then I suddenly came to read a script, and you've got helicopter cranes lifting the whole bloody lot up.

AA: That was the West End version, which was never done and never could have been done. They said, 'We want something a bit more spectacular!' And at that time, Peter was putting on *Come Spy with Me* with Danny La Rue, who was flown in in a helicopter, and he said this would make a good ending. And obviously a dramatist of that experience and that age – and one looks back on oneself with horror: the unprotected boy! – was open to suggestions from the office cleaner onwards. Everybody wanted to get in on the act. I suppose there's a reaction now: I'm very wary about any suggestion from anyone, except people I trust very much. Eventually we did the play again at Stoke, in a modified version from Scarborough. I think it was quite a good show.

IW: Did Peter Bridge eventually drop it, or did you drop him?

AA: It never came off. It just went on and on and on, until I suppose everyone had tried to do it. He still tried – I gave up. I said, 'I'm absolutely exhausted. I cannot continue. I've been through three different directors, all of whom said, "Yes, I like it. I think this is what we want to do." I've gone and stayed at their houses, and . . .'

IW: Who were they?

AA: John Hale was one, in Bristol. There was an Irishman called Jim Fitzgerald. Oh, and I met Bob Chetwyn, I think. I met a lot of people: I went round the directors. But eventually I did the play again in Stoke, as I say, and that was that. I exorcized it.

IW: *Mr Whatnot* was the one which Peter Bridge did actually get into town.

AA: He was a stayer, Bridge. He came back for more. After that, many a management would have turned their back.

IW: *Mr Whatnot* was written for Stoke-on-Trent. Did you direct it there yourself?

AA: Yes. After reviving *Standing Room Only* at Stoke I wrote *Mr Whatnot* – which is actually the second original play I wrote for Stoke, after *Christmas v. Mastermind*.

IW: What was the basis of *Mr Whatnot*? Was it the actors you had in the company at Stoke? Or was it a hankering after a mime play?

AA: Several factors all came together. We had an actor, Peter King, in his first season, who had a natural ability for mime; he was a very clean, clear, in fact a very strong mime actor, and I always thought it would be nice to use him more in that context. Secondly, I've got a great fondness for silent film, all the old classics – particularly the Buster Keatons and the Harold Lloyds and people like that, rather more than Chaplin. I'd also seen a couple of films by René Clair, particularly *Le Million*, which I was terribly taken with, and which had wondrous sequences. A mackintosh becomes a rugby ball: he would take a sequence, elaborate it, and transform it into another sequence about something quite different, with just a wave of the hand and a sound effect. I rather like that. And *Whatnot* started by using common jargon from other media and transposing it into a theatre setting, something I've done quite a lot – things like the car chase and running across ploughed fields in the morning, and a lot of filmic sequences of lovers in the sunset, and operas, and people dining in restaurants with gypsy violinists. It was firstly based around Peter himself, as the actor: he was very much in my mind when I wrote it. I was also aware that we had (you can't not be aware after working with them for so long) a group of actors who would perhaps be very responsive to this. It was, significantly, the first play I wrote for myself as a director. It was when I was going through my 'If-I-can't-show-myself-off-as-an-actor-I'll-show-myself-off-as-a-director' phase.

IW: You weren't in it?

AA: I wasn't in it. It was the first one I wasn't in, which is also significant. And it was also significantly, in retrospect, my most successful play to date. It became a very, very successful production, in its Stoke form, and was the first original, major smash we had there. It pre-dated, of course, subsequent big hits like *The Knotty*, which Peter Cheeseman went on to do when he developed the house style.

IW: It's based on a really quite remarkable suspension of disbelief, because Mint is not actually dumb, is he?

AA: He just can't think of anything to say!

IW: But he's played mute throughout. Even in his telephone conversations, he doesn't say anything.

AA: Yes, I originally wanted to write it with no dialogue at all. And, in fact, when I wrote the dialogue, I asked the actors to learn it and then distort it, so that 'Jolly nice day!' would become 'Wah-wah wah wah!' and so on. However, when they were playing the dialogue, it actually was quite funny, and they were rather reluctant to let some of it go. So, in the end, not altogether sorry, I conceded that they could keep the dialogue that was there. Yes, it was interesting to have a totally silent hero. My instructions to the actors were that they shouldn't really notice he hadn't spoken. I didn't want to make a great issue of him being a silent man, but it seemed to me that silence in a character creates a richness of its own. I mean, I would be crestfallen had I ever heard Buster Keaton speak, let's put it that way. It's rather like seeing your favourite radio actor in the flesh. We all know what Dick Barton looked like. I never wanted to meet him, because he wouldn't have the right eyebrows, the right square shoulders. He was totally in the eye of the listener. And in the same way, the sound, and a lot of the personality, of a silent actor was in the eye of the watcher. And indeed, I've seen a great variety in the Whatnots over the years. Paul Moriarty played him: it was a wonderful performance, he was a very good Whatnot. But it was a totally different, more dangerous, manic Whatnot that he played. Peter King is Welsh – he was a Welsh Whatnot. They're very rapacious and his was a very sexy Whatnot.

IW: How can he be a Welsh Whatnot if he's totally silent?

AA: Ah, he had Welsh looks and he had that dark, Celtic lust. He was very lustful. The thing that the successful productions did, and that the London production did not do, was to remain always fairly salacious. There was a danger that Amanda was going to get some horrific come-uppance when she did get into bed with Whatnot, because he would stop at nothing. And that was the nice thing about it – he didn't have a romantic image of her at all; he wanted her body. And as long as that happened, it gave the play a sort of balls, I think, which it totally lacked when he wanted to give her a flower. Cecil wanted to give her flowers and chocolates; Whatnot wanted to give her what-for! And indeed, one has suggested that this is all she was really wanting as well. She was certainly looking around hoping that something was going to happen. And in that sense our heroes both had their feet on the ground.

IW: When it's produced, presumably it can run anything from about fifty minutes to two hours.

AA: Yes, it's very flexible. What I've always said is that the script is there as a basis. In fact, the basis is very workable and one should beware of throwing things out or over-embroidering. Certainly there's a greater danger of over-embroidering than of throwing things out. But it is best, I think, played when the subordinate parts are kept very well set and the things like the tennis sequence are highly rehearsed, and allow set cadenzas for the Whatnot. If you've got a Whatnot who does handstands, it's useful to put them in somewhere. Peter was extremely nimble and obviously his Whatnot had more than a great fear of dogs, and it was nice to use that side of him. I've seen more ferocious and large Whatnots being able to cope with the other dog better, and had to find other ways round it.

IW: Peter King went to London with it, didn't he? What went wrong with the London production?

AA: Oh Lord, almost everything went wrong with the London production. Peter Bridge bought it. He first of all suggested we take the whole production down. Peter Cheeseman was less than enthusiastic about taking the whole cast, but agreed. But Peter Bridge then went back on that and said, 'No, perhaps this is bit risky. Perhaps we should think about getting a slightly better-known cast. And perhaps, on second thoughts, the director shouldn't also be the writer, because writer–directors are not a good idea.' So, could I think of anybody? And I said, 'Well, yes, why not Clifford Williams?' because he, after all, had done two of my earlier shows and I liked him. Clifford came up: he was at the Royal Shakespeare Company by then. He was heavily involved, I think quite liked the show but said he couldn't do it himself, and suggested another Welshman – Welshmen stick together, you see – Warren Jenkins. Warren I didn't know, but he was then directing at Cardiff.

Where it didn't work, to put it bluntly, was that he was not happy with the play and he was not happy with the company, which I think was the most extraordinary mixture of talents. There was a young Judy Cornwell, there was a youngish Ronnie Barker, as headstrong as Ronnie is now, a very talented Ronnie Stevens, who also wanted to go his own way; and Judy Campbell, who was a totally straight actress, and Diane Clare, totally straight – both in their way experienced. And then, in the middle of this, a very young actor straight from the provinces, thrown in as the lead, who was to dominate the whole thing; and a very young Chris Godwin also, playing the vicar and the pedestrian. The other member of the cast was Marie Lohr, a wonderful old lady who was actually the right age to play it – well, strictly she was too old to play it, she was in her seventies – and she gamely battled through the script, playing vigorous games of imaginary tennis, and broke her knee. So she was labouring under the most terrible handicap by the time we opened, with her knee strapped up. Anyway, that was the chemistry. That was the first thing: that the balance of cast and the director itself was wrong. The second thing that was wrong was that it was overproduced, and that far too much money was spent on it. Peter Rice, who'd done a lot of very nice designs for operas, came in and did some very, very decorative sets, none of which added to it. He added slides to a show that supposedly had to do with imagination.

The other thing I learned was that while theatre in the round can be quite small – every square inch of space is viable playing space – when you put something on to an equivalent quite small pros stage, there is no way you can get it all on. Warren had put in some very charming music by Vivian Ellis, which was totally wrong. I was looking for Ibert and Poulenc – those very French things. I wanted spiky little French tunes, and I was getting rather nice little English tunes. And the thing was rapidly becoming very chintzy and very charming. It was in fact, as I think one critic called it, a very gushy evening, very pretty, very winsome. I find Marcel Marceau slightly charming, but he opened the same week as us (which wasn't a very good omen), and by comparison his show was so butch it was unbelievable. We were fairytime, you know. If ever a show deserved to close, that one did.

IW: Were you able to rationalize it that way at the time? Were you sufficiently objective to do that?

AA: When a show goes wrong, it all goes wrong. I had actors coming and saying, 'You must get rid of this director.' We had emotional storms: the leading lady collapsed and cried all over me at the dress rehearsal. She was in a terrible state. Everything was dissolving and tensions were mounting.

IW: How old were you at this time?

AA: I was too young for that to happen. I was in my early twenties.

IW: Was Peter Bridge supportive?

AA: Like most producers, Peter wasn't able to help much in such a situation. He came in and made a few general suggestions for new jokes. But what we didn't want was new jokes: we wanted the old ones to be got right. I think the basic thing wrong was the ingredients. If you get the wrong ingredients, you can stir them round all you like, and shake them, but it isn't going to work. However, good things came of it.

IW: *Futtocks End*, the television film, grew out of it, didn't it?

AA: *Futtocks End*? Well, yes, but that was nothing to do with me. That was Ronnie Barker's. The best thing that came of *Whatnot* was that Michael Hordern's wife saw it and liked it, and some years later when Peter Bridge sent a script of *Relatively Speaking* to Michael to consider, his wife said, 'Oh, if it's by that man who wrote that play, it'll be wonderful. Do read it.' And it certainly helped in the cause. And a lot of people saw *Whatnot* who subsequently felt they really had jumped on it rather hard, and I've been lucky enough to get a sort of guilt vote back again.

IW: You revived it for the opening at Scarborough of what is now the Stephen Joseph Theatre. Is it due for any more revivals ever?

AA: No. I don't know that I should revive my plays. I think other people should do that.

IW: You gave up your job at Stoke to see the play into town, didn't you?

AA: Everyone had convinced me that this was going to be the big one. Again, young days. What one tries to say to writers is: wait.

IW: Yes. Why on earth had you given up your job, because you weren't directing the show, you weren't in the show in town?

AA: There were other reasons for leaving Stoke, although this provided a spur. The theatre was not able to contain both Peter Cheeseman and me. I was co-directing alongside him. I had been directing long before he joined – I'd probably been directing long before he started directing. And it was difficult for him to work with an associate director who in fact had introduced him to the round. And, as he developed – and he developed very fast – he got very strong ideas about what he wanted to do with that theatre, which didn't necessarily coincide with mine. The rift with Stephen didn't help, because he always felt, at that point (he certainly doesn't now) that I was a Stephen man and not a Cheeseman man.

IW: Surely the rift with Stephen didn't come until some time later?

AA: It was there early. Stephen asked me over to Scarborough one weekend from Stoke, and said to me, 'I want you to take over the theatre. I'm going to get rid of Peter.' And I said, 'I don't think I can do that.' It's something I've always been rather proud I said, because it was something I would love to have done, but I said, 'No, I don't think I can do that, Stephen, because I would actually lose all the people I'm working with.' It would have been such an act of awfulness, to have gone back and just ousted Peter – apart from the fact that I actually liked Peter very much and I did respect him, although I argued with him furiously about the round. But Stephen was obviously extremely frustrated and angry.

IW: What sort of arguments were you having with Peter? You say you argued with him incessantly about the round. Was this ideological?

AA: Yes, mainly. Peter was much more of an academic director and I, as it were, had risen through the ranks to direct. And I suppose it had something to do with my position as an actor–director. I was still in that peculiar position of acting in every other production, playing the lead more often than not, and then directing the next one. Peter didn't have that proximity. He just came in and directed every other play. Our main argument revolved around the fact that Peter believed essentially (and this is to put it a bit crudely) that no actor could do anything unless he fully understood the concept. That is to say, no actor could play a nuclear scientist unless he had read all the books about nuclear science. I said, 'No, that's not true: the most stupid actors can often play brilliant nuclear scientists. If the script is good, they convince you; and it isn't necessary always to break everything down and examine it to that extent, and iron out what is the truth.' And Stan Page and I, who were the two older-stagers, at the raw ages of about twenty-three and thirty, both insisted that there was such a thing as an actor's instinct, which must be allowed to flourish. Peter denied it, very strongly at that point, and said, 'No. If it isn't intellectually acceptable, then it can't be done emotionally.' And I suppose we shouted a lot about this.

Most of my work was done on the assumption that actors got there by instinct. Indeed, we had a boy in the company at that time – Peter King in fact – who worked entirely on instinct. He was, I think he would say himself, an extremely unschooled Welshman, who has since schooled himself enormously and read copiously and become really quite erudite. At that point, though, he could hardly join his letters together, and yet he remained a very fine instinctive actor. I think probably, in fact, his learning damned him as an actor. There is an old saying that a few coarse directors use: 'Give me a stupid actor and you'll find a good one.' And indeed, actors can be too clever for their own good. But Peter was a standing example of a man who could play anything. He could play Prime Minister, with a gravity and solemnity and authority, and apparent knowledge of politics which, of course, he didn't really have: he just had the script.

IW: How did Peter Cheeseman take this? Presumably he could see that Peter King could act?

AA: Yes, but he would say, 'Well, it's not true, because he doesn't. We know.' And I'd say, 'Well, no, but nobody else knows.' I suppose we were a little bit more showbiz than Peter. He was graduating rapidly towards the documentary, at that point, where he found it dramatic for real shop stewards to stand up and tell you about their day-to-day plight; which became dramatic because they were real shop stewards. I was moving rapidly in another direction.

IW: He was also moving towards the integration of actors into the community as ordinary members who ought to share the concerns of the community, wasn't he?

AA: Oh sure. It was the beginning of a very interesting rift. Are actors as other men, or are they not? I don't know. The public, I suspect, prefer them not to be.

IW: They'd rather have them glamorous, you mean?

AA: Yes. I run a theatre where the actors go and drink in the bar, but I'm sure that most of the public would love them to jump into the Rolls and steam off. They're all in variety now, those sorts of stars. There still are a few in Scarborough, and they're the people that the public is really fascinated by — when Danny La Rue arrives, there's a sort of air of glamour about. I think I believe a bit more in the illusion of theatre than Peter did, though he's come round to that more now. At that point we were poles apart: I think we're actually quite close now.

IW: Anyway, it was enough to push you out of the theatre.

AA: It was time to go. We all decided to go. New people were coming in, the old order was changing, you know. We were getting a bit dinosaur-like, really.

IW: So, you went to town, and you took this great critical drubbing. How — it's a daft question — but how hard did you actually take that critical reaction to *Mr Whatnot*?

AA: I took it very hard, actually. I was very, very upset, although I was cushioned by the fact that I sort of knew it was going to happen. But it was enough to stop me writing for quite a long time.

I gave up. I joined the BBC with no thought of writing again – certainly not for London or the stage.

IW: How did the radio job come about?

AA: Oh, that was funny. Everything happens by odd coincidences. I'd got an agent, of course, Peggy Ramsay, and I rang her a couple of days after *Whatnot* had opened, just for commiseration. Peggy is great on commiseration: she can bolster you up in no time. By chance, in the office was another client of hers at that time, Alfred Bradley (Senior Drama Producer for BBC North Region Radio), who was writing children's work mainly. He realized that his half-an-hour in London with Peggy was going to be absolutely wiped out if he allowed me to stay on the phone to her, because I needed half an hour at least with Peggy, while she told me that the critics were all bastards, and all that. So Alfred said, 'Get him off the phone. Tell him to write for the job.'

IW: You must have known Alfred at this time.

AA: Oh, I did, yes. Alfred I'd known because he'd come over and seen quite a few productions – mostly at Scarborough, some at Stoke. He was a friend of Stephen's. He said, 'Get him off the line. Tell him to apply for the job.' Peggy said, 'Alf's here.' I said, 'Alf who?' She said, 'Alf Bradley.' I said, 'Oh yes? Great.' She said, 'He says apply for the job in the *New Statesman*. Get a last week's *New Statesman*, and there's a good job in it, and he says you could stand a good chance if you apply.' And I said, 'Well, I . . .' 'Cheerio, now!' said Peggy, and, bang!, down went the phone. So I waited a few days, and then I thought, 'Oh well!' So I dug out an old *New Statesman*, and there was this job, so I wrote off. The BBC took ages and then they sent me an application form, and I wrote back again. And then I got the board. I travelled up to Leeds, got seen by this committee, and Alfred was very encouraging. I realized that they would interview the candidates and, provided they looked as if they weren't going to blow the building up, they would then ask Alfred which one he liked. At that point, I think I was probably the one with the most active directing experience, so he said to me, 'Well, unless Tyrone Guthrie applies, I think you're OK on the present showing.' Nicely the job did come my way with an astronomic salary. It was £38 a week: it was unbelievable.

IW: What were you being paid in the theatre at this time?

AA: Funnily enough, the highest I got to was in my swansong week as an actor at Rotherham, on £18. But at Stoke it was about £12.

IW: You stayed in the BBC for six years, but during that time Stephen Joseph coaxed you back into the theatre, didn't he, first as a writer and then as a director?

AA: Yes, Stephen asked me for a play for the 1965 summer season in Scarborough, and I did my well-made-play bit.

IW: That was *Meet My Father*, which, once again, Peter Bridge picked up for town. This time, though, he gave it a new title, *Relatively Speaking*, a cast with a chemistry which clearly worked wonderfully well – in Celia Johnson, Michael Hordern, Richard Briers and Jennifer Hilary – and it was a runaway success in the West End. I think a lot of people at that stage probably heaved a sigh of relief and said, 'Thank God! Ayckbourn's hit the winning formula at last.' Noël Coward sent you a telegram of congratulation after seeing the show, and you were clearly being groomed to assume his mantle. But your next show for Scarborough – to which Peter Bridge and Nigel Patrick (who had directed *Relatively*) came running – was *The Sparrow*, a straight chronological narrative, devoid of deft plot manipulation, about four distinctly unglamorous young people in a grotty flat. I suppose, in retrospect, it was the first of your more sour examinations of the state of marriage. It played to full houses during the summer in Scarborough, but I vividly remember – because I worked as stage director on the production – the brittle smile on Nigel Patrick's face as he greeted the actors after the show. 'Many congratulations!' he said to each of them in turn, and then moved grimly on as quickly as he could. He obviously couldn't get back to town fast enough! The show never made the West End.

AA: No. I don't believe, in retrospect, that it's as good a play as *Relatively*, but it's only had three weeks in its life, those three weeks at Scarborough. It's probably worth a little more than that.

At the time, the only reason it was suppressed was that somebody said it was a bit like *The Knack*. Since I hadn't seen *The Knack*, I didn't realize. I've seen *The Knack* since. It *is* a bit like *The Knack* — it's got a girl in the lead, that's what it was. But then, so has *Antony and Cleopatra*.

IW: And then came *How the Other Half Loves*, which got star-parted with Robert Morley and ran for ages. What did Morley do to it?

AA: Well, he started honestly enough: he did play it down the middle. He's an actor who rapidly gets very bored, and in order to refresh himself and to engage himself he always treats the theatre as one huge game organized by himself. The joy of the man is that he does have great enjoyment for what he does, an infectious, playful enthusiasm. Unfortunately, the people who suffer are the people who are on stage with him, or who are attempting to get on stage with him. And there's a few working actors ploughing doggedly through their script, clutching on to their characterization, which he almost delights in bombarding and trying to upset — hiding their props and locking the door and jumping out at them from cupboards. Which is all right but it tends to make them look awfully ropey. It also tends to make the play look a little bit ropey. In the case of *How the Other Half*, he tended to improvise round the theme quite a lot, but — because it was such a complex plot — he was unable to do perhaps as much as he would like to have done with it. I believe people like Peter Ustinov have rather stronger views about what he did to *Halfway up a Tree*, but with *How the Other Half*, I didn't actually go to see it after a bit, because there was no point in getting unnecessarily upset. I was a younger, more vulnerable author then. The night I did see it, I was terribly upset, because nothing seemed to be as we had originally arranged it.

IW: Did you clash with him personally?

AA: I would have done if I'd been stronger and had the nerve. I would do now, certainly. At that point, I was a very new author with a very new play, and I tended to sit rather quietly and weep in corners. But certainly the director, Robin Midgley, clashed with him on notable occasions before we opened — not necessarily with Robert, but with what Robert wanted. The trouble with Robert's area of interest is that it doesn't stop at his own performance. He was very insistent that, for instance, his leading lady should play it this way, and that somebody else should play it that way. He is in a sense an actor-manager. He wanted all the parts played as he wanted to play it. Now that wasn't necessarily the way that Robin wanted them or I wanted them. Fiona, in *How the Other Half*, is really a quite vicious character: she's not as vicious as some of her later versions, but she's an unfaithful wife who deceives her husband and plays a very sly game. Robert wouldn't have any of that. Her attitude to her husband up to the end was one of crushing and withering sarcasm a lot of the time. Robert insisted that anyone who was on stage with him should look as if they loved him; so, luckless Joan Tetzel and more luckless Jan Holden were forced to play against what the character was actually doing. I remember him quite vehemently saying, 'Look, nobody wants to come to the theatre and see people squabbling' – which dismissed about three-quarters of English drama, I should have thought. But he said, 'We don't want all these nasty cross people, and people shouting at each other.' A lot of *How the Other Half Loves* is about people getting extremely angry with each other, and when you get into the realms of Bob and Terry, whose whole relationship is teetering on the edge of disaster, and you start laying down the law and saying, 'No, you must love each other', then you aren't left with a lot of the mainspring of the play. In that sense the quarrel was there, but as to his performance, he turned in a lovely performance of Frank. If he'd actually had the courage to stick to the script – or perhaps the faith to stick to the script – a little bit more closely, it could have been an even better one. But I learned one great maxim from Robert, and that was that you can't argue with the system. Eighty per cent of that audience had paid to see Robert Morley, and I, as an unknown dramatist, had really no right to stand between that process if I wanted to take the money. If I could have suffocated Robert to the extent of preventing him from doing his own thing, I think I would have actually offended many punters. They would have walked away awfully offended.

IW: Though it needs to be said that by this time you were already through *Relatively Speaking*, which had been a tremendous success.

AA: Well, it was only my second. But the lesson itself was learned even more vigorously and vividly with *Me Times Me* when Celia Johnson toured it, with Roland Culver. Celia was, quite naturally, the star of the evening and had, rather against her better judgement, accepted the part due to the soft-forked tongue of Michael Codron, who had promised her the moon if she came into it. And she'd agreed, with fond memories, I think, of *Relatively*, which was a great performance by her. The part was considerably smaller, the stage time that she occupied was quite small. We took it on a tour, which included Brighton. In Brighton, again 80 per cent of the audience came to see Celia Johnson. But they didn't see Celia Johnson: they saw seven or eight other actors, with occasional appearances by Celia Johnson, and you could feel the temperature drop in that theatre when she went off. They said, 'Oh, this can't be an important scene because the star isn't on.' And I learned very quickly that, if you're going to have a star, it's got to be in a star part. There's actually quite a damaging thing in trying to persuade a star to play a part that isn't a star part. It seems quite an obvious truism, but you have to learn it the hard way.

IW: Yes, once again, *Me Times Me* never made it to the West End, despite going out on tour twice – though Sam Walters revived it as *Family Circles* at the Orange Tree in Richmond in 1978. You don't write star parts; you said that before.

AA: No.

IW: And, really, *How the Other Half Loves* was rehabilitated by the Actors Company, wasn't it?

AA: Yes, it was quite recently with Moray Watson, Barbara Murray, Stephanie Turner and Simon Cadell. It was very good; it was done by the right people. In fact, it restored the play. A lot of critics re-reviewed it – or critics who weren't around when it was first done, including people like Levin, I think, and Cushman, certainly – and it got nice notices, and it was very nice to see the old play restored. One of the most extraordinary things about the whole West End experience, the first time around, was that while it contained elaborately sophisticated time shifts, and was an extraordinary piece of staging – with that superimposed stage – not a single critic, to my knowledge, ever mentioned it. So something had got blurred! It's not normal, I'd have thought – it certainly wasn't normal in our time – for people to do English light comedy with superimposed time scales and, at one point, there were three sets of people on stage, two of them living at different time levels and one pair living at both time levels. It really is quite complicated, and nobody even mentioned it.

IW: *How the Other Half* introduced you to Broadway, didn't it?

AA: Yes. It was an experiment. *Relatively* had never come off in America, because I'd quarrelled vigorously with their attempts to Americanize it. In this one, I did meet a marvellous man called Gene Saks who was directing it, and with whom I hit it off immediately. We sat down, and with his advice I Americanized the script myself. It didn't help the play, in retrospect. At the time it was a very painless way to do it, because he just said, 'We would say that round the other way.' And as we did it, slowly we began to thin the language out and narrow down the subtleties. Sometimes he would add something very useful, but he was not a writer, he was a director, and I was not fluent in American. So the version was an unhappy compromise in many ways, although it worked, up to a point. The plot was the strong thing, and the machinations of that, and that certainly worked. We had a very good cast. It had a good tour, but it rose and fell really on its first night on Broadway, and it didn't pass the post. It got a lukewarm review from Clive Barnes, who at that point was the be-all and end-all of New York, and it ran a hundred performances, with a little help from its producers, which was quite respectable. It wasn't enough to make it any sort of money, but it didn't do me too much harm, personally. And it certainly restored Phil Silvers, who went on to do bigger and better things.

But I wouldn't want to ever go round on tour again with a pre-New York run. The tensions are enormous. There's so much at stake, a fantastic amount at stake, in money and in reputations. You see American actors, particularly the less starry ones, who realize that a Broadway chance may come once, and it matters so much. The most painful part was the auditioning for the smaller parts, particularly for the girl playing Mary. We chose a girl called Jeanne Hepple eventually. We went through an enormous number of girls, and it was heartbreaking the amount it mattered to them:

there were tears and all sorts of things. It's not very nice, auditioning, anyway, saying, 'Sorry, but no.' But in this case, because we wanted to be sure, we kept calling people back, then we got down to two. By that time, they were bringing their own props, their own costumes, changing in the loo and everything, and we both, Gene and I, sat there when we'd finished and chosen Jeanne and we were so depressed we got absolutely smashed at Frankie and Johnnie's. 'What an awful business we're in,' said Gene.

IW: How was Phil Silvers?

AA: Well, Phil was an amazing figure. This is the fate of the star system: Robert Morley having shaped the play as it was, we then looked for a man to play it on Broadway. And eventually, after going through an awful lot of people, somebody came up with the idea of Phil Silvers. He had disappeared for a bit; he hadn't been in the public eye. Sergeant Bilko he was still well loved for, and he'd got one or two Broadway successes like *Top Banana* under his belt, but that was some time ago, and nobody knew much about him. We found out about Phil that he was (a) an extremely nervous man and (b) an extremely nice man. But he'd had some form of nervous breakdown. He'd had – what can I call it? – a relapse, anyway. His marriage had broken up and it had upset him enormously, and he'd got a lot of daughters, all of whom he adored and never saw, because he wasn't allowed to. Anyway, he saw in this a chance – and I think everyone else saw in it a chance for him – to reconstitute himself. But it was a bit therapeutic, like all these occasions.

First of all, what had gone was his memory: he couldn't remember any of the lines. *How the Other Half* was a tour I followed very, very closely. I was with the play more than I would ever be nowadays – I know better. I came over for the early rehearsals and Gene Saks was a man who worked day and night really hard. Anyway, I left them in the early part of rehearsals, and it all looked pretty good. I came back at the beginning of the last week and I saw a run, and it didn't look any different from when I left it. So Gene and I went out and had a cup of coffee, and he said, 'What do you think?' And I said, 'Well, er, what's been going on for three weeks?' He sat there for a very long time and I thought I'd really upset him. He suddenly thumped the table and said, 'I don't know what's been going on for three weeks. What the blazes *has* been going on for three weeks?' He said, 'Nothing's been going on for three weeks! I'm going to go in there and tell them nothing's been going on for three weeks.' So he went back and said, 'Listen! This man has come back from England, and he's just said, "Nothing's been going on for three weeks." We're opening in a week, for God's sake.' And it turned out that one of the things that hadn't been happening for three weeks was that Phil hadn't learned his lines yet. They'd delegated an associate director to work with him – a man who crops up a lot in my life: he first cropped up as Peter Bridge's assistant, then turned up as Gene Saks's assistant, and is now Peggy Ramsay's assistant, Tom Erhardt. Tom is like a sort of lucky mascot; he turns up in various disguises. At this point he was in his native America, assisting Gene Saks. And assisting Gene Saks mainly meant sitting up with Phil Silvers every night and hearing his lines, until he was absolutely cross-eyed with them. Phil was in an extremely neurotic state. We found he was taking valium, which wasn't helping.

The first date on the tour was Palm Beach, the Playhouse there. And we'd got Phil as far as the third act, the last scene. So we had three scenes which we felt he could get through, with a little bit of help from his friends, but after that . . . So we said, 'Well, OK, we'll get there. We can rely on the prompter for a week.' Palm Beach has the reputation of being the worst place anywhere. The whole audience is made up of socialites, all of whom leave after interval: they never see the second half. The thing was that their chauffeurs were ordered back at the interval. They'd have their champagne reception when they were photographed extensively, and then they'd all leave. It was a terrible place. But it was my first taste of Florida, and it was very interesting to get there, suddenly zooming out of New York – in I suppose it was January – into sunshine.

We were a little flummoxed when we saw the stage, because it did not allow for a prompter. It was, like a lot of American stages, about 180 feet across. It was enormously wide, with an enormous forestage, and a big, billowing curtain like a maternity dress that came round the front. There was nowhere that you could have a prompter without a loud hailer, because the prompt corner was miles from the centre of the stage. So we looked at it, and this very old producer we had, called Michael Myerberg – one of those men who would be played by Gabby Hayes, you know, and who'd seen everything before; a marvellous old boy, but one of those men who just couldn't be told – said, 'Well, we'll cut a hole in the forestage.' But the carpenter said, 'No, you can't cut a hole in the forestage: it's aluminium. It's an aluminium stage. You're cutting through pure aluminium there.' Myerberg said, 'I don't care about the cost. We're having a trap, like an opera box, in the front of the stage.' So they cut this hole, amidst great protest, and down into this hole went Tom Erhardt with the book, because we'd made no allowance for a prompter. And when he went down this hole, he was down there from the beginning to the end, because there was no way he could get out. Well, Tom is blond and fair and thinning, and when they put the lights on, you had this bright, shining head in the middle of the forestage, and it looked slightly prominent! Everyone said, 'What's that?' Myerberg said, 'We've got to darken down his head: it's reflecting the light.' So Tom was equipped with a black beret, which made him look not unlike a Provisional IRA man, crouching in a slit trench. And there he is with his script when we get to the first night. Phil's going great guns: he's doing very well. And the play is going so well that quite a lot of the chauffeurs are actually told to hold on at the interval. And the manager is ecstatic. But to show the sort of people they were, they'd actually failed to reserve a seat for the director or the author: we had nowhere to sit. Gene was furious. He said, 'How are we going to get this play right when we're not allowed to see it?' So there's a great kerfuffle. He said, 'I demand that the author and I see the first night. We want to see it. We want to know how to do the second night!' So they find us a place, and it's way, way up behind the front-of-house lights, which are in a sort of loft. Behind wire mesh we sat crouching by these big beasts that were burning up – 5000 kilowatt lamps! – sweating and peering through the mesh, clinging on, feeling slightly giddy, and we were back, a long way back. And the big maternity dress draws round again in the scene change before the last scene, and it's a thin dress, it's not a thick curtain. And you can hear through the curtain Phil's voice shouting down to Tom in his hole, 'I need you now, baby!' Which, of course, comes ringing into the auditorium.

We'd had one marvellous incident just before that, when Bernice Massi, who played Fiona, had brought on the frigadella and served it, and parked her trolley without allowing for the rake. It had rolled away from her, very slowly tipped off the end of the forestage and covered two of the most beautiful American people – a blonde in a strapless evening dress and her escort in full dinner jacket – covered them in frigadella. That was tremendous, and that stopped the show for some minutes while they mopped themselves down and put this whole trolley back on the stage. The audience loved that, they thought it was terrific. They thought it was meant.

So, the curtains drew and Phil starts the last scene, and certainly cues are coming thick and fast and people are covering, and then he gets to one line, which was one of those lines that nobody could help him on. He says, 'Well, I . . . I . . . I . . . think, Bob, that . . . I think, Bob, that . . . that . . .' And Tom, the prompter, is not a prompter. There's a great art in prompting, to give the right key word and to give it quickly and cleanly. And Tom has a very loud voice, and a very slow voice. So Tom gives him, 'Possibly.' Phil, by then, you can see, has got buzzing noises in his ears, and he couldn't hear if you actually screamed it at him. He said, 'I think . . . I think, Bob . . . I . . . I . . .' And Tom's voice comes again, equally loudly, 'Possibly!' 'Just that . . . I think . . . I think, Bob . . . er . . . you know, Bob . . .' And a man, right at the back of the theatre shouts, 'Possibly!' Gene says, 'Oh my God, the audience are prompting him now!' At the end of the show, we walked round and round the block. Phil was prostrate. 'The humiliation! I'm a man who made millions laugh on *Bilko*.' 'It's all right, Phil, don't worry, we all have bad nights.' 'Bad night! I've been prompted by the audience!'

Eventually we get into Washington, and he's pretty well on the script, he's looking good. But by this time, he's being such a menace that nobody actually wants to know Phil, because he keeps telling you about his problems. So I'm with Phil a lot of the time. And I'm not sure if it is the Daughters of the American Revolution, but it's something similar, who have a luncheon, which they customarily invite the stars of the National Theater, Washington, to come along to. So they want, obviously, the lovely Mr Silvers and somebody else. The short straw is drawn and I get it, and I go with Phil. I said, 'Look, Phil is there. Phil will stand up. Phil will do the talk. You just sit there. And all Phil will forget to mention is that there's a show on. You tell them the dates, and where we're playing, and the ticket prices, and where they can buy tickets.' So I'm sitting next to Phil, and the chairwoman gets up – and Phil, I can see, is going into one of his lows. She says, 'Ladies, we have here today a man who I think can honestly be described as one of the funniest men in America, if not in the world. I'm very, very proud to present Mr Phil Silvers.' Applause. Phil got up. He always wore his glasses with his contact lenses below them, because he was always recognized as Bilko, but he didn't need to wear them. He took off his glasses and said, 'Ladies, I know you think of me as one of the funniest men in America, and I thank you for it. But underneath this, I'm a very sad and lonely man. I suppose any man who had four darling little girls, all of whom he adored and is now unable to see . . .' And he went on in this vein. '. . . and a wife who refuses to let him see them, so he's left alone in a hotel room . . .' And there's a drawing out of handkerchiefs, and mascara is running, and sniffing. Phil goes on for some ten minutes in this vein. The funniest man in America reduces the entire audience to tears. He says, 'All I can say is, if any of you are mothers who have children, God bless you. I love you all. Thank you.' And sits down. And then he turns to me, and he says, 'Knock 'em dead, baby!' I floundered on, but nobody could revive that audience.

Later on, I got very fond of Phil. Just before we went into New York, Sandy Dennis said, 'We must do something about Phil. He looks so terrible. He dresses so badly. Can't we get him into some decent clothes?' Phil's heard this eventually and he's very hurt. So we're driving into New York. He said, 'You realize you're working with a man who's unbalanced. I mean, I am unbalanced, I admit it.' I said, 'No, you're not unbalanced, Phil. You're nervous, because you're going into New York and you don't know what's going to happen to you.' He said, 'I tell you I'm unbalanced.' I said, 'No, you're not.' He said, 'What man who wasn't unbalanced would wear this tie with these socks?'

He opened, and the play got reasonable reviews. He was very good eventually, but it was such hard work to get Phil to that pitch. What one was pleased about was that we reconstituted a very funny artist. I saw him some three years later, still the fall guy. He was playing in Bournemouth – *A Funny Thing Happened on the Way to the Forum*. And I happened to be there, visiting my kids at school. I said, 'It can't be Phil Silvers.' And I went along, and there was old Phil, with an audience, I suppose, a quarter full, giving absolutely everything. It was a super evening. And so I whistled round to see him. Kenneth Tynan was also round there. He knew Phil and admired him. I said, 'Terrific to see you. I'd no idea you were in Bournemouth.' He said, 'Well, there's been a foul-up, baby. You see, I'd understood I was coming over here to tour prior to a West End appearance.' I said, 'Oh, you're going to bring this into town?' He said, 'Well, I understood this.' I said, 'But it's been in, with Bob Monkhouse.' He said, 'I know. I didn't find that out till I got to Norwich.' Poor old Phil.

The Business of Writing

IAN WATSON: You schedule a new play up to a year ahead, don't you? How much do you know at that stage about what the play's going to be?

ALAN AYCKBOURN: I have an idea. As soon as I've finished a play – once I finished, say, *Suburban Strains*, I was raring to go on another, keyed up and ready. You get on a tremendous high – I do – from writing, when you think, 'Wow! I can write for ever!' Actually, somebody at the back of you says, 'Oh no, you can't!' But nevertheless, that's the time I schedule the next one and say, 'I must get another one done.' And at that point there's a few sketched ideas. It may be off-the-shelf ideas.

IW: What do you mean by that? Things you've filed away over the years?

AA: Filed away. The *Taking Steps* idea was an idea that had been on that bloody shelf for years. The thing that was missing was the three floors. Once I'd got the three floors, then the other idea went *dooiing!* – about a man whose wife left him and another guy read the farewell letter. It sounds like the crudest idea in the world, but that was the nub of the whole play.

IW: So at what stage do you decide that you're going to take something off the shelf, or look for something totally new?

AA: Not until I get there.

IW: In the intervening period, which one might think of as a gestation period and which can indeed be exactly nine months, nothing happens, does it? You don't start making notes or drawing complicated plans?

AA: No. I usually treasure a sort of surrogate child, who gets thrown out of the nest as the time gets closer. I say, 'This is a wonderful idea.' I get closer to it, and the wonderful idea suddenly, as I sit down with a new sheet of paper, appears to be nothing but useless. And then I scramble round for the other idea that may have been lurking behind it. I've sat down with certain ideas time and again and never written them. I've written the idea that's been behind them. Things keep happening. Things add to an idea. It feels like a stone and it rolls, and little things stick on it. I need about eight ideas – well, not quite eight, but I need several – to make a play. I'm not happy when there's just one sitting there. For instance, take the example I gave you about *Taking Steps*: I'm not happy when I just have an idea about a wife leaving a man and him inviting another bloke in to read the letter. I need two more, like the bedrooms, and the man who drives everyone to sleep, and when I've got those three going together, then I think, 'Now we'll be able to get something to happen. Now the chemistry's flowing for a play, as opposed to a sketch.' And often the ideas I've got are sketch ideas: they don't attract other ideas like chemistry. So I dump them or shelve them until such time as they attract little friends, who together make a whole! That seems to be what happens. And it's often just a matter of assembling the right sequence of things together.

IW: Have you got any formula for getting these ideas in the first place? Presumably they accrete quite in spite of yourself a lot of the time. But where do they come from in the first place?

AA: God knows. They come in the most extraordinary ways. But I forget a lot of them actually.

IW: You don't write them down?

AA: No. I'm just annoyed at the moment, as I'm talking to you: something wonderful struck me the other day, and I can't remember what the hell it was. Ah, never mind, it'll come back.

IW: You don't often lose them forever?

AA: It's somewhere locked in here. Somewhere. The trouble is, because I don't tell anyone else, I can't actually check it! I always suspect that a new one will pop up if it's right.

IW: Most of your plays, quite apart from their ostensible subject matter, got a very strong craft element in them. On one level at least, they're about the whole nature of theatrical artifice. The sort of things I'm thinking of are the combination stagescape, as in

How the Other Half Loves and *Taking Steps*; equally the dumb-show in Act II of *Absurd Person Singular*, which is actually credible only as a stage device. Is it possible to separate the craft element from the evolution of the plays themselves? In other words, when the play's germinating, do you tend to work from thematic ideas or from some technical challenge that you've got to overcome?

AA: Well, they seem to go together; I think *how* to tell the story to me is always very important. And I always look for new ways. I am peculiarly attracted to the stage. Probably more than most writers, I write exclusively for one medium. I love the permutations that it possesses and I love exploring them. And particularly I'm fascinated by things like how it presents time, and how its space can be changed, and the peculiarity which it possesses that, when you warp time on stage, you're warping time for an audience as well as for the actors – you're doing it positively, in front of people's eyes. It's not like television when one's used to jumping three years. On stage, the way you do it is much more immediate. All these elements are very important. And I think, in the best plays, the idea and the technique come together. One wants to write something, the idea is glimmering, then the how presents itself – how do I tell this story? In *Sisterly Feelings*, I wanted to write about choice, and then came the thought that this was the time to use that particular device, precisely because it was about choice.

IW: The device of tossing the coin?

AA: Tossing the coin and choosing, and thus varying the play. I'm also, I suppose, reacting to my own peculiar theatre, where I couldn't have written *Rookery Nook* even if I'd wanted to, because I haven't got any doors. And so I've got to find some farcical equivalent. The thing with plays is selection: you've got to find how to tell your story best. It may be you do it with one set, continuous action (as in *Absent Friends*), and real time (moving from point A to, an hour and a half later, point B – that's the simplest). Then there are things like *Suburban Strains*, where I wanted to tell a very complex story – well, it's actually very simple, but I wanted to highlight it in a different way. I've always had this ambition to run parallel times, and here was the chance to do that, by starting a story simultaneously in the middle and at the beginning and running parallel.

IW: The technique is basically filmic there, isn't it?

AA: Yes, a lot of my stuff is obviously filched from film. The thing about film is that it's developed its own tense flexibility: what I do is pre-edit, as it were, with plays. I'm fascinated by techniques and by being aware that what I want to say is relatively simple, that is, it's usually telling about people and about their relationships. In order to throw any light – or at least fresh slants – it's necessary to find new ways to tell the stories.

IW: I wonder if there's a risk involved. Thinking again of *Absurd Person Singular*, which is a play about social reversal – social and professional reversal – is there any danger that the use of tricks, which is basically what the second act was, can in some way devalue what it is you're saying through the theme of the play? In other words, is there a danger that the craft can negate the theme of the play, simply by being too bloody clever?

AA: Oh yes, I think so. One's in this Scylla and Charybdis situation, because if I tell my stories terribly solemnly and seriously, or without any of this stuff, nobody wants to see them. I've really got to make them entertaining. I've really got to make them eye-catching, not in a garish sense, but in an absorbing sense so that people say, 'Golly, I was held from beginning to end.' And it's up to me to employ whatever technical resources I have; but I always try to be extremely careful that the technical resources do not deny the characters their true destinies. I hope that they always proceed with a certain dignity, so that their destinies are fulfilled without unnecessary author's interruptions and awful detours in order to get cheap laughs. I hope that rarely do characters say things that they would not normally say, in order to make a laugh. A lot of my writing is involved in actually avoiding such tempting moments, when you could, for the sake of five more lines, get a very big laugh, but would then leave the character without one leg to stand on later in the scene – I'm desperately trying to avoid these moments. If I do use a device, I hope it enhances rather than detracts, that's all I can say.

IW: The classic example of that was the device which came halfway through the writing of *Absurd Person Singular*. What happened there? You started by setting it in the sitting room?

AA: Yes, and swapped it to the kitchen. That comes back to selection. The whole of playwriting for me is, if you like: you get your idea, you get your sequence of events – which, if written literally, would take, say, four days at least to perform on stage – and you then have to select what you want your audience to see, preferably the minimum to allow them to understand the events. It seems to me that economy in writing is more and more desirable. If you could tell a story or draw a picture with four lines, then so be it, let's do it, let's make it the ultimate short story. Unfortunately, no one's quite clever enough – certainly I'm not clever enough – to do that yet.

IW: I suppose one of the great paradoxes about you – since I guess you're probably the most prolific living playwright in English – is that you spend very little time indeed actually writing, don't you? You spend – what? – at most about two weeks over the writing of a play?

AA: I lay aside four and write for two.

IW: And you don't work from notes made over a longer period. Can we just take it step by step? What occurs during your period of creative retreat? First of all, you pay all the bills, you shut the doors, close the windows and you don't see anyone. Is that right?

AA: Yes. I say, 'Look, loves. I'm out of commission for a month.' I suppose for about the first week or ten days I don't do anything very much. I wander around and read and sharpen pencils, watch telly. I do all the normal things – fix shelves, things like that. I go for walks, moon around . . .

IW: Is this a thought process?

AA: Yes, a thought process; a sort of sifting process, really.

IW: It's not just avoiding the issue?

AA: It is avoiding the issue, partly, yes. But it's also knowing it's going to come, but there's no hurry. That's the sort of feeling.

IW: Well how do you know it's going to come, and why is there no hurry? Because manifestly there is, when at this stage you're already scheduled to get into rehearsal on a specific date at a specific hour in four weeks' time. Why are you not suffering the most appalling pressures and taking all sorts of tranquillizing medicaments?

AA: Well, one's worrying, in a sort of way. But I know that there's no way I'd start a play four weeks before it's due to go on. That just isn't the way I write. I know I've got to be within single figures of the opening date before there's any chance. So, really, with twenty-eight days, I've got eighteen days at least to go before I start to write.

IW: Why?

AA: I don't know. I've got to finish it just before it starts.

IW: You can't start it earlier and take longer over the process?

AA: No. If I get time for rethinking – I'm a really ferocious critic of my own work, I really am – I would destroy it. There's no way it would survive if it didn't have to survive just in order for there to be something there.

IW: Right, so you're pottering around, watching television and putting shelves up and so on. And getting irritable?

AA: A bit. Not too bad, to start with. I usually have a notepad at hand on which I draw primitive designs. Probably the shape I'm working on is the shape of the aforesaid original idea, that I was thinking about eight months ago and trying to work. Nine times out of ten, that idea will be jettisoned like some old skin, and I just hope to God there's something underneath. Occasionally, I then have a frenzied ferret through the shelves of my mind for other previously rejected ideas which suddenly spring forward – as, after desperate raking, I came across the old *Taking Steps* idea which had been thrown out before. An idea keeps popping up like a weed in the garden: you lop its head off and next year back it is again! There are other times when I'm actually much more committed to an idea, as with *Bedroom Farce*. I was committed to writing a play

[73]

about bedrooms, though I didn't actually know what to write about bedrooms until I started.

IW: How, committed?

AA: Well, I'd said I wanted to write about bedrooms and I'd announced the title.

IW: The title's something I wanted to ask you about, because the first thing anyone ever hears of any of your plays is the title, which seems to come at a very early stage of your retreat.

AA: Yes.

IW: And some of your tiles are very weird anyway. Though they're very memorable as titles, they don't necessarily have anything very much to do with what's in the play. You once told me that *Absurd Person Singular* was actually the title of a totally different play; you kept the title and changed the play.

AA: Yes, I liked the title.

IW: It's a smashing title, but it hasn't actually got anything to do with the play. Do you think of the titles as a totally separate game?

AA: Sometimes. Some of them are quite easy to come by, and some of them are more difficult. Sometimes the titles arrive halfway through the play, sometimes they arrive before the play's even thought of. It depends. *Joking Apart* was before the play was thought of; *Bedroom Farce* way before the play was written; *Suburban Strains* halfway through; *Taking Steps* – oh yes – after it had started, so, in fact, quite apt.

IW: Do you have a deadline when you say, 'Right, I'm actually going to sit down, and that paper in front of me is going to start being filled'?

AA: I have two or three nights when I realize I'm getting very close. It's always nights. I don't start until the sun's gone down, probably ten o'clock at night.

IW: And you write through the night?

AA: I try to. I tend to get later and later. Probably, the first night, I sit down at ten and go to bed at two, very disgruntled because I've written nothing. The next night, after a frustrating day moping around, I sit down at ten and I might work till three, and still have written nothing. And then one night, I might write half an act, a third of a play; it depends how it goes. Normally, I probably start quite slowly – write a quarter of a play; if the play isn't working, I tend to start the second draft before I've finished the first, in an attempt to shake it.

IW: That is all in longhand, is it?

AA: The first draft is in longhand. But, for instance, with *Ten Times Table*, I was getting very stuck. I was into page 90 on my foolscap, thinking, 'I can't get this clear.' So I said to Heather, my assistant, 'I think I'll want to dictate tonight.' Heather always keeps herself clear. And so we sat down and I started to dictate from the notes, through all the dialogue. And that's the second draft.

IW: How different is it from the first draft?

AA: Oh, vastly. Unrecognizable. You can pick up a page and, if you could read it, you might recognize where it came from in the play – you might not.

IW: You dictate it to Heather, and Heather types it straight off.

AA: Yes, quite slowly. What might happen is that she types during the night, she goes to bed, and by that time – I've found of late – I can actually work during the daytime. I sit down and write, perhaps, some more during the day.

IW: Of the first draft?

AA: Yes, and then dictate it to her as a second draft. That's quite a nice way of working: it's less lonely. I'm always finding ways not to be quite so alone writing. As soon as I can get on to the second draft, I'm actually kidding myself that I've finished it. Although, of course, I haven't. In fact, I've been known quite often to throw out a whole act of a second draft and the thing remains very fluid until the moment when it's bound and delivered. Anyway the excitement from doing the second draft stimulates me into doing more of the first draft. And actually talking about the characters, there come points when you *can* talk about the play. I remember having dictated the second draft of the first act of *Absurd Person Singular* and Heather asking, 'Where are we going next?' I said, 'We're going into the Jacksons' kitchen, and I thought I'd have this dog outside the door.' By that stage, one is sharing the idea. Then I went off and wrote that. That was a strange play. I wrote that while I was rehearsing during the day. I was much younger then.

IW: Rehearsing what?

AA: I was rehearsing the first play of the Scarborough season, called *Carmilla*, by David Campton. *Absurd Person* was the second play to go in. I remember going into a rehearsal of *Carmilla* and saying, 'Anybody know any forfeits?' And somebody said, 'Orange between the knees.' And I said, 'Oh, thanks very much!' People in the cast wondered what was going on! That's how that was done. So that's the second draft: dictation.

IW: And you get right the way through and finish the play in second draft form?

AA: Yes. It's then a pile of typescript. Then I have to brace myself because we're getting very near, probably, to rehearsal by now.

IW: In fact, you might be there by now.

AA: Yes, I might be, indeed, into the first day. I then sit down and read it through. Probably there's quite a lot to do on it – not vast rewrites in the sense that we pull out fifty pages, but every page has probably got something to be altered on it. I generally find this with dictating. Occasionally it's very good for effect, but obviously you don't want to use the same word eight times in a sentence, just because you're not aware what you've said, or because you've lost the thread.

IW: Do you do the voices and the accents as you dictate?

AA: Yes, I tend to. I certainly soften off on the women. Heather says occasionally, 'I can always hear the way you dictated that: they never played it quite the same.' Fortunately, I personally lose those rhythms very quickly, otherwise it would be unbearable to work with an actor on them. That's the crucial draft, the dictated one, and that just takes off.

IW: And the third draft is . . .

AA: Correction. Musing upon it, shaping it, clearing up the odd bit, clarifying it. Correcting silly things, like calling a bloke Gordon in the first act and Geoffrey in the second — little things like that. And then, just the duplication.

IW: And how sacrosanct is the script thereafter? Is it freeze-dried or is the company allowed — do you allow yourself — to make revisions within rehearsal?

AA: It very rarely changes, I must say. I suppose, to be fair, the actors are rather wary now. At one stage, when I was very new, the actors wanted to change everything. They all wanted to put their three ha'p'orth in. Now they learn my spelling mistakes! So I have to say, 'No, no, I didn't actually mean that, love. That's the name of the play next week — it got printed at the bottom by mistake!' Of course there are occasions when I change things. But I have the same attitude to my plays as I suppose someone who's just finished a picture must have — that the composition is as it is because it is as it is. While I was writing it, I very carefully put my figures in this particular landscape in this particular order. And one must assume certain things: my technique by now must be fairly good, and therefore the figures are recognizable, and if they're there where they are, it's because that's how I painted them. In a sense, if I have to do something radical like move a figure, I'd sooner rewrite the play. So, no, nothing gets changed very much in rehearsal. Things get clarified, things get explored. There are occasionally additions, as when I took *Absent Friends* away and wrote two or three pages; in the case of *Just Between Ourselves* I inserted a whole scene.

IW: In rehearsal?

AA: After it had been read. There's a scene in Act II with Pam and Dennis, in which she says, 'Do you think I'm attractive, Dennis?' And he replies, 'Ah, well, I'd certainly fancy you, but I'm a married man.' That scene wasn't there initially. I don't quite know how it worked without it, but at the time that's how it was. I think what happens sometimes is that something's in my head but it's not on the page! That was a very odd case of a whole scene I certainly thought I'd written: I looked and it wasn't there. The actors read it quite happily, but I think they might have questioned it when they started to work on it.

In *Absent Friends* I rewrote something that didn't work. I wrote something rather sentimental by mistake and snatched it back, then wrote the proper scene: the scene between Paul and Colin towards the end. If I make my character voluble and eloquent, I'm always doomed. I gave Paul a sort of manic laugh, which did the whole thing for me and said what I wanted to say. That's where one learns about playwriting, to say, 'Oh, come on, the audience already knows that, you've told them that.' The nice thing is to spread clues and spread them quite thinly, and allow the audience to gather them. I think an audience responds to that. It's a joy to put something down, then see it picked up. And maybe you don't know it's being picked up until twenty minutes later, when some reference is made and the audience reacts. You say, 'They did get that. That's marvellous!' And you're never quite sure. You hope they do, and you set it up so that it should work.

There's a very interesting example in *Bedroom Farce*, I remember, which you could perhaps say is a crude one. Trevor goes into the bedroom at the end, and Kate says, 'Look what Malcolm made for me.' And it's that chest of drawers. We did it on the first night – and we'd pissed ourselves laughing in rehearsal about this collapsing chest of drawers – and Chris Godwin crossed to it and picked it up, and it all fell to bits. And there's a very desultory laugh. And we said, 'What happened? What happened to our expensive prop and no laugh?' Then it occurred to me that you must give the audience just enough time to anticipate what he was going to do. What was going on in their minds could never be capped by what was going to happen to four pieces of timber. So on the second night, I just said, 'Be nearer that piece of furniture and put your hands on it *before* . . . and then they're with you.' And he did that and it was a belter.

IW: Yes, the alternative to that, of course, is the second act of *Absurd Person Singular*, where everybody in the audience knows, a full twenty minutes before it happens, that someone's going to get drenched underneath that sink, because you set that one up. Yet when it eventually happens, it's at a beautiful moment.

AA: Yes, that's always fun. Try and mislead them twice, and then make out you're not going to play the gag, then do it. *Taking Steps* is full of running gags – there are thousands of them, all running at once. Somebody called them repetitive, which I thought was a bit rude. But audiences love running gags.

IW: When you talk about your writing, you sound as if you're not terribly fond of it and writing is actually just another way of directing.

AA: Well, I don't like a lot of writing. When things are working, it's extraordinary. And quite often I find when I'm writing a play, for the first half I'm spewing out things which I then reap later. Mark, in *Taking Steps*, for example, has a characteristic where, whenever he talks earnestly and seriously about his relationship, everybody else falls asleep: his voice gets duller and duller. It's sort of tragic and slightly removed from the truth, but none the less everyone knows people like that – you are aware they are talking seriously but your mind wanders. So here he is, this tragic man, who is doomed like some Ancient Mariner to see people nodding off as he speaks, and I thought, 'This is fun.' So I put him into the first scene. I had no idea how I was going to use it again, but was joyous when I got later on, into a scene where Roland has taken sleeping pills and they have to keep him awake, and I said, 'Oh! I've got a man who sends people to sleep in this scene! This is wonderful!' I was so pleased that the two elements had been on collision course, but I had no idea when I started the play that would happen. That was terribly enjoyable.

But on the whole it's a lone and boring business. I don't know how novelists manage, because they never get to share their business with anybody. I actually get in there – admittedly, I also stand to be knocked down – with a group of actors. You share your writing with them and discuss it and work it and, hopefully, if things are going well, they get fond of it too and find the things funny that you found funny. Then, eventually, an audience – and that's marvellous.

IW: Did radio never appeal to you as a medium?

AA: No. Frankly, I didn't know what the job was when I applied to join the BBC. I thought I was going to be sorting out Alfred Bradley's filing. But it seemed quite a good way to pass a little bit of time while I thought about what to do after *Whatnot*. When I got there I found that, far from sorting out Alfred's filing, I was going to be doing my own programmes and running with a great deal more responsibility than I'd had in the theatre. I think the single most important thing it gave me was the moment when, with a little bit of guidance from knowledgeable secretaries and other people, I was actually going to put a whole show together. I was to book the artists, book the studio, and do all that sort of business: it was almost like a finishing school.

Radio itself, I must say, I went into without enormous enthusiasm, although I'd been a great listener as a child. But once in, I found it was a magic place. At that particular point in the history of the BBC, it was such a backwater (television was the place) that you could work totally unobserved doing the most interesting things. It did two things: it gave me a great opportunity to do far more plays – I did more plays in a year than I'd done in ten years in the theatre – and it also foisted upon me the occasional plays that I didn't want to do, which, of course, in the theatre you can generally avoid because you don't accept them. And it's quite good occasionally to do a play you don't want to do. You actually have to learn a little bit of technique: you've got to keep the actors going, just for the length of the play. They know it's bad, you know it's bad, but if you ever admit it, it's gone. And some of my best work was done on those things.

IW: It wasn't at that stage as technical a medium as it is now, in so far as it wasn't stereo, was it? It was purely monaural. Did you feel that you explored the medium as a medium?

AA: Oh, yes, very much, because I was fascinated by sound. I had, of course, with *Whatnot*, been a tape-recorder freak. There was some wonderful equipment there and we had great fun with the gear.

IW: Were you at all influenced by Alfred?

AA: Not production-wise, though I was influenced by him in other ways. Alfred's strongest point was obviously his relationship with his writers. And I suppose I learned from him a certain amount about how to treat writers, and how to draw them out, though I don't think I've got the perseverance or the dedication to do what he does. There were the maxims he had: if you want a play, you've got to go and get it. The unsolicited scripts are never any good: nobody ever sends you *Under Milk Wood*. You've got to go out and sit in Dylan Thomas's pub until he writes it. And all his plays came that way, of course, as a result of his doggedly driving around in his large Rover and parking on people's doorsteps. I'd already been working with actors, of course, and I suppose I had learned the hard way about directing them. But now I learned something about writers.

IW: But you never felt moved to write for radio yourself?

AA: No. I think I was dealing so actively all day with writers that I felt first it would almost be cheating to write my own plays for radio. And I also wasn't actually very inspired to do so. I did try one script, which I sent to Colin Shaw (the Head of North Region, now at the IBA) when I'd just joined, but he wasn't very keen, and I wasn't very keen on it either, so I gave it up.

IW: Since leaving, the medium hasn't attracted you at all?

AA: No. It's a narrative medium, it's a different sort of medium, it's not mine. I'm really too basically a visual writer for that.

IW: You did once write – and this was ten years later – a television play. And only one.

AA: Oh, that was ridiculous. I happen to have a very close friend who comes to all our first nights, called Herbert Wise. He's a well-known television director, who'd been landed with a series for BBC2, called *Masquerade*. Some boffin in the back room had this great idea. He said, 'Let's ask about half a dozen jolly writers to write a play around a fixed theme – like a fancy-dress party.' So Herbie said, 'Look, it's half an hour: here's the theme. Please, I'd love to do your first telly.' And I said, 'Well, it's very nice of you, Herbie.' And half an hour, actually, is twenty-eight pages: it's really a night's work. So I said, 'Well, look, I must see the producers. I must talk about this, because I don't know anything about it.' So they dutifully showed me round the studios. And I said, 'Well, could you just give me some idea of the cast requirements and the set?' And they said, 'We've got this wonderful new lightweight video camera, so really, don't worry about the sets. You write what you want to do in half an hour: we will film it.' I said, 'Oh, that's wonderful. What about cast?' They said, 'You write what you want: we will cast it. We don't want you to be hampered by physical conditions. Just write.' So I went away and I wrote this play for twenty-four people. It roved all over this bloody hotel: there were about thirty-eight sets. So, silence. 'Ah,' they said. 'Well, we didn't think you'd write twenty-four people.' So I cut it down to eighteen and simplified the sets. But, of course, the budget of the series was already costed and so the whole thing was pitifully under-financed. And, because of the technical complexities which I'd set, Herbie, on location – two days in a pub in Berkshire – was having his work cut out. Some scenes he never got in the can at all, because he had no time! So, it was OK, but it was very far from what it was intended originally to be – a waiter's eye view of a dreadful office party.

IW: You gave up after that, did you?

AA: I didn't find it very enjoyable. At the point when the thing was being done and I was used to being most involved, I was sitting in a van with a bloke who was recording it. He was watching the budget on ITV, and watching my play out of the corner of his eye, just to see when they said, 'Roll VTR.' Then he went back to the budget again. He said, 'What is all this?' I said, 'Well, it's a play, actually.' 'Oh yes? What's it about then?' I said, 'Well, I wrote it.' He said, 'Oh, did you? Is it any good?' I said, 'Well, yes, it's about this . . .' and I actually talked to him for about half an hour about it. By the end, he was shouting ideas down the line, and they were saying, 'Thank you very much, VTR, we can manage, thank you.' It wasn't a very good way to spend your play.

I only want to be up there directing – and I really can't be bothered to start taking television directors' courses at this time of life – or I don't want to know. The interesting bit's directing, not writing.

IW: And to date, anyway, no film screenplays.

AA: The British film industry's nearly dead: that's the only one I could ever have written for. I suppose if Ealing Studios had been going at full flourish, and if they'd been interested enough to approach me and say, 'Would you like to be another Tibby Clark and write a few *Lavender Hill Mobs*?' with the studio of talents they had at that time, it would have been quite exciting to write for

Alec Guinness and people. But films now seem to be either one-man shows — director's concepts which grow — or they're blockbusters. Neither of which appeals to me. All the stories you hear about the film industry are to do with compromise. I suppose, artistically, I'm lucky enough to have reached a level where I don't have to do a lot of that any more, and I don't want to go back to it.

IW: So you don't see yourself moving out of the theatre at all, do you?

AA: No. I don't want my work tampered with by some half-pint shit in a front office. I don't need him. I'll do it my way.

Plays and Themes

IAN WATSON: You started writing very soon after the angry revolution – John Osborne, John Arden, Ann Jellicoe. That crew suddenly hit the Royal Court in 1956 and were making really rather a lot of noise in the British theatre. You seem to have been affected not at all by them in what you were writing at that time. Were you aware of them and what they were doing?

ALAN AYCKBOURN: Yes, I think I was, but not immediately, perhaps. Although they were writing then, I was starting in rep where they hadn't yet arrived. We were still tending to do Agatha and *The Grand National Night*, and all those sorts of thrillers: we'd alternate thriller–comedy–thriller–comedy. So I suppose that my instant exposure was to the more conventional drama of the time. It wasn't until I ran personally into people like H. Pinter that things really began to take a grip. He certainly did affect me. I was also influenced by boyhood fads of the time. At this point, I remember – it doesn't show either – I was influenced a lot by Pirandello and Ionesco and Anouilh. I was very keen on Anouilh. I liked the way he constructed. I was very drawn to the craftsmen of the business. Although I liked the content, I was perhaps slightly less impressed by the techniques displayed by some of the new wave, because it did seem that a lot of things were thrown out simply because they smacked of Rattigan, who, poor man, went to his grave with 'well-made play' being shouted at him. But occasionally, when you sat through one, you thought, 'Thank God for the well-made play', because the evening did at least come to a successful resolution, even if one quibbled with some of the content.

Priestley I liked. But it was only later that I began to see the other side. Pinter was enormously influential, simply because his history is that of an actor and of a poet, then a writer, a playwright. And I sense that the actor–poet is still what he is; his use of language and his careful selection of words (which is something I was very impressed by and have tried to copy), is so fascinating and yet so eloquent, so delicate, that it had an immediate effect on me. My selection of words is far more, I suppose, sly than his: he will use a word more stylistically. I'll bury words. But on occasions you'll find, I think, similarities.

IW: In the earlier plays, the critics in Yorkshire, anyway, were tending to talk about you in terms of Noël Coward.

AA: Well, there's a similarity, but it came after *Relatively Speaking*. And at that point I really was still formulating a style. I always say to writers, although sometimes they don't believe me, I don't honestly think there's any harm in being influenced by, and indeed in copying to a certain extent, people you admire. I didn't actually copy Noël Coward; I mean, I didn't intend to. Looking back on it, I can quite see why *Relatively Speaking* was compared to Noël Coward. But what I was trying to do was something that Stephen Joseph had told me to do: 'For once in your life, try and write a well-made play.'

However, I suppose a lot that influenced me has nothing to do with the theatre at all. *Whatnot* is the outstanding example, which was totally to do with films – people like René Clair and Renoir, and going back to Buster Keaton and Laurel and Hardy, who still remain, I suppose, my major comic influence. If I could write a latterday Laurel and Hardy film, I'd be absolutely delighted; or a latterday Laurel and Hardy play. A lot of my stuff is actually closer to that and to Keaton than I suspect it is to my contemporary comic dramatists.

IW: You talk about your work as belonging to the popular theatre. That term needs a certain amount of definition, doesn't it, because the Popular Theatre, I guess, is what the left-wing writers would say they were writing for – a working-class theatre: a working-class and intellectual audience, perhaps, which is not in any sense what you're meaning by popular theatre, is it?

AA: No, but I don't actually think that established theatres have anything to do with the working class anyway. Of course, there's a sizeable minority of people from the working class who go to the theatre, but I don't in general think the working class want to know much about it. It smacks to them of culture and exclusiveness.

It's not so much a matter of class as of sex at the moment: the theatre is predominantly a middle-class woman's occupation. The men in Scarborough that I meet say, 'I don't go, but the wife does' – it's the famous phrase. You say, 'Why don't you go?' 'Well, it's a bit highbrow for me,' they say. And you say, 'Oh, so you think your wife is more highbrow than you; I mean, that your wife is more intelligent than you?' 'No, of course she isn't.' I say, 'Well, what makes it so that she can understand it. . . ?' 'Well, she's into art, you know.' Art is such a dirty word in England, it really is. It's like it's poofy, it's female, it's élite, it's exclusive – I suppose that view has been encouraged because we're a nation of snobs, and we tend to make art exclusive. It's quite extraordinary to go to New York, for instance, in a fairly egalitarian artistic society, and see policemen going in to buy a seat in the theatre, in uniform – I thought we were being raided! And not feeling stupid about it. And cab drivers saying, 'Oh, I saw that.' Ask an English cab driver to take you to the Lyric and he'll say, 'Where? Oh, it's a theatre, is it?'

I'm on a crusade to try and persuade people that theatre can be fun, but every time I start doing that, some hairy bugger from the Left comes in and tells them it's instructive, and drives them all out again. If I want to be instructed, I go to night school. I may be instructed in the theatre, but I don't go in there predominantly for instruction: I go in there for entertainment, and of course all the best plays instruct me, or enlighten me – it's a better word than instruct. But if you put a label on a whisky bottle with 'For medicinal use only' on it, it rather puts you off the drink.

IW: The canvas you take in your plays tends therefore to reflect the people that you reckon are going to be coming into the theatre?

AA: No, that sounds as if I deliberately try and reflect the audience. I'm very lucky that my particular level of writing, class-wise, is slap-bang in the middle of the English theatre-going public. If I was a working-class dramatist, I'd have a much harder time of it because my reflected audience would be that much smaller; I could overcome it, but it's a tougher battle. Then I'd be better off writing for television. People will watch unbelievable things on television – unbelievably deep, absorbing plays that they would never dream of going to the theatre to see. It's nothing to do with the play itself, I suspect, it's to do with the social act of going to the theatre.

Theatres go through awful convolutions trying to attract the

working class. They make the theatre very dirty and very unpleasant and smelly, and they say, 'Well, this will encourage
people: they won't think it's stuck-up rubbish.' But then, that's not
the answer, because most people in the working class, particularly
if they go out for the evening, want to put on their very best clothes
and want to go somewhere very nice — hence their working men's
clubs, which are some of the most magnificent buildings in the
north, and the best appointed. So that's a myth. So, you then try
and make it very comfortable and very pleasant, but then it begins
to look a bit snooty, so I don't know quite how on earth you win
the audience. The first thing you've got to do is to have very good
draught beer. But where is the art in all this? Then the chaps will
stay in the bar anyway! Stephen Joseph circled it for a long time,
with his fish-and-chip theatre. But what you're then doing is
actually not providing theatre: you're providing a *sort* of theatre.
To me, theatre *is* an art; it has to be something that takes 90 per
cent of your concentration, not 8 per cent, otherwise you're
providing music-hall, variety or something else. They of course are
very valid, very important forms of theatre, but it's not the same
thing. All the plays I admire require at least silence.

IW: So you're in there, up to your elbows in the English middle
class — or rather the English middle classes, because one of the
things you do like is to find the internal hierarchies. I wonder where,
in fact, you get them from nowadays? You spend so much time — in
fact, you seem to spend all your time — in the theatre, rather than out
in the suburban dining rooms which your plays examine.

AA: I get about a bit, because I live in a small enough town to do it.
In London I probably wouldn't. In London, one tends to go from
box A to box B. In Scarborough one tends to go to intermediate
boxes and, because I am willy-nilly drawn into some of the social
life, because a lot of the people there know me by sight, a lot of chat
goes on, a lot of socializing with audiences, a lot of opening of
fêtes. So I do hear English spoken, which is really the name of the
game. And, of course, actors are, after all, human beings too: one
sometimes tends to forget that. I would be wrong to say they have
more complicated lives, but they have lives every bit as complicated
as people who aren't actors. Running a theatre means that you are
forced to share a building with twenty-five other people, eight of

whom are actors, and the rest of whom are in various classes of trade – wardrobe maintenance through to electrics. The company is very aware that a lot of what they do is picked up and used: there are a lot of smiles when we first read one of my new plays. The Vera syndrome, the knocking everything over: there were at least two actors who looked rather – well, they didn't look upset, but they smiled thinly.

The thing that I don't often stress is of course that – I don't know quite what the percentage is, but I suspect it's very large – most of it is me. Now, I happen to have just about every single phobia and fault that anybody's ever had: I have them all. And I also am possessed, fortunately, with a sort of enormous detachment from myself, so that I can actually see myself doing it. As Tom says in *The Norman Conquests*, 'I let her down. I can feel myself doing it while I'm doing it.' I do a lot of that. And a lot of it's me.

IW: Would you accept that in *Relatively Speaking*, and perhaps other plays around that time, the natural habitat of the people was actually Shaftesbury Avenue rather than the world? In other words, that they owed more to a theatrical atmosphere than to any real world?

AA: Yes, I suppose they were slightly more stylized than later. I think, too, it takes a long time to have the courage to write people. It's not easy. You start – I started – with plot very much. It was round about the *Norman*s that suddenly, because of the scale of them, I was unable to keep plotting. There was one scene that I started to write in the *Norman*s, and I realized that it just had to be there because it was there, and nothing was actually going to happen in it. It was the beginning of the second act of *Living Together* when they all come in from washing up, and there was just this lagoon of peace. I had to sit down and write a play where people just sat and talked; it sounds very naive, but I'd never actually written people sitting and just chatting. I was very nervous about doing it. And I suppose out of all the *Norman Conquests* that, to me, was my big achievement, and it was that which led on to *Absent Friends*. I thought, 'Wow! I can write a play where everyone just sits down and has a talk.' Which is really what happens in *Absent Friends*: a person gets up once and pours some cream over another, but the rest of the time they really are pretty static. You only move them round to keep the eye from getting totally bored. I'm always dismayed by people who claim that my writing hasn't moved at all since *Relatively*.

IW: Your plays clearly gain from being seen as a sequence, a development, an organism which is still growing and developing.

AA: I'm very conscious myself of using the experience of each play to go forward, and in my own mind I'm perfectly clear how it develops. In pulling one out off the shelf, as I pulled *Relatively* off the shelf to redirect, it's a very curious experience I wouldn't want to repeat too quickly, because it's most throwing chronologically.

IW: Did you feel inclined to rewrite it?

AA: Well, I either had to do that, or just close my eyes; which I did, and carried on with it, saying, 'Sorry about this.'

IW: You get yourself a historical perspective, I suppose.

AA: Yes. But I always describe my plays as a receding galaxy: when I've written them, they immediately shoot away and they go into a band of disfavour. Then, if they're lucky, they pass through that and come out again. But there's a certain point at which I'm really rather fed up with them, except for the wan little sickly children that one tends to keep a fond eye on. I'm rather cheesed off with *Bedroom Farce* at the moment: I've had quite enough of that.

IW: Why particularly?

AA: Oh, I don't know. I never really liked *Bedroom Farce* very much. Yes, I did: I got to like it quite a lot. I felt rather extraordinary when I wrote it, though. I didn't quite know why I'd written it. It was very strange. It cropped up in the middle of my serious phase. This rather jolly play suddenly arrived. And I think I was rather rude to it. I said to it, 'I'm an *Absent Friends* man now, a much more serious dramatist.' I always liked *Absent Friends*, but that's just blatant prejudice for a play that's had fewer productions than any other.

IW: Only in this country. All these dark Scandinavian and Teutonic countries seem to have latched on to *Absent Friends*.

AA: The extraordinary thing about the theatre in England is that the West End still, to a certain extent, is the watershed. Your play is scuppered if you don't get a particularly good showing – which I claim, sadly, *Absent Friends* didn't have. As a result it fell totally into disfavour. Three or four reps have done it, but one senses they did it because there wasn't anything else around.

But I think I'm very lucky really. I think now I'm accepted, if not warmly congratulated, on the fact that I do have at least two separate levels that I write on. The ones that are slightly darker, in general, don't get any public and win awards. And the ones that are jolly probably get a lot more people coming to them. I'll have to wait until I write another harrowing piece that empties a theatre in Shaftesbury Avenue before I get another award.

IW: It was 1974, wasn't it, the year of *Absent Friends* in Scarborough, that Michael Billington in the *Guardian* came out with his splendid headline about you: 'Ayckbourn is a left-wing writer using a right-wing form.' Which is directly contradictory to John Osborne's terse summing-up of Alan Ayckbourn sitting there as 'a right-wing boulevardier'. How do you react to that sort of attempt to classify you in left and right?

AA: It's all meaningless, isn't it? Of course, everyone has politics and everyone has attitudes to politics. I'm certainly anti-extremist; I'm very English. But again, I sit, I suspect, in the middle of most English opinion. The Tory party right wing fills me with total despair, as indeed does the Labour party left wing. I suppose the nearest I get to being political is that I'm rather attracted to things like the Social Democrats. That's the sort of area I'm after. It sounds awful, but I really like things to be fair. I think people should treat each other well. And unfortunately, in this world, it's getting more and more difficult to treat people nicely, because the suspicions are growing rather than diminishing. That is greatly sad.

IW: I think all Billington was actually meaning, when he used that phrase, was that you take the form of middle-class comedy and you use it not as, say, Rattigan or Coward have done in many of their plays, to confirm the complacency of that cosy little world, but actually to question and tear apart, as often as not, the people you place within it.

AA: Yes. In trying to write a rounded character, one obviously writes quite often the very unpleasant side of them. All my characters have flaws and are pock-marked, and I don't do a cosmetic job on them. I don't honestly want to make judgements.

IW: But I do think you ask them questions which the standard light-comedy writer would protect them from. And one of the techniques for doing this would seem to be, in the classic phrase of Jake Thackray, chucking a bit of grit into their life's vaseline. In quite a number of your plays, you've got this maverick character. It starts with Mint, in *Mr Whatnot*, goes through to Tony in *The Sparrow* perhaps; even in *Ernie's Incredible Illucinations*, Ernie is creating absolute bloody chaos all round him; Leonard in *Time and Time Again*; Norman in the *Conquests*.

AA: Yes, it is a theme: it creates the conflict. And one can isolate the conflict because what one is trying to portray is normality, but you've got to have something to contrast it with, and indeed to upset it.

IW: Linked with that, the subject of many of your plays seems to revolve around destruction — I mean personal destruction in one form or another. You start examining factors within personal relationships which actually inhibit those relationships and start destroying them. Yes?

AA: Yes.

IW: The destructive factors come in various forms. There's daft things like sheer social machinery: you are fascinated by mealtimes and picnics and parties and things like that.

AA: Yes, I am. Meals are convenient times when people are willy-nilly forced to sit opposite each other and possibly exchange conversation.

IW: Yes, and they're crowded around with all sorts of silly little conventions.

AA: Yes — who sits at the top of the table, to start with. I'm also quite fond of extending that: there's always somebody in my plays — well, not always, but often — who wants to do things properly, according to the way they think they ought to do it. In the

*Norman*s, Sarah's attempt to have an embassy banquet in that naff house, with only lettuce in the fridge – it serves her right, really.

IW: She is surely protecting herself from any sort of relationship with anyone by hiding within the form.

AA: Yes, and the best thing to do is to formalize it all with everyone sitting around the table, well dressed, and having jolly conversation. And then you can be reassured that everything is normal, because the one person who is about to crash is her. She fancies Norman more than any of them, so she's fighting herself, and she's also fighting the sins of her sisters-in-law. She's really trying to touch a safe base, and the safe base is rolled napkins, and knives and forks, and man–woman–man–woman, and 'Hasn't it been a lovely day?'

IW: The internal hierarchy of the middle class is fascinating within your plays, and the boss–employee relationship is one which recurs a bit with its sexual concomitants, which make for some really quite comical things.

AA: There's John and Paul in *Absent Friends*. Paul is John's boss and has had Evelyn. And John, who is married to Evelyn, bites his lip about it and says nothing, because he needs a contract. John's very much a parasite on the back of Paul, only Paul is himself a parasite. Big fleas have little fleas . . .

IW: In *Time and Time Again*, there's a complicated situation too.

AA: Graham and Peter: yes, indeed. In some employers – and it's American thinking, but it's come over in a half-baked way into England – the enthusiastic employer always feels he'd like to know his men as well, and by 'his men' he also means his men's women – or, if he's employing women, then his women's men. (I haven't written about a female employer yet: I must do that and remedy that situation. Now she is very much a prominent figure on the scene, and getting more so, that tension would be quite fascinating in reverse.) I know that I'm always interested to know quite how far employees go in some of these organizations to appease their employer. Would they actually hand their wife over? They probably would, actually, if they thought that it would help them on their way.

IW: There is in several plays an almost shadowy presence of brothers and sisters – the sibling relationship, if you like. Obviously in *Family Circles*, *Time and Time Again*, the *Normans*; there's a brother in *Sisterly Feelings* and there's a brother again in *Taking Steps*.

AA: There's a whole family in *Sisterly Feelings*. I'm very fascinated by the style of relationships there, because it is totally different from that of a chosen relationship. It is enforced, you're with someone you didn't ask to be with.

IW: You throw them together in a way which I find strange.

AA: I usually use a focal point to get them together. In the case of *Sisterly*, I've implied that Dorcas probably lives away from home for a lot of the time, but that the father, particularly now that he's lost the mother, would need visiting more. All the scenes take place at weekends, so one assumes that that's the time she comes back. And Abigail lives near – none of them actually lives with him – so that's how they're foisted together. In fact, we see them in untypical proximity, because that's the relationship I'm interested in exploring. But I find there is in many relationships – certainly parental ones, also I suspect with brothers and sisters – a sort of love-hate. There probably is a great deal of animosity, but there are moments when they just touch and react as one, because they both have the same attitude. It's a closeness that can't be touched by an outsider.

IW: The other relationship which you have foisted upon you rather than choose is the parent–child relationship, and that doesn't feature very much.

AA: Not as much as it probably will do. My own childhood is now in quite good perspective; and also, having a nineteen- and a twenty-year-old son now, that relationship is beginning to be distant enough to look back on. I'm tempted to write very soon – it was there in *Joking Apart* to a certain extent – the parents of younger children. But my great objective is never to see them: I don't want the children around at all. It's the parents I'm interested in. Then one day it would be nice to write parents with older children. That remains to be explored.

IW: The area that you've been into in enormous detail – and I suspect you're going to continue going into it in even more detail – is marriage, of course. And if anyone did a computer analysis of Ayckbourn's canon, I suspect you would end up as the greatest threat in the British theatre to Christian marriage. You really don't have any time at all for it, in the plays anyway.

AA: Well, I only write what I see.

IW: I don't believe that.

AA: Well, let's say this: the marriages I do see are either fraught or dull. There are one or two very happy ones, but that's probably because they're new. In general, I don't think people were meant to live with each other for too long – although, having said that, there are millions of exceptions. As soon as people feel that they are married, there's a sense of entrapment. That was certainly my reaction: I signed a document to say, 'I will love you for the rest of my life' – which, at that time being less than twenty, I suppose I optimistically reckoned as at least fifty-five years. I suddenly became attacked with a great sense of claustrophobia: 'My God, what have I promised?'

But I'm less interested in marriages than I am in just man–woman relationships. Men and women are much nearer than they sometimes say they are, but at the same time they do think quite differently and their attitudes are quite different. And it's not just hereditary or environmental pressures. Of course those are there; but even so, I am absolutely sure that, if you took two new babies and brought them up identically, you could spot their attitudes as male or female. They're just, thank God, different: I don't say there's anything better about one or the other. I suppose if they were brought up in totally equal circumstances, they would probably live very harmoniously, but they're not: they're brought up with the most extraordinary expectations. As long as we continue to make the promises we do about the opposite sex – that is to say, mostly sexual – we're going to be permanently disappointed. There aren't any page three *Sun* women, apart from on page three of the *Sun*. They don't arrive at breakfast; they arrive sort of smudgy and a bit dirty. Nor are there those super blokes that step out of the screen: they're actually sweaty and spotty. And they're much more ordinary than that. And I think that's where the tensions come these days; it's in leading us to expect beautiful people. There are about twenty-five beautiful people.

IW: So the collapse of marriage is all to do with the collapse of fantasy, is it?

AA: I think to a certain extent, yes. I certainly went into my marriage with the most extraordinary ideas about what it was all going to be about, even though what we were setting out to do on our honeymoon wasn't a totally new experience. All the same, it was going to be marvellous. And there's a great conspiracy, because nasty old middle-aged people like oneself – I hope I don't: I've been so careful not to – gather round to perpetuate the myth. They say, 'Your mother and I have never had a cross word.' And you think, 'You lying sod, you were hitting her when the relationship mattered and it was full of passion, as it was early on, and you bothered to shout at each other. The only reason you don't shout at her now is not because you like her any better, it's that you really can't be bothered.' I think that's quite a nice state to be in, really. I don't quarrel with my relationship now, because we know all those alleyways: we've been down the shouting. In fact, I think in second relationships you can often avoid going down all those alleyways.

My biggest recurrent theme is that people do care about each other; it's just that they handle each other in boxing gloves half the time, and not with kid gloves. And I remember that all the screaming and shouting and hurling of food against walls that happened in my early relationship had to do with wanting to get closer to the person I wanted to share my life with. It wasn't that I wanted to hurt them (although occasionally I did, because I felt they were hurting me). It was to do with caring and loving: it wasn't to do with anything destructive.

IW: Yes, but your more objective self, looking at marriages within your plays, is quite clearly saying, 'Marriage is destroying these people.'

AA: I think it often is. I think a big piece of us dies in a marriage. We enter it, often spoilt, only children and, in general, it goes one of two ways: we're either very bad at adjusting at all – we say, 'Yes, I don't mind marrying you, but I do object to the fact that you want this over there.' Or one personality, being stronger, will eclipse the other. Sometimes that happens by slow erosion – in the woman's case it's usually a long-term marathon: she'll just whittle away. One sees in Scarborough the man in the garden, smoking by the shed – I've seen that quite a lot – because his wife won't have tobacco smoke in the house. And you think, 'Go up to the house and say, "This is half my sodding house, and if I want to smoke a cigarette in my lounge, which I'm paying my mortgage for. . . !" ' But no, he's standing by his shed having a fag because he's not allowed in the house, poor little sod. And that's a case of one personality having just gently established a superiority.

IW: Is there any sense in which you're mellowing slightly in the plays? Both in *Sisterly Feelings* and in *Suburban Strains*, you seem to come to the conclusion: 'It's not perfect, it's not what it was supposed to be, but it's all we've got, so let's do something with it.'

AA: Yes, I am mellowing. The fire's gone out of me a bit, in that I'm not longer as indignant as I was. I was so rudely hurled into a so-called permanent relationship so early, I became very angry about the fact that nobody told us. Why should they? But now one side of me says, 'If you can get through all that fire and water . . .'; while the other side of me is saying, 'You're becoming exactly like those people who say, "You'll come through it and, you know, if you give a little and take a little, it'll be all right!" ' I think, as you get older, you get a bit more tolerant. I hope so.

IW: With *Absurd Person*, even more so with *Absent Friends* and also in *Just Between Ourselves* and *Joking Apart*, you started tapping a new well. You started getting into the dark comedy, which took a lot of people by surprise at the time and still hasn't quite found an audience.

AA: Yes, the dark seam is there. I think it really came about as I began to explore the characters. As my confidence grew in holding an audience if you like. I discovered that I could start to strip the layers off the people a little bit and find, perhaps, less typical emotions than you find in your average light comedy, like anger and jealousy and fear and rage and lust: I mean real, burning, destructive desire, all those sorts of thing that one normally associates with Tennessee Williams and the swampland. Once

[96]

you're into that, then obviously there are going to be some dark things, because you can't really write about it without them.

IW: By the time you get to *Joking Apart*, you've got a really very gloomy play indeed. It manages to be funny but in the process it blasts the hell out of Christian marriage, the work ethic, and several other things.

AA: I've related why I started to write it. Somebody said, 'Why don't you write about a really nice couple? I'm fed up with all these bloody awful marriages.' I said, 'Yes, I really must get this couple together.' And I suddenly realized that, in creating a happy couple – and there are people on the fringes of our lives: they're never in the centre of our lives, they're people we faintly know, which is why they're quite nebulous – they're not the central people, but they're very important to the play. I don't believe that, if we investigated Richard and Anthea beyond a certain level, we could keep up the image I wanted of them which was of perfect happiness, because it obviously doesn't exist anywhere: there must be knots. But I was interested in seeing them from our other characters' point of view. And from their point of view, as Sven says, 'Every bloody thing he touches goes right!' The misunderstanding of the play is that people often think I was writing a play about Richard and Anthea: I was writing a play about Sven, about us, about the inequalities of life. Why the hell should someone be born with less ability than another? Some people seem, in our lives, to have a natural aptitude for everything – everything they touch.

IW: A small point made in the play is that Richard and Anthea are living together, not married: is that particularly significant?

AA: I wanted to avoid a 'happy marriage'. I wanted to give them a grounding of less than conventionality. There's a suspicion that Anthea wasn't happy in the past, that things haven't always been that incredible: it was the mating of Richard and Anthea – a second-time-around, in fact – that fused into a sort of ideal oneness where everything came right for her. That's the only reason for that – and the fact that it gave Hugh, the vicar who destroys himself in love, a glimmer of hope. Sometimes he thinks, 'Well, if my wife dies, or she leaves me, or we get divorced, I could give up the church and I could go off with Anthea; she could leave

Richard.' There's a little door with just a chink of light – awful, really.

IW: *Joking Apart* disappointed you greatly in town by the fact that it didn't run. The audiences didn't come in sufficient numbers. You went straight from that disappointment into writing *Taking Steps*, and I'm interested to know whether there was a strong element of reaction in that?

AA: I just wanted to write something fun for a change. Just as, at one point, I didn't want to be known as the king of the giggle business, I didn't want to be known as a writer who'd suddenly gone gloomy. I want to be able to write whatever I want to write. I don't ever sit down and consciously say, 'Here comes a jolly!' The company was braced for a very grim play, because they'd already realized that I wrote alternately something rather jolly and something rather dark, and *Sisterly Feelings* had been a very sunny, light, merry sort of evening – so they said: 'Ah-ha! The next one's about the axe murderer!' And, in fact, out came old *Taking Steps*, which is, in some ways, a strange mixture. It's actually quite a savage play. I always find it's much more savage than others do.

But, this was a farce. I know Frank Marcus argues over what is a farce. He would claim *The Norman Conquests* were farces – I'd disagree with him; or *Absurd Person* – I think the second act is getting very near it. But I don't think I've written a farce for a very long time – *Bedroom Farce* certainly wasn't. *Absurd* possibly was the nearest to a black farce that I've written. And I think *Taking Steps* is a return to that momentarily. It's nice to do. Hopefully, if I get time, I shall write two or three more.

IW: Farces?

AA: Yes. I love doing them, but they're bloody hard work. They're much the hardest thing to write, and you can't do more than one every five years, simply because the technique involved is phenomenal. It's like playing a very difficult Liszt sonata: you need to have so much muscle and ingenuity. And you have to use up a stockpile: I won't have that much ingenuity again for another five years. I've got gentle ingenuity for things like *Just Between Ourselves*, but not this massive construction job that has to go on, because the more unlikely the events you wish to portray, the more credible you have to make them, and that requires an enormous amount of artifice.

IW: Your plays are translated into something like twenty-four different languages and played pretty well everywhere in the world including almost every country in the Eastern bloc. I tried to find out whether there was any record of your having been played in the USSR. I think Tom Erhardt is convinced that you've been pirated over there.

AA: Yes, you don't get many royalty cheques from the USSR.

IW: When you were doing *How the Other Half Loves* in America, I think you said you had to Americanize somewhat. Are you conscious of foreign translations of your plays having been bowdlerized in any way?

AA: There are two ways of approaching them, really, as far as I can see. They either decide to play, as we often do, say, a French farce, or a French comedy, where we carry on behaving as if French. Or we do the other thing, which is to make it into an English play. In Europe, what they do is to retain the Englishness of them. What they tend to do, I suppose, is to put all the men into bowler hats, metaphorically, because a lot of my plays confirm what they already think about England.

IW: Does that imply that they're broadening them too much, that they're caricaturing them?

AA: Not always. It's very hard to tell if you don't speak the language. I saw a production once of *Relatively*, when they seemed to play it in an orange grove: there were a lot of oranges all over the place. But that, they assumed, was an English orchard, I suppose.

IW: That was where?

AA: Berlin. Often the productions have just been lifted – the sets and the costumes and the images – from London, and they're very, very similar. But I have also seen new productions in Germany as well.

IW: Yes, the Germans are very fond of you, aren't they? They've translated virtually all your plays and play them a lot.

AA: I've got a very good agent there, Klaus Juncker. He is always ringing up with reports of how many productions he's sold and how he's doing. It's a great challenge for him. In other countries, in Italy for example, where you haven't got that service and probably not that response for that sort of theatre, it's more difficult. But I do well in Germany and the Scandinavian countries, and Holland, too – although they all have their own peculiar problems – Spain, to a certain extent; and France, again, pretty well. The other thing that helps the plays, of course, is that my very limits are also my strengths, in that I tend to write about human relationships. And one can see quite easily in *Season's Greetings* – provided they like the play – the characters are very easy. Wherever in the world there are Christians who have Christmas – or even non-Christians who have Christmas – they have family staying with them. And it's the family coming together that the play is about. And when you have family, you possibly have an eccentric uncle and you possibly have a couple that are having a rather difficult relationship in their marriage. And so, immediately, you're nine-tenths there. What you do with the details of it – whether they all drink sherry or Manhattan cocktails – is really immaterial.

IW: Have you seen them played in Germany a lot?

AA: More so than elsewhere, yes.

IW: And do they get the productions about right?

AA: Sometimes, not always. I have seen one, in Hamburg, which was marvellous of *Relatively*, and one of *Absurd Person* that was really very poor.

IW: In what way poor?

AA: *Absurd Person*? Oh, well, they played it like a jolly comedy. It had no balls to it at all. And you say, 'Oh well, they don't understand that play' – then along comes another production of it that's marvellous. But in Germany, it's the sort of theatre I rather approve of. I made the crass blunder when I first went there of asking when the production transferred to Berlin. They said, 'Berlin? You're joking! They can do their own bloody production, and it won't be as good as ours, thank you very much.'

IW: Where else abroad have you seen productions of your work?

AA: I've seen a Spanish production of *How the Other Half*. They're completely berserk in the Spanish theatre. It may have changed a little: I saw it during Franco. Because it's a non-union theatre, totally non-union, the hours they work are extraordinary, extraordinary. They have a second house that doesn't go up till about eleven o'clock – they do twice nightly, including Sunday – so they come down on the second house something like half-past one, two o'clock. I saw it on New Year's Eve, and they had this strange business of interrupting the play with the equivalent of Big Ben, Big Maria, which they played over the loudspeakers. The play stopped, the cast ran on, champagne was poured, streamers were thrown at the audience – a little junketing for about quarter of an hour, twenty minutes. Then, almost to the line, 'As I was saying . . .', and the play goes on again. That was very extra-ordinary. At the end of the show – I came on the stage for the streamers, then went off again – my translator, a nice guy called Nacho, said, 'Would you like to meet the company?' I said, 'Very much.' I came round, and they were setting up on stage with the standard sort of rehearsal furniture – chairs, tables and stuff – and moving the rest of the set back. And I said, 'Oh, tomorrow morning?' And they said, 'No, now!' So I said, 'Rehearsing now?' They said, 'Oh yes. Tomorrow the actors are doing radio in the morning, so they have to.'

IW: The Dutch?

AA: It's curious: they're very short of actors, the Dutch. It's a small country. You have to book your actors. It's fascinating seeing how the different theatres run. The German theatres each have their own company of actors who are, as far as I can make out, contracted until they die; they are permanent members of that company: an extraordinary system of growing up through the ranks and taking over a part if the leading man dies. In Holland, on the other hand, which has its national theatres, its subsidized theatres, I've dealt mainly with commercial management. Commercial management has to plan its productions years ahead, just to get hold of the actors; but the shows that I've seen there have been quite good.

IW: Paris, though, played funny games with you.

AA: Yes, they played funny games with *How the Other Half*, and I got quite nasty about that. The director suddenly thought it would be nice to have an extra scene with Bob on the phone to his mother! After the play was over, the producer said, 'What do you think?' I said, 'I didn't like that scene you put in, I must say.' 'Oh, well, a little adaptation!' So I said, 'Yes, well, I don't think I'm going to let that happen any more.' One of the other strange things about it was the clothing. All those people are from different social strata: Frank and Fiona are very wealthy and they have no children, and they're successful, and he's a managing director. But Bob and Terry Phillips are struggling – they've got a young baby, and they mis-spend their money. Bob drinks a lot of it and she gives the rest to Oxfam; so they really are in quite reduced circumstances. And the whole point of their household is that she doesn't care about clothes anyway! And then Mary, in the third of the couples, is tremendously naff, and William does buy her dresses, but they're always horrible. And in the Paris production, there were three really elegant, very chic women: they looked glorious in their clothes from Dior. And I said, 'Couldn't we have them a little bit more like Mary and Terry?' And he said, 'In Paris, we do not wish to see ugly women on the stage. This is Paris.' So that was the end of that question!

Absurd Person, on the other hand, was a very good production. Ironically, they had done everything I asked – it was tough, it was real, there were no elegant, chic Evas in beautiful négligés – and it ran the shortest of any of them, because they then said, 'This is not boulevard comedy. What is it doing on the boulevard?' The people who would have enjoyed it shunned it because it was on the boulevard, and the boulevardiers backed off it because it was not jolly enough.

Relatively was another slightly strange production in Paris; they filmed the first scene. There's a curtain, and you think, 'We're going to see a play', and you sit down. And the curtain goes up, and there's a cinema screen which says: '*Pantoufle par* Alan Ayckbourn' and all the credits. And then it starts. Everyone but me seemed to be very happy with it. Then, a marvellous *coup de théâtre*: at the end of the first scene, the girl does something and then there's a mix into a hand on a teapot, and then a track back and back and back on the camera, until slowly it encompasses first the two at the table, then the garden itself, which is palpably by now a stage set, then the proscenium arch, so that the screen fills with proscenium arch; and the screen rolls up and, damn as make any difference, there's the real scene behind. It's an amazing piece; but again, nobody seemed to take any notice. Nobody clapped or anything: it was the blasé French. The English would have been leaping around, saying, 'That's tremendous!'

IW: I'm told there was a legendary production – I don't know if it ever happened – in the States of *How the Other Half Loves*.

AA: Oh, the Gay Lib one, yes. I got a very sweet letter from this company, saying, 'We are a gay company operating in California, and we think your play *How the Other Half Loves* is marvellous. We would like to adapt it for our company, which will be, in this case, an all-male cast. And we would make Frank and Fiona, Bob and Terry, and William and Mary into gays.' So I wrote back, 'Look, you really mustn't think I'm prejudiced in any way: this is a wonderful, wonderful idea. And I think your theatre is marvellous and serves an enormous section, I'm sure, of California. But the fact is, I think you're really picking the wrong play, because there are certain central things in these relationships which are heterosexual. For instance, I suppose, just about, Frank and Fiona could be played gay, with a big pinch of salt. But certainly Bob and Terry could never be gay, because the whole action round that pair is about their baby. Terry is saying, "I'm trapped, I'm trapped with a kid, and I can't get out. And I'm a woman with a brain." Are you going to suggest that there is some way they have adopted a baby? It doesn't sound right: if they've adopted a baby, then they've done it voluntarily, and . . .' 'No, no, we've solved that,' they wrote back. 'We're going to make it a chimp.' So there's a man, trapped at home, looking after a chimp! I wrote back and said, 'No, I really don't think I can give my permission for this. I'm sure there must be many more plays that are more suitable. I just don't think it'll work.' So I've probably blotted my copybook.

IW: Any other foreign productions which have been hair-raising at all?

AA: Well, the American producers of *Absurd Person Singular* tried to switch the second and third acts, because audiences were laughing more at the second and they wanted to end on a high. Then there was a note from somewhere like Hungary: '*Relatively Speaking* has opened and is running very successfully now, and we're sending you royalties. P.S. The musical version is also doing very well.' We never heard any more of it.

IW: Another musical, *Jeeves*, which you did with Andrew Lloyd Webber, was not a success, but I believe you met Wodehouse.

AA: Yes. There was a sort of mooted plot afoot that it would be nice to have his approval of the show. Not a plot by Andrew and me, I hasten to add, but a plot by some managerial whiz-kids, probably up in the Stigwood Organisation somewhere. Plum lived at that time out on Long Island. He didn't have a piano, but there was a convenient young millionaire composer within a stone's throw who did. So the idea was that we'd go over to Plum's house, pick him and his wife, Ethel, up in a sort of cortège of cars and go on to this composer's house. So we arrived, and we drove through Long Island, which is very like Surrey – it gets more and more like Surrey the further you go – and the first sign that we were in Wodehouse-land was that we passed a sign saying, 'The Bide-A-Wee Cats and Dogs Home', which indeed was run by Ethel. And Ethel was, as we arrived, finishing boiling fifteen chickens for the stray dogs and cats.

IW: Ethel was his age, was she?

AA: I think she was probably about seventy. He was about ninety, so she was quite a stripling. He was very, very deaf, and he wore a deaf aid, but one suspected immediately that, like some of his characters, he wore it as a defence. He seemed to be able to hear everyone except Ethel quite well. Ethel would scream at him and he wouldn't take any notice, but you could say, 'It's a lovely morning.' 'Yes,' he'd say. Anyway, he came shuffling out. He was working on his new novel. He smiled and nodded and shook hands with us and smiled. And we got into the car and started to drive. Ethel said, 'Be careful over the bumps. He doesn't like bumps.' So we drove quite slowly, and this house turned out to be quite a long way away. Plum was muttering away in the front there about how it was lovely to be out in the open air, and said, 'Jolly good, this, jolly nice. I'd like to meet the chap who wrote the words in this.

That would have been very nice.' 'HE'S SITTING BEHIND YOU, PLUM! YOU'VE JUST MET HIM! HE'S SITTING BEHIND YOU!' screamed Ethel. He said, 'Oh, he's sitting behind me? Oh, that's nice. Didn't know you'd written the words.'

Well, we got there and we had our photographs taken outside. We went in, and Andrew sat down to play the score. We sat Plum by the piano, and I sat next to him to hand him the sheets of lyrics, because it was quite apparent he wasn't going to hear very much. And Andrew – I remember very clearly – put the music up, and turned round, and he went, 'Aaaah!' He looked sort of desperate. I turned round, and there were about sixty people in this room. They'd all filtered in – sort of casuals from the composer's relations and odd, very bearded, woolly Americans with Afro haircuts who were all sitting cross-legged. Suddenly, Andrew was playing a concert performance and P. G. Wodehouse was the last of the people to play to. The whole of the newer wave, modern American composers were there. The man who owned the place turned out to be the foremost electronic composer. So Andrew played through the score and sang it quite well, even if he kept missing my words because he was trying to play it right. And Plum was nodding and saying, 'Jolly nice, jolly nice.' At the end of the music, our hostess had absolutely excelled herself. She'd laid on the full English tea: cucumber sandwiches, tomato sandwiches, pots of tea, scones, a full table. And Plum said, 'Ah, tea!' and absolutely beamed. And Ethel seized him by the arm and said, 'No! Time for home, Plum!' and whisked him away, and that's the last we ever saw of him.

IW: Having worked on *Jeeves*, you actually got the taste for musicals, I think.

AA: Yes, but it's very difficult, I had to find someone who'd work my way. Initially, I appointed Paul Todd as the theatre's musical director. The writing collaboration grew from this. It soon became apparent that he works at very high speed, is extremely flexible and complies with how I'm working extremely well. For instance, we work musically to lyrics rather than lyrics to music. With *Suburban Strains*, he was the last one to know what the play was about. I would say, as it got later, 'I think we need a big I-hate-you-and-I'm-leaving-you song, something like . . .' and I'd give him a rough lyric line, and he'd bang out a melody for it. And that worked very well. Having said that, there's obviously a tremendous amount of give and take.

IW: Most of the work you've done with him is in fact revue stuff, apart from *Suburban Strains*. Are you actually hankering after the great British musical?

AA: No, I'm hankering after *Suburban Strains* and developing in that line. There was a very interesting development: it was only a minor one, but it's a small seed, if you like. In the second of our lunchtime shows, there were two or three songs which I call one-act songs. There was the 'Fancy Meeting You' song, where the man meets the old girlfriend and she says, 'I'm married now' – which is one of the more successful. There's nothing dazzlingly original about the situation, it's a miniature one-act play set to music; I've just used his music and written dialogue to it. Well, that interested me a lot, and I think we might continue writing some one-act songs. If he provided me with thirty minutes of music, the next step would be to write a one-act play on top of that. I've asked for a well-structured piece, with a developing theme; possibly a return-ing theme would be nice. And then I'd take that and use it as a format for writing a play round. And it'll be an opera. And then if that works, we might write a two-hour one.

IW: Music theatre.

AA: Music theatre. Maybe it will have dialogue interspersed, or I may come back and say, 'This tune's very successful, but I need it again, because this is the way the dramatic flow is going.' I'll try, as far as possible, not to misshape his images. So he's writing an overture – not an overture, it'll be more of a sort of sinfonietta. And that can only work really in the sort of theatre we're at, because he's taking a lot on trust. He's turning out thirty minutes of music which could finish up on the rubbish tip, if it doesn't work. But Paul's got a great generosity of music: if you ask for a tune, he'll give you nine. Which is nice. I like that.

IW: Do you envisage music taking over your work, or just becoming another strand of it?

AA: I think it might complement it. I don't think I'll ever become a 'musical writer'. But I would like to think that if the play stream ever did dry up, that would be there. It's only when I feel I'm definitely repeating myself that I'll want to move on to another strand. But I do think the music strand is very nice: it acts as a sort of buffer. And writing songs has been like using other muscles and incidentally buffing up one's lyric writing, and actually learning a lot about it by practising it and hearing the results. And hearing the results of those twenty songs, I know the ones that I think work. You know, I could finish up being quite a good lyric writer, if I keep at it long enough; and indeed, I'm learning about music. Not about chords and notes, but about what it does to words, which is very important.

The Scarborough Dimension

IAN WATSON: On your passport, where it asks for 'occupation', what does it say?

ALAN AYCKBOURN: 'Writer.' It sounds grander on a passport.

IW: Yet you consider yourself primarily as a director rather than a writer?

AA: Yes, I do. Forty-eight weeks of the year are spent directing, or thereabouts. And really only a tiny minority of the year is spent in the physical business of writing. Directing really occupies my whole working life.

IW: And pays you nothing.

AA: No, it doesn't pay anything at all. A salary is earmarked: what I choose to do with it, or whether I choose to draw it, is up to me. Actually, I don't because I regard Scarborough as something rather special and am quite happy to refuse payment.

IW: There are two aspects of directing, and we'd better take them separately. One is being the director of the theatre, and the other is directing shows. First of all, the theatre. Perhaps we've got to clear something up, for the history books. Everybody, as a sort of shorthand, talks about the theatre in Scarborough either as Stephen Joseph's theatre or Alan Ayckbourn's theatre. It needs to be said, I think, that had it been left simply to the pair of you, that theatre wouldn't be there, because Stephen abandoned it at one stage while he was still alive, and when he died, you were working elsewhere.

AA: Oh yes, there's a third member of the triumvirate who never gets mentioned, and that's Ken Boden. He was, I think, when Stephen first came here, secretary of the local branch of the British Drama League. Stephen believed quite strongly that amateur theatre should be drawn into the professional theatre, and, indeed, made allies of rather quickly. So Stephen did quite a lot early on to cement our good relations with the local groups, and they've remained. And out of that, one of the people who emerged was Ken, who in time became front-of-house manager for the theatre. He was also – another shrewd step by Stephen – a local man, and at that time an insurance agent, who sold insurance to practically everyone – or attempted to – in Scarborough. He was therefore in an excellent position to welcome practically every local face that came to the theatre. So he was a very good plank in our PR drive, if you like.

Later on, in 1967 when Stephen died, Ken just picked up the reins and kept a caretaker government going until the time I started to take over in the seventies. It's quite amazing how he managed to cope at all, because one thing Stephen was was totally unconventional. He ran the theatre as he ran theatres and as nobody else ran them, in an extraordinary robbing-from-Peter-to-save-Paul-and-back-again way. His books were idiosyncratic, to say the least. I think it took Ken about fifteen years even to begin to understand how a normal theatre functions. As the theatre grew, so Ken grew with it. But the theatre he started running for Stephen was on a totally different scale to the one we've finished up with now.

IW: Ken was actually the head of a sort of little mafia which ran the theatre, wasn't he? There was Margaret, his wife, who ran the box office and there was Dorothy Ruff and Joan Gregory on front of house, who were there, it seemed, since the year dot.

AA: Yes, they were; they grew up with the theatre. And, of course, the people we added, since we moved into the new theatre, were Stan and Doreen Lawton. Stan was the caretaker, and he was also barman, and he was also everything else. And Doreen, his wife, did all the catering. They're another gold-plated couple. I don't know where Ken found them, but they were marvellous. And they became a very central plank in the family. Ken was extraordinarily successful in incorporating people like that.

IW: So in that sense, the theatre is following on a Stephen Joseph policy. In two other important ways, you're very much pursuing policies which Stephen stood for. One is the policy of having a permanent company, and the other is the policy of running effectively a theatre for new writing. The concept of the permanent company has become unfashionable. There must be very few theatres left in the country which are pursuing that policy. I think the argument against it is that, with a permanent company, you are inevitably constantly casting against the nature of the actors in the company. What's the argument for it?

AA: Well, one really ought to say first that the theatre's changed radically in one way from Stephen's. When Stephen ran the company, it was very natural that it should be a permanent company, in the same way that, say, Hull Truck or any of those companies where the identity springs from the group are permanent companies. We were then, I suppose, the first of the fringe theatres. And, as all fringe groups are, we were all suspect communists and suspect everything else! At that time, as an actor, you didn't mention you worked for that company if you were auditioning for another, because eyebrows went up and you could feel the black marks being added to your name; you were working with a sort of subversive.

IW: That was because it was theatre in the round, though, wasn't it?

AA: Also because it was Stephen. There was something anarchic about Stephen, and the image he gave was one of wishing to overthrow existing standards, and so, perhaps, the more conventional members of the theatre felt slightly threatened.

Anyway, establishing a company theatre, as Stephen did, was a quite normal thing to do. What's become less normal is that, as we've grown — and it really happened when we became a year-round company and got our own building — we became an established company. We became on a par, if not on a financial par, with, say York Repertory Company, and, in that sense, it became perhaps abnormal that the permanent company should continue. And that, I believe, is entirely my doing.

I believe a permanent company works, for me and for this theatre, for several reasons. Firstly, because our work — a lot of it — is original work, one needs actors with the muscle and the preparedness to tackle new work. And it isn't possible to do this with every actor: many are too slow; many actors don't react quickly enough with each other. With a new play you are asking people to do twice the work — you're asking them not only to learn the lines, but also to be prepared to test out a new, completely untried product, to take changes and alterations, and to accept a certain air of nebulousness. If you're tackling an established classic, at least you know at the back of your mind that it's going to work if you do it half well. With some of these plays you just don't know until the first night. And you really do need a sort of crack SAS team to tackle this. That's one aspect.

The other aspect is that, on the level of theatre I'm running – I mean, the financial level, where it would be impractical to expect star actors to come up – you've got to get the best actors available, and most actors feel happier and respond more readily to a company situation. It's far more interesting for them to feel a security in their working relationships, where they just respond better. And I've found that actors who've come have grown visibly under this system: their work's relaxed. Obviously, there comes a point of no return when they should leave, because their work becomes too relaxed and too easy-going, and indeed they begin to believe perhaps that they're better than they are – partly because I probably get lax enough to believe they're better than they are – and then they ought to go away and do something else. Sometimes it's six months, sometimes it's years.

It's also to do with the nature of the director I am, which is a slow one. It's probably to do with my own personality. I'm a very slow person to get to know, and to get to know people. I tend, in my first production with anyone, to let them go very much their own way. Stephen always drummed into me: don't stamp on all the initiative of an actor until you've actually seen what he can do; he's got to show you his paces. And at the end of the first show, you can say, 'Ah-ha! You're one of those actors who does this, that and the other. You're one of these actors who goes over the top on first nights. You're one of these actors with a peculiar mannerism. You're one of these actors who's downright inaudible.' And then you start to work on it, and in the second production it gets more interesting. Obviously you can't give him *no* production in the first show you do, but you give him a much laxer production, and then you begin to close in, rather like a doctor who's begun to diagnose, not only on the faults of an actor, but also on the strengths, and you attempt to build on them. And that's a long-term working relationship, and the fascination and the excitement of finding something new in someone is exactly paralleled by one's exploration of one's own writing.

IW: The other side is the audience. What has the permanent company got to offer the audience, which is where it's got to show?

AA: It's got that rather dubious side, the fact that audiences love the known. They love the known element. They miss actors when they leave. And we do try to let the organism develop with the individuals. I always say to new people coming in – and I hope it isn't a load of old cobblers that one trots out – that this is an entity which I hope is flexible enough that anyone who comes and has reasonable ideas, which can be accepted by a majority – and that's the important thing – can effectively alter the organization and bend it. When Bob Eaton came along and joined us as a part-director, part-actor, he gave us roadshows and gave us our first bar shows. I, for my part, I think, developed his acting to an extent that he'd never developed while he was at Stoke. So he gave and we gave, and when he left the relationship had blossomed to the extent that he knew where he wanted to go from there. That's a very clear example of someone adding to the company from within it, which I hope is the way it works. And that's the value of a company. I think one's only obligation is to make sure that the thing is fluid enough, and that means constantly changing. There's always a 20 per cent addition to, and subtraction from, the company each year.

IW: Obviously a very delicate organism. What's the error rate? How many people do you employ that you regret and have to get rid of fast?

AA: Oh, there's quite a lot. My associate director and I go to endless trouble when we audition. I'm talking about actors particularly, and of course they are the most delicate. What you cannot tell is how an actor will socialize. You look and hope he isn't a heavy drinker, and you check with a few people, and you look at the references, but ultimately you employ him because you like the look of him and because he looks as if he can act. I have little faith in auditions, and I loathe those big workshop sessions that go on for days. It's an awful thing to say, but I tend to like people when they walk in the door. And, of course, this occasionally leads to disasters. We've had some extremely inferior actors in the company from time to time; we've had actors who've drunk, and we've had some that have been so anti-social and so unpleasant that people longed to get rid of them, because you are in fact asking people to live in each other's pockets for twelve hours a day, and in a very small concern of eight, nine actors with a communal men's, communal women's dressing room. So it is tricky, and obviously we make mistakes. You can't hope that they'll all love each other: what you can hope is that you can gather people together who, although they may well see each other's errors, respect each other as artists.

IW: A writers' theatre: there have been subtle changes over the years in the policy of presenting new writing, but Stephen Joseph's policy itself remains; that a prime purpose of the theatre company should be to present new writing and the work of new writers. There was a time – and indeed you're a product of it – when the members of the company themselves, the actors in the company, were encouraged to be the writers for it. You continued that for a time, with people like Bob Eaton, Stephen Mallatratt, Stephen Lowe and Alison Skilbeck. It doesn't seem to be happening any more: you seem to be accepting the division of labour, as it were, and commissioning writers living away from the company.

AA: Yes, it's not a conscious decision, but nor do I particularly go around asking actors if they can write. I'm obviously looking for actors primarily. Stephen often would look for writers primarily, and then ask if they could act. I don't think I can do that, because now, whereas Stephen was running at the most a thirteen-week season, I'm hoping for an actor's commitment of up to a year, maybe two years, and during that time I'm going to be putting enormous strains on that person's capabilities as an actor, because the casting is likely to be extremely wide. I can't really get by with an actor of narrow abilities, however kooky his personality is: a little charmer with one performance isn't going to last too long – it's going to get rather thin round about Christmas time! So I am looking for really a very experienced actor. As a result of asking for this level of experience, perhaps I haven't found any actor–writers. In general, although there are exceptions, the better the writer the less good they become as an actor, because they become rather like directors and like a lot of actor–directors they become more and more removed from their performance, rather detached. Certainly, as my writing improved, my acting slowly faded away. At one time I wasn't bad. I always say I'm a very bad actor, but at one time I wasn't really that bad. I certainly got worse as my writing took over.

IW: Sure, but the fact of having been an actor and having been an ASM and a stage manager, and a technical stage manager at that, has informed your writing to such a degree that it couldn't actually have happened without it. I wonder whether the sort of writing which you're going to get from 'writers' is going to be that informed about what the theatre is. Isn't there a danger there that, because they haven't got the theatre background that you have, they rely on yours to tell them how to write for the theatre – that you work with writers in such a way as to show them how to become Alan Ayckbourn?

AA: It's possible, I suppose. But I try when directing someone else's work to tackle it as a director, not a playwright. I try and keep the two functions separate.

IW: Robert Cushman, I think it was, divided current British playwrights into the domestics and the state-of-the-nations. And you were either the head, or very near the head, of the domestics. I suppose the nearest to a state-of-the-nation you've put on was *The Crucible*, which happened to be a set book – and I guess that was the motive for doing it. Does this imply that you don't approve of the other strain of writing in the British theatre at the moment? Do you not like the Brentons, the Barkers, the Snoo Wilsons, the David Edgars?

AA: They're fine. I just don't want to do them myself, that's all – any more than they'd want to direct my plays.

IW: Do you accept that the repertoire of the Stephen Joseph Theatre in Scarborough is actually a fairly narrow one? It's not what any other rep in the country would regard as a very balanced programme. You don't do Shakespeare, you do very little costume drama – *The Crucible* really was something out of the ordinary, wasn't it?

AA: Yes. We're very limited financially. We tend to do the set book we can afford to do. And so much of our stuff's new.

IW: But new in a certain mould.

AA: Well, it's that way because I like it! I suppose that's what makes it narrow. I present a theatre for a community, what I think the community wants to see. I also do what I think my actors want to do. And somewhere between the two, we've got to get the balance right. Our theatre's a small one; we don't have very many people, and I don't feel our resources are up to doing certain plays as well as we might. I don't see any point in us doing *King Lear*. It would be *Lear* with a lot of ASMs, and the carpenter coming on as Gloucester. It would just be awful. It seems to me that we ought to do what we do best, and undoubtedly what we do best is the domestic-scale play – partly because the theatre is scaled that way, and partly because we are in the midst of that sort of audience. People in general seem to want to see themselves, or reflections of themselves. They want to see things that reflect their own particular dilemmas.

IW: As director of the theatre, how much of a problem would you have if you didn't have a house writer called Alan Ayckbourn?

AA: Oh, quite a lot, I think. It certainly helps. I'm an enormous subsidy to the theatre – not only financial, but also artistic. It allows me to take chances with other people's work, which we do. We take writers at quite early stages and take devastating risks in putting them on.

IW: Do you not worry about the time when you're going to have to find a dauphin? When Stephen went, there was a ready dauphin around, someone who was ready just to step into his shoes – or very nearly ready. What is going to happen to that theatre when it hasn't got Alan Ayckbourn?

AA: I think what'll happen is what happens anywhere: the thing will go into a period of decline. It might go on; if one were incredibly unlucky they'd just produce your plays every year so it became a sort of memorial theatre, extremely boring. But with any luck that won't happen. Theatre to me is nothing whatever to do with buildings. It's to do with the people in it, or the person in it:

very often, the person. When John Neville ran Nottingham, it was sensational for that period, and it was then somewhere else's turn. Quite a lot of reps in this country are being run simply because there's a building there, and there's a group of chaps who've gone and filled it and said, 'We must do some theatre in it', instead of the other way round. In fact, they should have said, 'Look, this is the sort of theatre I want to do: now let's find somewhere to do it in.'

When I leave, there may or may not be someone of equally strong identity. I suppose ideally, if there isn't, they should close the place and say, 'You've had your theatre, Scarborough, and that's it.' And the Arts Council should bundle up their grant and look round for someone else they fancy. And it should always be a person or, better still, a group of people. It shouldn't be a building.

IW: You are rather talking about your theatre as a sort of personal fiefdom.

AA: Because I'm the nucleus of the darned thing. But having said that, rolling along as I have, I've picked up a lot of extremely talented moss, which has become more than moss: it's become a group of talents, and all I do is act as a flashing beacon, now, and attract people of like views. How long they stay, or whether they choose to branch off and become their own beacons, is up to them. But I think that's what I'm doing. Actors, in general, work best when there is a director around the place. I'm talking of me as a director now, not as a writer.

My writing is a sort of gold hook, but I hope that the actors actually like to work in the theatre because they like working with me as a director. And I think that, in terms of the theatre that I run here, I'm not bad at it. I'm less of a West End director, because I don't like the system, and I don't enjoy the way they work.

IW: It's fairly clear how you feed that theatre. The relationship is actually symbiotic, isn't it? You feed that theatre and that theatre feeds you. In what way does it feed you? By laying an obligation on you to produce a certain amount of work?

AA: Yes, it does that. I am very conscious that my pen is largely responsible for the theatre remaining solvent. There's got to be a play of mine floating in repertoire, or we're going to be very heavily down. And that is the main reason for writing. It also gives me the right small horizon to work for. I can't work on big horizons. I couldn't write for New York and London. I find it quite sufficient to write something to fill the space I've got, and that, I find, is quite interesting. It's interesting also to write, not for the individual members of the company, but to write for the feel that's coming off the company as a whole. It's a very nebulous thing, but, as the company changes, with new members joining it, so I get different feels – I sometimes get a very morose company, and I tend to write moroser plays.

IW: Would you have written as much had you not been director of the company?

AA: Probably not so much, because I'm very easily discouraged. I've got a terrible mixture of total confidence when attacked, and total lack of confidence when praised. The more people praise me, the more depressed I become, and the more uncertain I get of what my own work is like. And the more people go knocking it, the more confident I become that it's OK. I'm just cussed, really. I've never been, for instance, more certain that *Taking Steps* is a very good play than now the London critics have torn it up, and I'm certainly less convinced that *The Norman Conquests* ever were any good, simply because they were so overpraised that I've come to dislike them intensely. Undoubtedly there's nothing like criticism to concentrate the mind wonderfully and, indeed, you have to rally under it. And Scarborough provides me protection from too much hammer: I can simply get it produced relatively quietly.

I was thinking today about this when I was directing my new play – that what I'm actually having (and I don't see any harm in this sort of theatre) is an enormous amount of fun, creating a game, if you like, which the actors, I hope, can play with the audience. Because I want the game to be a good game and I want it to have a lot of other facets to it, I've taken a lot of care, I hope, to make it quite a deep game. But I do really treat theatre as pure art. That's why I don't like intrusions like heavy political themes. Of course one can write a play about women's liberation – it's a very important topic – but I don't think it's very satisfying when they stand on a chair and tell the men in the audience that they're pigs. And that's where I differ from agit-prop theatre, in that I hate being told things. I hated it at school and I hate it in theatres.

IW: You're not objecting to the subject-matter; you're objecting to the didacticism with which it's presented.

AA: That's well put, yes.

IW: The pressure on you, then, is to produce a new piece for every season. Are you actually scared of the block, the writing block?

AA: Yes, I am. I'm worried about everything. I'm worried about repeating myself; I'm worried about the fact that the more plays I write, the narrower the options get. I've used certain things that I wouldn't want to repeat, and I am worried that there might come a time when I'm not satisfied with what I'm writing. And in that case I'll stop. The censor in me will arrive and say, 'No, this isn't good enough' — as he has arrived in the past.

IW: To what extent does the state of affairs in the Stephen Joseph Theatre affect the content of what you write? By which I mean, if the theatre is having a rough year financially, does that force you (a) to think of writing a smaller-cast play, and (b) to think of writing a more obviously commercial type of play?

AA: Well, I don't think I can do (b). I can do (a), but that happens simply because there is a smaller cast: full stop. If we're in a bad way, I'll have wound the company down by the time I'm writing. Often it's quite a problem. This time I had nine, and I was writing a play and I could only find eight! And I was saying, 'Where the hell am I going to get this other character from?'

IW: One of the slightly unusual things about your company is that once a year you go on the road and tour. What's the function of touring?

AA: It makes us money. It also — and this is the most important — gives the company a change of air, a change of audience, a change of vantage point, and, I think, a bit of an artistic rethink. The other thing is that it gives a continuity of employment, which means I can hold my actors together. They now get a month's break in the spring which they deserve and need — and nobody ever gripes about that, although, in fact, their holiday pay is only for three weeks and they have a week on the dole. And they have a two-week break in the autumn. So an actor who wishes to remain with us for a period of a year, two years, can be guaranteed continuity of employment during that time, with six weeks' break over a full year. And that's the real value of touring, because we can't yet stay in Scarborough all the time.

IW: Is there an element of not being a prophet in your own country? That is to say, if the company stays in Scarborough it's actually going to get devalued by the people of Scarborough, whereas if you can come back with great notices from Amsterdam, and indeed London, it's going to make them value what they've got rather more? In purely financial terms, does it help you to raise sponsorship for productions?

AA: I don't think so. Scarborough's terribly unimpressed by anything that happens anywhere else. It's an amazingly insular place. Unless you've been on ITV, you really aren't very much good. And I've only been on occasionally, so I'm really not that much. People still think we're amateurs. Of course, rather like your football team, they like to check up on your away games, and they're very cross – and it's nice to see people coming to our defence – if we are, for instance, criticized by anyone nationally. The company tends to get good notices, particularly in Europe, because of course English actors are actually very good. English acting, and indeed all British theatre, is held in high esteem (it's about the only thing that is) abroad.

IW: Do you consider yourself a fairly authoritarian director?

AA: I don't think I'm authoritarian. I tend to suggest, and I tend to organize quite well. But I do allow actors enormous leeway. I do that because I believe that what they're likely to give me, if they've made a decision themselves, will be better than if I've made it. I resist such things as demonstrating – a thing which I hate, and I never have a play blocked when I arrive at a rehearsal: I have absolutely no idea how the moves will go.

IW: You and Peter Cheeseman must be the two longest-serving directors, in the same theatres, in the country. You've been in Scarborough eighteen years, Cheeseman's been in Stoke a little longer. Do you see yourself staying here to retirement? Or do you get itchy about it?

AA: I don't see myself moving. The thing is that the theatre at the moment is flexible enough to keep me occupied. I've still got enough to explore here. I haven't got a lot of ambitions to run anything bigger, so that's out. I don't think I'd care to work freelance, because I find that inconvenient and rather boring. I like what I'm doing. It's nice working with people like we've got here. So I shall stay here. So there!

Conversations: 1987

Plays 1980 to 1988

IAN WATSON: Was *Season's Greetings*, in 1980, any sort of watershed?

ALAN AYCKBOURN: It was the twenty-fifth of my plays. I remember, because we had the silver poster! It was a funny old play, *Season's*, because it nearly went down the spout. It was at a time when I was getting a bit disenchanted with the West End for various reasons, and I wanted to try and do something for the Scarborough company. I forged a deal with Thelma Holt, who was running the Roundhouse at the time, under which we went down there and did – as it turned out – two plays: *Season's Greetings* and *Suburban Strains*. As it transpired, the Roundhouse was a hopeless venue for anything we did: it was a bit like a baseball field. Certainly for *Season's Greetings* it was huge, and the play totally disappeared. It stood no chance at all and was written off by most critics. It was Greenwich that came to the rescue of the play, in the form of Alan Strachan, who suggested I might like to do it there with a new cast. (Although the play itself was quite successful in Scarborough, Michael Codron didn't have much interest in it after its Roundhouse débâcle.) In the end, we did it with a marvellous cast – put together mainly by Alan – directed by me. And it was a whacking success. At Greenwich it was a sell-out. Then Michael Codron – as ever – leapt in and transferred it. It ran OK, but it was one of those tricky things with a huge success. I always mistrust transfers very much. Everyone says, 'It's doing so well here, let's move it.' And in the moving, something happens. It did pretty well, but it was never quite the same as it was at Greenwich. It was the same with the *Norman*s. I don't think they really transferred totally blissfully to the Globe. I was beginning to recognize that buildings are actually very important for plays.

IW: *Season's Greetings* has been much played, hasn't it?

AA: Yes. It's the first time anybody really got shot in a play of mine! It's quite dark, but it's quite fun as well, and it seems to catch

[123]

on with people at Christmas. Everyone seemed to warm to this play. Michael Billington was very enthusiastic, comparing it to Ibsen and things like that, which was rather nice.

IW: It does end on a distinct down beat, although I have seen productions that have played totally against that. In Calgary, where it had its Canadian première, it was played as farce, with a very gigglesome end: the two had a little giggle and ran upstairs to bed together!

AA: Oh God! However many stage directions you write in, you can't change the way people do it. Some directors set out to so imprint their own image on a show that you think, 'I don't know how you reach those conclusions.' Sometimes it can be interesting. If you want to do *A Midsummer Night's Dream* as an ice ballet, it can be quite interesting. But when you're actually inverting the meaning, it's wrong. And one hears of people who go out of their way to play the thing in reverse from what it obviously means. It's not as if they misinterpret; it's that they are saying, 'It would be better if this was made into a feminist statement' or 'This could be made to fit this.' I just think it's nonsense.

IW: It's intriguing, though, isn't it? You would say that it was legitimate to emphasize the comic elements in *King Lear*, for example.

AA: Yes, if they were there. But what I wouldn't do is to get him to get up after he'd died and do a knees-up. Or bounce Cordelia across the stage; or use her as a glove puppet. If the dramatist is any good – and presumably, if you've chosen to do the play, you must think he's something – then it would be nice to enhance what he's saying, rather than to bring out what you want to say through him. If he's not any good, you shouldn't be doing him anyway.

IW: *Season's Greetings* was 1980. Since then, your output of full-length plays has been *Way Upstream, Making Tracks, A Trip to Scarborough, Intimate Exchanges, It Could Be Any One of Us, A Chorus of Disapproval, Woman in Mind, A Small Family Business, Henceforward* . . . and *Man of the Moment*.

AA: A lot of plays!

IW: Is it true – since you were so off pat about *Season's Greetings* being number 25 and we know that *Man of the Moment* was for months scheduled on your word processor simply as 'AA35' – that you are actually counting and measuring yourself against Mr Shakespeare's canon?

AA: No.

IW: How many plays did he write?

AA: I don't know. Quite a lot. Heather knows: she may be counting. But I'm not.

IW: With the benefit of hindsight, do you discern any particular shift in yourself over those plays since *Season's Greetings*?

AA: There is a certain slow movement, but it's a bit like an iceberg. I don't think it's something I'm really in control of. It just happens that the plays, in general, are becoming slightly more 'social'. They seem to have a slightly more outward-looking view.

IW: *Way Upstream*, which came next, was actually christened by one reviewer your SDP play.

AA: Oh God, yes! Well, it was inevitable.

IW: It was almost an unavoidable conclusion, wasn't it? The play was written in some frustration, I gather.

AA: It was written for two things, really. First was that question which every comfortable, middle-class person asks himself at some stage, especially when he sees the news and reads the papers: 'If danger threatens, how will I react?' And second, I wanted to investigate the nature of why some people lead others – leadership, and all that business. Yes, it was much more of an allegorical play than I normally write. It was an attempt to get away from what I had been writing. It's also an adventure story. I was beginning to be – and I very strongly still am – of the opinion that the theatre's salvation lies in a move away from the over-emphasis on the verbal, back towards the visual. The perfect play is a combination of both, which is, of course, what we had in our theatre tradition until, alas, some of the dramatists I admire most came drifting into view – the Ibsen–Chekhov school of writing, which reduced theatre very much to a verbal level. Shaw, too. And it has held on for a long time, except for people like John Arden, who did try something different.

IW: Do you read Arden?

AA: Yes, I was reading his *Workhouse Donkey* only a few days ago, when I was looking at plays I might be able to do at the National. He is one of the few dramatists who try a different approach, but generally we've still got the feeling that theatre's there purely to present arguments. It seems to me that your play is failing whenever you see someone with his eyes closed, listening with a serene smile on his face. It can't happen all the time, but I would love to feel people were saying, 'I'd better watch this, because I may miss something.' And certainly in *Way Upstream* there's a conscious tug towards the visual, and the excitement of it. It's something I've made a conscious decision to put in a memo to any writer who produces anything for us. I say to people, just very gently, 'Do bear in mind that it's a visual medium. Please do not present me with plays that, as a director, I read and say, "How the hell do I make this interesting to watch?" It's much nicer if a script says, "I defy you to try and do me!" '

IW: I take it you would never have considered putting Michael Frayn's *Benefactors* on the stage, then.

AA: No. It's a radio play: I can't remember anything visual about it at all. It's a completely auditory experience. It's a good piece of writing, and Michael Frayn has done plays that are very visual, like *Noises Off*. I suppose we can't always be doing that, but I was aware that I had nothing to watch. As you perfect your craft, it's very easy to relax that element and say, 'Well, now I'm in control of my characters, I can allow them to sit still.' But physical structure is very important, and I always try, once the idea is there, to start searching around for an interesting visual way to tell the story. At the moment I've got what I think is quite a good idea for a play, but I'm not sure how to tell it yet, and that is as big a problem. Something dramatically visual has to happen; some event has to occur to make the audience sit up. Increasingly over the years, theatregoing has become a special occasion, just in that the effort required is greater even than it used to be, when perhaps it had less to compete with. So the event has got to be something a bit special.

I've done a lot of tricks with *Intimate Exchanges*, and with *The Norman Conquests*, and with *Sisterly Feelings*: each is special, and each is a bit different. You can't indefinitely do that, but each play must have its focus. And that's what happened with *Way Upstream*.

It has terribly unfortunate connotations as a result of all the disasters at the National, but in its simplest terms, in Scarborough, it was a terrific event, and people really enjoyed it. Indeed, even at the National, once the old ballyhoo had died down, people just came because it was on. One front-of-house lady said to me, 'My God, your public are faithful! Some of them have rebooked three times for this, because of cancelled previews.' And, you know, the audience cheered and shouted and booed the villain. It was really a plea for reasonable people and wasn't actually to do with David Owen particularly. I just find extremely narrow-minded, aggressive trade unionists as objectionable as extremely narrow-minded, bigoted bosses. And while those two are busy chewing each other's heads off – particularly when you looked at those two locked in mortal combat in the miners' strike – you despair for the reasonable miner who is getting caught up in all that mess of violent picketing. The play was really saying that there ought to be another way; and it's a bit difficult to say, without being accused of being a wishy-washy liberal. But I still think there is, and if there isn't, then we'll all get blown up anyway. One cheers the feeling that is current, of a slight *détente* in the world. I don't think that was due to *Way Upstream* – more likely Mr Gorbachev!

IW: You're altogether too modest! But what about the ending of *Way Upstream*? It's one of your weirder endings, as you go under Armageddon Bridge, and flags are run up and bands start playing, and God knows what.

AA: Well, that was just as they were going along. It's really a love story again inside there. A relationship between a man and a woman – Alistair and Emma – was dying because of lack of purpose: they were a purposeless couple. He had lost his will to decide, and because she, for better or worse, had locked her destiny to his, she had lost her purpose. By the end, it says that, provided he's prepared to make decisions, she can make them with him and they can stand and fight together. There's a great coming together by the end of the play. At the beginning, they're drifting hopelessly apart, because their whole sex life has broken down and everything. And it's then that they're put to the test. I was very careful not to say that the man becomes strong and therefore the woman becomes strong, but that the one leads the other. In fact, his act of heroism is matched by an act of heroism of hers and they both grow together. It was the first optimistic play I'd written for some time. It is saying that men and women can learn to respect each other and also live together, and if, for some reason, one of them loses self-respect, it's very hard for the other to do anything about it. It's also, I suppose, a morality play.

I carefully balanced the forces of darkness to be coming from both ends of the political spectrum: there is a violently right-wing girl, and a violently left-wing man of some nebulous type, but they're both, in a sense, river spirits of evil who come literally out of the water and probably go back into it again. The flawed people like Keith and June – they're not born that way, they've developed – are doomed because they are flawed with pride and vanity and self-interest, while the goodies like Emma and Alistair – basically good people, although they've got all sorts of things wrong with them – can survive, particularly if they stand together. There was that sort of morality in it: Keith goes completely mad and June follows him soon after. It's quite bizarre, but it is quite a funny play: these complete maniacs slowly grow into these huge monsters! It's got a touch of J. M. Barrie and *Peter Pan* about it. What was nice was things like the plank-walking scene, which was my first foray into a really big scale 'how-the-hell-did-we-get-here?' exercise. This started off as a cabin-cruising holiday, and all of a sudden the boat's been taken over by pirates and our heroine is walking the plank blindfold over a huge river – which is quite physically dangerous anyway – while her husband is hopping around on the bank, uncertain whether to pluck up courage to rescue her or to wait hopefully for it to blow over. In the end, he rescues her, but in doing so nearly gets murdered by this man who is fifty pounds his superior in terms of physical strength. For the audience, it presents a double interest, because it is comedy set against a huge, dramatic and quite dangerous moment. It was fun, an exploration.

IW: Next was *Making Tracks*, which was your last – to date – major musical project with Paul Todd.

AA: Yes, I don't know what happened with that. I thought it was quite a good idea, but it never took off in quite the way that we meant it to. I think it works within its own scale, but I wonder sometimes whether maybe I ought to have let somebody else direct it.

IW: Why?

AA: I have a love-hate thing with a musical. I like it, but I hate some of the things it has in it. I hate all the schmaltz and all the phoney glamour of it. And I was really trying with Toddy to write a musical that was as hard-nosed as possible. I don't like a lot of the magic that goes with musicals. My favourite musical is *Guys and Dolls*, but even that I find a bit soft occasionally. I hate where they all get married at the end – I think that's disgusting. Up to that point, it's great fun. In the end, though, it seems that people only go to musicals to be reassured, and the musicals that don't reassure – and some of Sondheim's don't – are the ones that are not very successful. Sondheim's got a huge cult following, but his great joke is that he's the most unsuccessful successful musical writer in the world. He's had one hit song in his life, which was his schmaltziest song by far and the only one I personally would want to burn. In *Making Tracks* I wanted to write a musical which said it wasn't OK out there, really. But then I tried to compromise a bit by giving her a big number at the end, where it all came right – and that didn't work. Actually, I think the musical and I are doomed not to get together very much more, because my instincts are fairly pessimistic – too pessimistic for the musical.

IW: Yes, but back in 1980, we were already speaking not about musicals so much as about music theatre, which is somewhat different.

AA: Well, I may move into that more. That is a possibility. The use of music within theatre is interesting. I use it in *Henceforward* . . . , and that is probably the most satisfactory blend I've had, because it's got an irony and a non-sentimentality about it, which is what I was looking for. But it's not a conventional musical. I must stop trying to get my characters to burst into song, because people don't naturally do that. But there's nothing to say that music can't enter their lives somewhere. One day we shall see if we can't use it again.

IW: Was *Making Tracks* intended to be a major operation?

AA: No, it was really because Paul and I were looking for a second theme, and I suddenly had the idea that I wanted to incorporate the music on the stage. Then I decided to use my experience in the recording studios of Leeds, and it came to me that it might be quite fun to set it all in this place, with the glass between studio and control room as another device, so that you could use the silence of the sound-proofing between the two sections. I had actually had an experience with a singer, whom I booked while rather drunk one night in a club, and when we'd got her into the studio, she couldn't sing at all!

IW: Was it disillusion at the end of *Making Tracks* that stopped you pursuing the major music work?

AA: Yes. I was also having quite a lot of trouble finding actors who could sing and singers who could act. The other problem – and that was not entirely his fault – was that Paul does write incredibly difficult music. Most trained singers have a hell of a job with him. He writes for vast ranges, and it's not normal actor-singing music. But I can't ask a man, 'Would you mind writing simpler music, slightly more boring?'

IW: It was round about this time that you interfered with R. B. Sheridan's *A Trip to Scarborough*. How much did you change it?

AA: Well, it was there. It needed to be done, just because of the title really, and I kept picking it up. It's actually a reworking of *The Relapse* by Vanbrugh, but he took all the balls out of it. It is a cosmeticized and rather inferior version, and if you're going to spend out money to do *A Trip to Scarborough*, you might as well spend it to do *The Relapse*. The Sheridan has no quality and isn't much fun. It did occur to me to do it as a musical, but I wasn't at that time really interested in adapting that sort of thing. And then it occurred to me that the story itself was quite interesting, and I had the idea of splitting it into three, so that I took a third of the play, cut a lot of the sub-plots and then ran two other plots parallel with it.

IW: New ones of your own?

AA: Yes – one set in the early 1940s, in wartime, and one set today. What it really set out to do was to explore the decline of the hero, from Tom Fashion – the buck who rushed around seducing the ladies, begad – to the very disillusioned forties fighter-pilot hero, who is in fact a nervous wreck, to the very sleazy modern businessman with the rubber goods in his suitcase – up on the town, away from the little woman, looking for a bit of sport in Scarborough. It's also the story of how London folk come up to Scarborough to take advantage of the yokels, and how the yokels have the last laugh on them. The London antique dealer comes up to buy a manuscript of Sheridan's original *Trip to Scarborough*, and buys it for a fantastically deflated price, and then finds he's been swindled anyway, because it doesn't belong to the person who sold it to him. It finished up with a sort of Royal Shakespeare-like dance, and they danced through the three periods, starting with a stately minuet and finishing with a rock 'n' roll number. It went rather well.

IW: *A Trip to Scarborough* was actually written in the middle of your writing marathon for *Intimate Exchanges*, wasn't it?

AA: Yes, it was. I had a summer of *Intimate*, followed by the autumn when I took on a company for *Saturday, Sunday, Monday* (which I was able to do because I had only two actors all summer), then I did *A Trip to Scarborough*, and then I came back and wrote the last *Intimate* after Christmas. It was a very fertile time.

IW: It's difficult to know where to start on *Intimate Exchanges*!

AA: I think *Intimate* was a tremendous exercise in nostalgia for me. It's a complete Laurie Lee of a play. Most of the characters are drawn from my childhood and it's set around my prep school. Toby and Celia are images of my old headmaster and his wife.

IW: Was he an alcoholic?

AA: He did drink a bit. He went to Spain and died, eventually. I remember them having terrible rows around the school. They ran out of money eventually, and we were the last five boys in this huge, huge school. When I'd joined it, there were about seventy or eighty. They were very sweet to us, and when we left, this whole school closed. It was like their dream had finished, and they went and moved into a small bungalow. I populated the play with 'village characters', and it was what I call completely closed-circuit writing: it all gathered in around one tiny area. It was meant to be like a big picture book. It was never intended that anyone should sit and solemnly watch all sixteen versions, but that you could dip in occasionally and have a look at it.

IW: Nostalgia was the starting point, was it?

AA: Well, the starting point really was that we'd just done *Way Upstream* in Houston, Texas, and it became apparent that most of the company wanted to leave. I was just left with two of the most experienced actors, and the rumour had been going around for a long time that I was thinking of writing a two-hander.

IW: A rumour started by you, one hastens to add.

AA: Yes, I started it. But they all got a bit nervous, because they all thought that this meant six people were going to get fired! I'd always thought, 'I won't write this two-hander while the company's together, because that would be terribly mean.' But finding myself with two actors — and two actors who knew each other quite well and worked well together — it seemed the perfect moment to do what I wanted. I'd also had this whim for a long time to write something larger with the alternative-endings idea.

IW: The history of those started with *Sisterly Feelings*.

AA: Yes. I think it was something to do with not having a lot to do in Houston, really. I was supposedly directing *Absent Friends*, but I couldn't direct it a lot of the time because they were performing *Way Upstream*. So I began to dream up this idea. It could only have been done in the Scarborough situation, because it meant just announcing a blanket title for the summer — scrapping the season that we were going to do — and then seeing how much we could actually manage.

IW: You started with the structure?

AA: Yes, I drew that up first.

IW: Can we just talk that through, because it is incredibly complicated. You start with one moment . . .

AA: It's about a thirty-second moment. A woman comes on and she makes a very small decision, about whether or not to have a cigarette. If she does, she sits and has one, and therefore hears the doorbell. If she decides not to have one, she goes on her way to the garden shed to get a pair of step-ladders, and she misses hearing the doorbell. She therefore misses the person who is ringing the bell, and instead meets somebody else. The idea of the play was that it started with this tiny moment of no consequence, which knocked on to moments of increasing consequence, and finished up with variations in a churchyard (rather aptly) on births, deaths and marriages. So, you had that moment, followed by a choice from two ten-to-fifteen-minute scenes, when she met either Mr Hepplewick the gardener, or Miles Coombes, who had come to tell her indirectly that he loved her. That then split to what is Act I Scene 2 – there was a choice of four of those – and, just before the interval, they split yet again, giving us a choice of eight Scene 3s, which were quite large, some thirty to forty minutes into the second half. Then there was a ten-, twelve- or fifteen-minute last scene – of which there were sixteen leading off the eight.

IW: So what's all that equivalent to?

AA: About five or six full-length plays, I think.

IW: Are all those scenes mutually compatible?

AA: No, they're choices. The two actors play nine or ten roles between them, about six of which are key, important ones. I felt each character had a choice of destiny through it, that's all. None of them behaves inconsistently within that, but things happen to them in one story that couldn't happen in another. You can't cross over once you're set on a course.

IW: So you cannot, when you go a second time, retain what you saw the first time.

AA: You'd know more about them. Sometimes there are back-references. Sylvie Bell is an interesting case. What's interesting about the plays, as well, is that a character like her can actually make a three-minute appearance in a play and never be seen again.

You couldn't give that to a normal actor, because you wouldn't get anybody worthwhile to play it, but because it's only one of the doubles that the actress plays anyway, it's fine. You say to her, 'Just give us three minutes of your Sylvie tonight, then the story's really about Celia, or Rowena.' The other thing is that Rowena can vanish altogether, or be seen, very briefly, as a walk-on part in somebody else's life, and the story can encompass her. Sylvie has so many different possibilities, and her destiny is more cliff-hanging than most. She can be swamped by the awful Lionel and forced into marriage, with hundreds of awful, ginger-headed children, or – as in two instances – she can get adopted by Toby. They all have this Pygmalion complex about her, and they all want to change her, to get their own kicks. In one story, she actually breaks away from Toby and goes off into the world to become a girl reporter, returning very trendy with a new haircut. Miles is always trying to cast her as the perfect village maiden, but in fact she's far too cynical and down to earth and she really doesn't want all that nonsense. What the play explores, I suppose, are the options open and the great element of chance – how, by meeting different people, we are affected (and affect them) in different ways. Some situations are never resolved: Miles and his wife Rowena are a permanent mixture of unhappiness, partly because they are actually in love with each other. Toby and Celia eventually really loathe each other, but are held together by something. And there's something horribly fascinating about Lionel Hepplewick for Sylvie. They're all relationships under some sort of strain.

IW: The writing process here took a year in itself, didn't it?

AA: Yes. I wrote two before the season started, and then another two during the course of the summer. (When I say two, I'm talking about the eight main scenes at the beginning of the second act.) Then I wrote the other four main scenes and eight endings over the course of the winter, while doing other plays. It became increasingly easy to write, because the characters were really talking for themselves once the theme was there.

IW: Didn't it get to feel as though you were writing soap opera?

AA: Oh yes, I suppose so. But it was nice.

IW: Or did you, on the contrary, feel that you wanted to write even more of it?

AA: I was very fond of them. We all were, I think. I remember Robin Herford's reaction was to be a little bit wary about some of the characters. When I wrote for them, I wrote them each a part which I knew they were capable of playing, to reassure them – well within the middle of their range, as a singer would say. One was Celia, and one was Miles. And then I also gave them one that was very difficult, which for Robin Herford was Toby and for Lavinia Bertram was Rowena. Funnily, Robin didn't like Toby at all when he started, but by the end he was by far and away his favourite.

IW: More than usually, you were very much writing for two specific actors, and it was conceived as a two-hander. It's not essentially a two-hander none the less, is it? You will permit it to be played by more.

AA: Yes, but I don't see there's much fun in it, and it's curiously constructed to be done by more, because there are these essential soliloquies to cover quick changes. It'd be a bit like two pianists playing a piece of music that was designed for one – they could play it a bit faster, but the fun really is that one guy does it all. And it's not accidental that each of the three main characters of each sex is an element of perhaps one bigger character. There is, if you like, the 'air' side of the man's character – which is Miles – and there's the 'fire' side – which is Toby – and there's the 'earth' side – which is Hepplewick, a sort of Caliban-like creature. And all three are complementary, all three lack something the others have. Miles is a hopeless dreamer, an idealist who is born to be hurt. Toby is so determined not to be hurt that he's lost all his dreams of everything and is really – although he's quite a funny man – a very, very sad and bitter man. And Lionel is Lionel, the jackal of the pack who goes around picking up the leavings and opening fast-food restaurants. And the same with the women: Celia, who is the most frigid woman in the world, and Rowena, who is all body and a making-clay-models-on-the-kitchen-table-growing-watercress-in-the-kitchen-sink type of woman – a big earth-mother, but in the end not able to behave within the confines of what her husband expects of her. And then, of course, there's Sylvie . . .

IW: Has anyone else, anywhere in the world, attempted to perform the entire project?

AA: Not yet. Three is the most they've done. I think it will have to be when three people get together who want to do it – whether it's a director who finds two actors, or an actor who says, 'I'd love to have a go at this.' But it's actually the logistics of setting it up. You could do it in a big company if you could afford to let two actors float free. You could do it, say, at the National, in the Cottesloe, and it would be rather fun. But even when it was reviewed, a lot of people didn't actually believe it existed: they didn't come to more than one version. The *Scarborough Evening News* refused to let their reviewer come to more than one. They said, 'We've reviewed it for the summer,' and we said, 'Well, it's rather different from that.' But they never came again. Very odd.

IW: After the two-hander, you reverted to another of your long-touted projects, the thriller. *It Could Be Any One of Us* is undoubtedly the least known of your plays since *The Sparrow*. After reading it, I don't know whether it's pastiche or parody.

AA: It's a mixture. In the end it didn't work, because it didn't satisfy either party. It didn't satisfy the thriller lobby . . .

IW: Because it was too jokey?

AA: Yes. You've got to kill somebody in a thriller.

IW: I have to confess I was very miserable at the lack of total death.

AA: But I didn't really want to do that. I wanted to write a whodunit in which three or four people could equally have killed somebody, and it suddenly occurred to me that, to do that, they'd all got to be potentially homicidal. And I don't think that, in any one room, there are necessarily four homicidal maniacs. To impute all four with homicidal motives struck me as being rather boring.

IW: But that's why you didn't write it first time around, when you finally came up with *Season's Greetings* (in which, of course, you came very close to having a body!). You said at the time that you'd started writing the whodunit and just got bored with the characters.

AA: Yes, I tried it again. I had to get it out of my system. Having said that, there was a lot of stuff that was salvageable from it: there was a lot of fun, and people did quite enjoy it. Norris was a good fun character, a sort of English Clouseau, and his summing up at the end, with a completely wrong set of facts, was tremendous fun. And it did have moments in it which interested me. There's a scene where two of them are in the house alone, and there's thunder and lightning around, and a large (doll's) head comes down the stairs. The whole audience used to leap several feet, and I always felt it would be fun to do something really horrific – fun horrific, not where you go home frightened of the dark. Like a good horror film, where you know you're being frightened but love being frightened despite it. One day, I might use the experience of that play to do something that makes people jump.

IW: Did you, having done it, kill it?

AA: Michael Codron read it and wanted a body. Somebody else wanted to do it, but I didn't want them to. I've put a block on it now. There are so many of my plays flying around that it seems silly to put out a less than satisfactory one, when I might well, one day, come out with a more interesting version of it.

IW: I get the impression that this was a particularly difficult time for you, because after that came *The Seven Deadly Virtues*, which I believe was another not entirely happy experience.

AA: Oh no! *Seven Deadly Virtues* was the real nadir of our musical collaboration. We got into really deep waters. I set Paul a brief, saying I wanted to write seven pieces for seven actors, all of whom would appear in all but one; so it was really seven pieces for six actors – with a total of seven actors! It was the ultimate complication and complexity of the music – which was unsingable except by, I suspect, highly trained opera singers – combined with lyrics of such density that made it very, very complicated and very unsatisfactory.

IW: Why did you do it?

AA: I don't know. I think we were trying to find something new to say, something new to do. But it was a blind alley. In the end it was like a concert piece, and that was the wrong way to go. We should have been getting simpler and we were actually getting more complicated. It seemed that we were almost saying, 'To hell with it: let's try and do something a bit more avant-garde!' In the end, it was an unsatisfactory blend, and I wrote to Paul afterwards and said, 'I think we ought to just sit and rethink what we're doing for a bit.' And I went back into full-scale straight writing.

IW: Well, yes, *A Chorus of Disapproval*. Not exactly a complete departure from the musical.

AA: No, indeed not. But that was a curious tale. It started with a conceit I had for writing a play set in an amateur operatic society, and utilizing a large amateur choir, who would be scattered through the auditorium, reducing the auditorium capacity from its usual 303 to about 215 seats. There'd be about eighty-five singers, completely incognito, sitting in scattered seats, and at various points starting to sing from their seats – thus causing the person next to them to look absolutely alarmed. They probably wouldn't join in for about the first twenty-five minutes, and I wanted to use not new music, but old music. I set about some of the texts and I found *The Vagabond King*, which is just a wondrous text. It's also one of the funniest Samuel French scripts in existence, because the songs have all got very, very painstakingly detailed stage directions on choreography: 'Man 2 and Man 13 run five paces down L. and kneel, while Woman 15 dashes across to Man 4 and grasps him by the hand.' I had this image of this director, trying to direct the thing from a French's edition. As with all amateur societies, five of them haven't turned up, two of them are standing in for others – you know, the comic results could be enormous! But inside that, again, a love story. I was also chasing the theme of inner corruption inside a society, and how an honest man in a dishonest society looks like the biggest rogue of all. It was a forerunner, in some ways, to *A Small Family Business*, except that Guy doesn't get drawn in, he just acts with really not much moral conscience at all – he just doesn't say 'no' very much.

However, there were two drawbacks. The first was that Equity refused to allow me to employ any amateur singers at all. They said they all must be professional – which knocked the idea firmly on the head. The second drawback was that Rudolf Friml's Estate refused point blank for me to do anything with *The Vagabond*

King, claiming there was a major revival in the offing. It was getting quite late – like two or three weeks before it was due to rehearse. We were getting a little desperate, and I suddenly thought, 'Well, the first thing to do is to find something that's out of copyright.' It then occurred to me – one of those happy solutions – that *The Beggar's Opera* was the play I ought to be using, because it was something I actually liked – unlike *The Vagabond King*, which I thought was a load of garbage. It is never good to work with something you despise, because in the end you don't get inspired by it, you just tread on it. But using *The Beggar's Opera*, which had all the things I'd been looking for – short songs, and a whole theme of corruption – the whole thing suddenly went click as if it was meant to happen. I bought all the records I could get and found the sheet music in the library; and the play started to work very, very quickly. I was actually able to build a structure of songs, and around it wove the story.

Paul, meanwhile, was very early on cast as Mr Ames, the pianist within the show, but also, more importantly, was doing arrangements of the songs I said I wanted. And the songs were starting to rehearse long before the script arrived, and it all gelled beautifully. It had been one of the plays that Peter Hall had asked me if I could be thinking of for the Olivier, and it was at the back of my mind that something like this might be suitable, which could have a bit of a gusset in it to let in a few more actors. And, indeed, we did, in London, employ all the understudies as part of PALOS (Pendon Amateur Light Opera Society), because the Olivier stage would have looked rather empty without them. It was a narrative play, and that was also very important. I was beginning to learn my lessons about the Olivier more strongly now: strong narrative plays were the answer there. So both the recent Olivier plays have had very strong story lines. Both the Olivier and the Lyttelton need strong narrative.

IW: It's not bad for any theatre, is it?

AA: No, it's a jolly good principle. But you can get away with a bit of mood down in the Cottesloe: you know, you can have two people in armchairs. In the other two, you really do need to keep it banging along with 'I wonder what's going to happen next.'

IW: *Chorus* gave us another slice of Pendon life. One day, we must put together a profile of Pendon from what we know of its ethnology and geography and groups – not to mention the peccadilloes of its populace. But *Woman in Mind* was not particularly Pendon, was it?

AA: Well, it probably was just down the road.

IW: *Woman in Mind* inspired another of Michael Billington's ten-yearly pronouncements. Having pronounced, about a decade ago, that Ayckbourn was 'a left-wing playwright using a right-wing form', he now gave us: 'Ayckbourn is our finest feminist writer.'

AA: Oh yes! The idea came to me of writing from inside somebody: that was the first thing. I thought it would be quite interesting to see events inside somebody else's head. It then made logical sense that the person would have a rather peculiar view of things, or otherwise it wouldn't be very interesting. Then it occurred to me that it might be nice to look inside someone whose perceptions were getting, for some reason, unrealistic and less and less sure.

IW: Was this consciously a progression from *Just Between Ourselves* and *Joking Apart*, which both had women falling to pieces?

AA: Yes. I wanted to get away from it being in any sense autobiographical, and it seemed to be a very personal play in many ways. I didn't want to make it a man and have everyone saying, 'Oh my goodness me, it's you!' – because it wasn't. I was also interested that the character of the woman would be slightly . . . well, I think people would treat a man differently in that situation. I wanted someone who was allowed to go progressively madder, because nobody really took any action about it, for various reasons. Not because they were particularly sadistic, but they just weren't prepared to acknowledge that it was happening. So she was left to dream. And it was also, I thought, interesting to try and lead an audience again to the how-the-hell-did-we-get-here syndrome, to lead them – at first assuming that this was our guide for the evening, and would therefore be quite safe – into dangerous water, where we were not sure ourselves any more. And like it or not, we were stuck with the bloody woman. She was actually giving us wrong information, because she was receiving wrong information. It wasn't her fault that she was getting more and more confused about reality.

I'd just read about the man who mistook his wife's head for a hat: it's when people fail to recognize everyday objects. The psychiatrist saw this man and said that he was unable to tell what certain things were any more. The brain had refused to accept the information. And when he left, he got up and seized hold of his wife's head and almost pulled it off her shoulders. The psychiatrist pulled him off and said, 'What the hell are you doing?' He said, 'I'm sorry, I thought it was my hat.' The psychiatrist said, 'No, it was your wife's head. You were pulling it off her shoulders!' He said, 'But that's awful!' And the psychiatrist would pick up a spoon and say, 'What is that?' And he'd say, 'I don't know.' 'Can you guess what it's used for?' 'Well, it's round at one end, so it could be used for hitting something. No? Picking something up?' They'd say, 'It's a spoon.' He'd say, 'It's a spoon?' And then he'd forget. What was interesting was that, reading the cases, you were standing inside another person's head, and you thought, 'I can't really imagine what it would be like.' Maybe the stage is a good place to go in there. And, of course, it's not that far away from a sci-fi idea: they're always sending people inside other people's brains to straighten them out and fight their fantasies and so on. But it had to end in tears: it was never going to end happily.

IW: It's not the sort of subject that one immediately thinks of when starting to write a comedy – or even a serious play with comedy in it.

AA: The extraordinary thing about it was the response it got, particularly from women, who recognized it and identified with it very strongly – then said quite a lot of strange things. 'I came out', one woman said, 'determined to assert myself as a woman much more.' Things like that.

IW: Was the writing of it very much an act of imagination, or did you go to some lengths to research it?

AA: Not really. I'd read certain books and, I suppose, if you're writing, you live with people like the dream family all the time. You may have a much more firm grip on them, but there is always the feeling that one day they'll actually become more real than the people you're talking to. And one knows that a lot of people have it in them to create imaginary people, or to have them around. Right from being kids you start with imaginary friends. It seemed to me it was something that could happen to me, and I've always hoped that what could happen to me could happen to other people, and other people would identify with it. I've never set out particularly to graft around.

IW: The effect of *Woman in Mind* on the actresses playing the part has been profound, I believe.

AA: Yes, Julia McKenzie and Ursula Jones, both. Julia got quite affected by it: she played it for six or seven months in the West End, and it did get to her, because it's an enormous outsurge of emotional energy through the evening. It's also one of the biggest parts, and certainly the most concentrated part. She's never off the stage – she can't be, as the first-person narrator. So it's a very arduous part. Julia was wonderful in it, because she has that essence of ordinariness. She's not ordinary at all – it would be very rude to call her that – but she comes over as a very ordinary, just-like-the-rest-of-us woman. Which is great, because immediately everybody says, 'Oh, I know her.' The danger would be to cast some abnormally strange actress, or one of our leading actresses whom everyone looks up to and says, 'This is someone rather exceptional.' Julia seemed to grow into the character more and more. She had a lot of good support from the two men – Martin Jarvis and Peter Blythe. They were very supportive of her off and on stage.

IW: But she finally couldn't take it any more?

AA: Well, she partly couldn't take it and she'd also got Stephen Sondheim's *Follies*! There was always a danger that she was going to have to do *Follies*. But she was going through a stage when I suspect she was glad to get out. She was also getting worried, because she said, 'I don't think I'll ever have a part like this again, and I don't quite know where I'm going.' *Follies* was a wonderful chance for her to do something totally different. She couldn't have done another straight play after that, not for a bit. It is quite a small-scale, very introverted play, and it suits the smaller auditoria.

It was a direct move away from things like *Chorus*, which were very robust.

IW: What sort of foreign interest do you get in a play like that?

AA: Well, it's been done off-Broadway, at the Manhattan Theater Club, with Stockard Channing. It's been done in Amsterdam, and Delphine Seyrig played it in Paris.

IW: *A Small Family Business* came next – the first play since *Mr Whatnot* that was not written for Scarborough.

AA: Yes, and the first play ever written a year in advance. That was what worried me. It was a good exercise for me, to see if it would work, to see if I could do it. And I did – I had to do it.

IW: What's the difficulty about writing a year in advance of production?

AA: There's no real compulsion to finish it.

IW: Except, presumably, the National gave you a deadline.

AA: Yes, but that was October, and it had to be done in April because I was directing *Woman in Mind* in the West End. But I enjoyed writing it. I felt I had to write it rather carefully, particularly the descriptions of how it would go together, because I was never sure that I would remember what I meant – normally, I know I'm going to be doing it in two days' time. So it was quite a weighty tome, in that it had all these dense directions. We blocked it reasonably slowly over a week or so, and when I'd finished the last moment I said, 'Thank God! Nothing needs changing.' It was all there: it was like digging up an old Sanskrit text.

IW: It was written for the National simply because you wanted a larger canvas on which to work? It's a thirteen-hander, isn't it?

AA: Yes. Peter Hall asked me to do a season, and his only other stipulation was that I should write one for the Olivier. I'd spoken to Michael Gambon way back when we were doing *Chorus*. I said, 'If Peter does ask me to do a season, would you like to do it, too?' And he said, 'Yes.' So I said, 'Well, would you like to do a new play by me?' And again he said, 'Yes.' So I wrote the play, and I sent it to Peter at the National – but he wasn't at the National, he was in Los

Angeles, so it was sent on out there in a bag. And I sent another copy to Mike Gambon, who was filming *The Singing Detective*. And neither of them replied. Mike Gambon has still to reply! Peter did, eventually, but I'd never felt such a silence. I'd never submitted a script to anyone since Stephen Joseph died.

IW: Nevertheless, you presumably didn't feel unconfident about it?

AA: Oh yes. I didn't know. There was a possibility that Peter would say, 'Look, this isn't really what I had in mind.'

IW: Fair enough, but you've still written a play which you have confidence in.

AA: Yes, but it would have been a bit eggy to have written a play for the National, which was already distantly in the schedules for production, and then find it had been turned down.

IW: However, Peter eventually wrote to you . . .

AA: . . . and said he liked it very much. So I kept ringing up Lynn to see if Mike had read it, and she said, 'He's knackered from doing all this filming, and all this make-up.' So then I wrote to the National and said, 'Well, I don't know if he wants to do it,' and they said, 'Well, he's signed the contract!' I think he'd actually – which is the sweetest act of confidence that any actor could do – signed the contract without reading the play. I think he read it months later.

IW: Were you able to put the play out of your mind in the period between writing it and the start of production?

AA: Oh yes, I just put it away: I didn't read it at all. Fortunately, I had *Woman in Mind*, then *Tons of Money*, then *A View from the Bridge* to direct, and they were quite powerful enough to occupy me. But I got quite encouraged by the fact that I had managed it, so I wrote *Henceforward* . . . in between the opening of *A View from the Bridge* and the start of rehearsals for *A Small Family Business*. So I'd distanced myself even further from *Business* by the time we started on it, because not only was I doing it for the first time, but I was actually doing an old play!

IW: Did it change at all when you came back to it?

AA: No. It was quite a joke, really. I changed one word and cut a line and a half. That was all.

IW: As a writing job, did you find it more difficult to work on that larger canvas, with rather more people to manoeuvre than you were used to?

AA: Yes, it was difficult. But they're all difficult: it's the problem of getting things to go in the direction you want them to go in, without making it look as if you're pushing in that direction. I knew I wanted to go from A to B, and I wanted a man to be increasingly involved in crime.

IW: It's a highly moralistic piece, about public morality.

AA: Yes, and our perception of it. While we all have different ideas about what is really moral, we all tend to chop corners off and say, 'Oh, that's OK. Income tax is fair game!'

IW: From pinching the office paper clip to the really massive Mafia operation.

AA: Well, this goes from one end to the other. I didn't know quite how far I would go with it. I knew we'd get into large-scale theft, and I thought we'd get into a murder – which seemed to me the ultimate crime at the time. But what I didn't find, until I was in it, was that the three women were going to do the murder – which was great fun. And it was very satisfying that, in fact, he should have involved his wife and daughters, whom he set out to protect, in the really ultimate crime. Then, finally, there is the final tie up with the drugs issue, which harks back to the beginning with the daughter: that was quite good. It's quite a dark piece, really, but again I hope it's driven forward by its laughter and its narrative momentum, so that people are into a situation to a point of no return before they can get off. That's the whole idea of it: we have a central character whose behaviour we condone, until we find that he, like us, has been sucked into the whole thing in a worse way.

IW: The point at which it ceases to be acceptable is a very fine one indeed.

AA: Oh yes, it is. And Gambon moved very subtly from small English businessman to Mafioso *capo*. When we were rehearsing it, the final thing we did was something I thought of at quite a late stage. Where the script has him and Russ Dixon, who was playing his brother, 'clasping hands', I suddenly said, 'I think you ought to kiss him.' And that really made it the final Mafioso embrace. What was lovely was that one thought: 'Well, I don't know, maybe that's a bit subtle'. But it was where the audience went 'Way-hey!' when they first saw it – like a great roar of recognition at where we'd come to. That was lovely.

IW: Which takes us on to *Henceforward* . . . It's not, I know, an entirely unprecedented occurrence, but very close to the end of your scheduled writing period for this, the wires suddenly became hot with the news that *Henceforward* . . . had now been abandoned, and that, in the two or three days remaining to you, you would write another new play for the Scarborough season, to be entitled . . . *meeting like this*. In the event, . . . *meeting like this* joins *The Silver Collection* in that canon of The Lost Plays Which Alan Ayckbourn Never Quite Wrote, and *Henceforward* . . . was rehabilitated. Do we gather you had some considerable difficulty getting it on to paper?

AA: I got it on, but it wasn't satisfactory when it was on. I've found in one or two cases that I have to write out the subtext, actually put it on to paper, a very black format of a play – and then find ways of telling it which are bearable to watch. Some of my plays are very, very dark, and if you wrote *Woman in Mind* without the humour (although there will always be people who will say, 'This is what should be happening'), I claim that people would not watch it. Or rather, the people who should be watching it wouldn't watch it. Those who are already converted to this sort of thing don't need to watch it anyway! You have to be careful how you get your laughter from a subject but, at the same time, a subject needs its laughter just to make it flow. In this case, in the end I was writing about one or two themes I have obviously touched on before: what people do to other people, particularly men to women, and also, something I haven't covered before, the nature of the creative artist, and his relationship with reality, and people, and those he purports to love.

IW: The context into which you place these themes is futuristic and horrifying. A very long way from Pendon.

AA: Yes, I wanted to go forward. Firstly, I had to go forward because of the robotics, which are very important to the nature of the story – the fact that Jerome had a mechanical woman, which had huge comic potential, but which was also a very telling image in itself.

IW: Huge, but very dangerous, comic potential.

AA: Dangerous, oh yes, that's right. Robots are great off-putters. They're also quite boring, if you're not careful. My biggest problem was to keep the technology logical, so that it wouldn't infuriate the average computer-user. The whole behaviour pattern of the robot was a logical one. The art of any sci-fi writing is somehow to keep the technology under control – just enough of it to convince the aficionado, but not too much to bore the majority of us who really don't want to know how many wires per circuit per soldering inch there are. But in fact, the whole thing is slightly allegorical anyway, so it wasn't that important. The important thing was that the man was having increasing difficulty telling real people from machines, and was really showing a more and more marked preference for the machine. What's quite interesting in our society, it struck me, is that, as we get more and more computer-literate, more and more little boys sit down in front of computer screens and find them much more satisfying than playing outside with their mates. And we could be moving into an age where people relate only to screens, and find them preferable, because, in fact, they are much more logical and much more reliable. Like many of us, at the moment, prefer cats – but at least cats do behave occasionally in a completely bananas way: they don't necessarily love you all the time. Computers are, on the one hand, quite reassuringly constant (unless they crash, as they say) but, on the other hand, they're awfully dangerous because you don't, in the end, get anything back from them. No conflict and no criticism.

IW: There is also the vision of total anarchy in the outside world. Is this your native gloom, or is it something you saw from the window of your flat in Wapping?

AA: Well, you do see it a bit. I don't think anybody who's lived in any urban society isn't convinced that at least it could happen – and, of course, the term 'inner cities' has been very much on everyone's lips since the 1987 General Election. There was a man who came over here at Christmas, and he was talking about where he lived, somewhere near Keighley, in West Yorkshire. Because of the depression and the lack of jobs, he said, it's become a sort of wasteland, and there are, as it were, primitive tribes roaming around outside his house. 'I run to the shops,' he said. He's an art historian, a strange, rather rarefied man who works on ancient hieroglyphics and runes. And I could picture him sitting there, doing this – in a sense, completely irrelevant – work. No, it isn't irrelevant – it is relevant – but irrelevant to that area. It's a completely fanciful image, because he probably isn't like that at all, but I still have this vivid image of this man, sitting up in his tower there, with these baying kids throwing bricks at one another down below – just fighting because there's nothing else to do. And I thought that could happen. There could be people attempting to keep a candle of civilization alight, saying, 'Well, somebody's got to be writing music, even if nobody wants to listen to it.'

IW: The isolation of the creative artist: is that something of an autobiographical scream?

AA: Well, yes. One is always, in a sense, cut off in that way. But the question is more: is it possible to be an artist – albeit a composer or a writer, particularly, I suspect – and still live a normal life, still have normal relationships? The deeper those relationships go, the more you are liable to use them in your work, simply because they're there and feature very strongly in the centre of your life. By using them in your work, does it make it easier or more difficult to live those relationships any further? I suspect much more difficult, because everything that is shared in the relationship gets some sort of airing; and most people – unless they have nerves of steel – would eventually be very wary about what they put into the relationship. Showing your vulnerability to each other is something that is essentially very private. It's rather like – to use a crude parallel – making love to your wife and then showing the snapshots round the bar afterwards, saying, 'This is what she's like, fellas.' There is a bit of that, although, of course, you do tend to hide it a little bit more carefully in plays.

IW: You disguise it?

AA: Yes. And people say, 'I wonder if that is him and her?' They can usually hazard a fairly accurate guess. And at any first night of mine, you can usually see members of my family looking at me reproachfully, and saying, 'But I thought that was a private moment.' And I say, 'It *is* private – nobody knows.' And as someone once said, 'I don't care if nobody else does know – *I* know, and that's the important thing.' It is a problem, it's a huge question, and in *Henceforward* . . . I've expressed it quite literally in a man who positively does record his subjects. Even painters who are obsessed with one model, though, put their feelings very much on show in their work.

IW: But in the case of a painter, it's not usually a warts-and-all game.

AA: No. We playwrights tend to concentrate on the warts for dramatic reasons. What goes wrong is more interesting than things going well.

IW: By the time it arrived in London, *Henceforward* . . . had already played to a remarkable variety of audiences. If we leave aside the English-as-a-Foreign-Language audiences it found in West Germany, Poland, Egypt and Turkey (simply because the language factor must play a large part in those cases), what trends do you discern in the way audiences are reacting to your work?

AA: One is so aware of the economic drain to the South, of affluence down there. There's almost a Restoration feeling to the audiences in London now, a feeling of 'We're here because we've heard it is right to be here, but we may, or may not, give you our full attention. We may leave at any moment, because there are several other things we would prefer to be doing.' The social spectrum in Scarborough audiences is slightly wider, but only marginally, but in Scarborough – thank God! – most of the time one still has the feeling that audiences have bought their seats and are determined to sit and enjoy every moment of the show. That's what they have paid to see, and their attention is on it.

IW: After Scarborough and before London, came your second production of *Henceforward* . . . in Houston, Texas, with George Segal and Judy Geeson. I gather that was not a happy experience, but it did lead you, I think, to some conclusions about the state of American theatre and the way it is funded.

AA: Oh yes. One saw what I've just been describing amplified further. If you like, there's Scarborough at one extreme and Houston at the other, with London somewhere in between, drifting, I fear, Houstonwards.

IW: If that is the case, with all British arts policy currently being modelled more and more on the American pattern, it's possibly a good moment to sound some warning bells.

AA: I feel so, very much. I think the thing that appalled me most, in my Houston experience, was the way in which the people at the theatre were forced willy-nilly to raise the money for the plays and for the continuous running of the theatre. Practically all the energies of the theatre went towards fund-raising evenings, gala events, and in anything one did there were pressures on the artists, and on everyone concerned with the show, to make public appearances and to be seen to socialize. You felt very much that the sponsors had bought not only their seats, but the show and all the people concerned with it.

IW: What sort of fund-raising evenings do they have?

AA: To an outsider there seems to be a core – quite a sizeable core – of people in Houston who move, often with the best intentions in the world, from one social event to the next. They're usually 80 per cent charitable, that has to be said, so an awful lot of energy goes into them, and the same people tend to turn up. They tend to wear, in terms of clothes, enough money to feed the Third World for about two years. The main object is to be seen, and to be seen wearing something new. They're usually very well stage-managed. At the Alley Theater gala, for instance (I didn't get round the whole thing), the main auditorium was handed over to an auction, with a sports star and a star from the local television station auctioning everything from flights to Europe, to the puppies of the great-granddaughter of Rin Tin Tin and basketballs from the Astros. There was a steel band on the top floor, a huge big band on the bottom floor and a fashion show in the studio theatre.

IW: Was all this just for *Henceforward . . .* ?

AA: No, this was for the Alley Theater generally: they have one every year. They spend out on it between $50,000 and $75,000, and they expect to get back in about a quarter of a million dollars in sponsorship, and auctions and people buying tickets, which are very, very expensive. It's big stuff. They built the opera house next door and they raised millions of dollars for it – the staircase alone had sculpture up either side which cost a million. But they didn't build a rehearsal hall for the ballet company, because it didn't interest the sponsors – who cares what happens behind the proscenium arch? So the front is very grand, and you come into the opera house up the escalator, past the million-dollars'-worth of sculpture, into this very, very big foyer – quite well made, quite well done, and then you can walk straight through the foyer to a series of doors, and you think this is the auditorium. But no, these are the sponsors' boxes and the grand boxes. The rest of the people go down some very narrow stairs to the stalls. It took us a quarter of an hour to get into the theatre on the first night, because of the bottleneck. The auditorium is fine, but again, the theatre has been designed for the very rich. It's back to exactly the theatre one used to have, and the stalls were in fact where the poor people sat.

IW: And the corollary of all this, I believe, is that seats are paid for, but not always occupied.

AA: It's a bit as though you're buying pardons from people in the Middle Ages: you buy a box at the ballet or a subscription for the theatre, just to improve your soul, I suspect. You probably turn up twice a year, but those seats remain empty because they're paid for. I was amazed: I never saw a full house for my show in the entire time I was there. It is a big auditorium but, at the same time, you'd have thought with a major film star like Segal and the première of a play by me – not terribly unknown – a place the size of Houston should have found at least one full house. But apparently not. And yet they have a 30,000 membership – the biggest single subscription list for a straight theatre in the whole of America. The other thing that I was talking to the theatre manager about is this new fad for instant everything: the thin novel, the short play, the tiny epic. Eventually, if we're not careful, all our arts will be down to the length of a commercial, because people actually can't sit and watch. Some evenings – and I'm sure it wasn't just the production – I lost about a third of the audience during *Henceforward* . . .

IW: Because of a lack of concentration?

AA: Well, they wanted to go on to other things. They came, they touched base, and they moved on. They were restless before the play even had a chance to bore them. They'd stand in the aisles chatting together in little huddled groups, and the house lights would go down, and the chatter would continue, and the stage lights would come up and then they'd finish their conversation. As the play was starting, they'd sit, and some people would come in from the back and wander down, with apparently no sense of apology for disturbing everybody, and some people from the front row would get up after ten minutes and walk to the back. There was a feeling all the time of movement, of just sheer bad manners.

IW: It's the brave new world – a thoroughly well-funded theatre that nobody actually wants to watch.

AA: No, because we've paid for it, and if we choose to watch it, it's entirely up to us. It's rent-a-video. The whole meaning of theatre, which is the communication of an actor with an audience, is made impossible because, for the actor to communicate, he does have to have at least token attention. One felt none at all: it could have been a video. And I know it's all subscription-sold, but I rehearsed there for five weeks, and for four weeks and six days there was no mention that my play was opening outside the theatre. Instead there was this big poster proclaiming the Alley Gala, which continued to be proclaimed long after it had finished, and you wondered occasionally whether to go to the box office to check that your play was actually going to open. But apparently it didn't matter: the seats were sold. But, you say, 'Doesn't anybody who's passing by, or someone who's moved into town, perhaps want to know?' Apparently not. The way they sell seats is to this circle of people, and in fact one need not advertise at all, presumably. You needn't even bother to tell people it's a theatre: it'll be a secret clique and it'll become almost totally exclusive. If you're not on the mailing list, how the hell will you ever know? The funding has totally gone mad: there is no government funding, and there is no opportunity for people who can't afford it to go at all.

IW: There doesn't seem to be a great deal of opportunity for any sort of creativity either.

AA: No. You are up against the hidden pressures of private sponsorship in what you choose to do, and they are quite subtle and insidious. Sometimes it is necessary to do a play, even though the theatre may halve its attendance, because that play one day will be filling theatres. If you can't do any play unless it is guaranteed universal approval, then you move forward at the pace of a glacier, because you don't actually ever do anything new. You look back to see what might possibly be successful.

IW: And what happens in the States is that the verbal arts get squeezed out. Sponsors will put money into the symphonies and into the ballet, because they're not going to be over-controversial.

AA: They're safe, they really are. And they're that much more high-profile glamour, too: you can wear even bigger jewels at the opera than you can at the theatre.

IW: I get the impression that you would not be exactly 100 per cent in favour of sponsorship-based theatre becoming the norm in Britain, too.

AA: No, I would not!

At the National Theatre and Back Again

IAN WATSON: Early in 1985, you suddenly announced that you were going to take some sabbatical leave from Scarborough. Rather later in 1985, it was announced that you were going to the National Theatre as a Company Director. Which came first – the negative decision, if you like, to get away from Scarborough, or the invitation to the National?

ALAN AYCKBOURN: It was almost simultaneous. Peter Hall made me the offer to form my own company. That followed on hot foot from the success of *A Chorus of Disapproval*. And then we vaguely talked about a time to start, which I followed up. But it was obviously a time to take a two-year break.

IW: Why was it obviously time to take a break?

AA: The quality of the work I was doing here was not up to what I consider to be my best standard. I was actually doing too much and age was beginning to tell. One of the things about running a place like Scarborough, for me, is not only that you've got to just make ends meet and run it from day to day, but, just to keep the thing going day in and day out, it does need a sort of game with yourself to find new adrenalin. I did a lot of things – some of them, looking back, positively detrimental to the theatre – in order to keep myself fresh: like removing the examination-set-book production from the annual programme, removing the kids' show and doing a season of American plays in mid-winter. They were all designed to keep me alive. The irony was that Peter Hall offered me a comparable operation on a considerably larger scale, but it didn't include in it the disadvantageous side – the slog – of running Scarborough. It was just the cream: going in and rehearsing – and a bit of casting, which is always hard work. But Scarborough also has in it a lot of administration and a lot of just trying to make ends meet on budgets – finding plays to fit the limits of what we have available, and just sheer economics. Although the National is still governed by certain parameters, it's obviously much, much wider. When you're talking about a £40,000 budget for a production in the Olivier, you're talking about bigger toys to play with, and you're talking about bigger companies.

Also, my plays have been getting bigger, and the final reason for moving away was a sort of daredevil in me because I felt my writing could do with a jolt, too. It was revolving around the Scarborough system, which has served me terribly well, but I wanted to see if I could write for somewhere else, and even a play like *Chorus* was essentially written for Scarborough and then enlarged for the National. The combination of moving away and having to write a play a year in advance, on a scale that meant I had no safety net, was absolutely unheard of. I went into the Olivier and I had to open it. I had to get it dead right first time, because you don't get a second chance. In Scarborough, there's always the possibility of something not quite right being remedied during the run, without too much damage to the reputation of the play in the future. Scarborough does give you a second chance.

IW: All the reasons you've given are perfectly legitimate artistic reasons, to do with personal and company development. Was there also any element of reaction to what you felt was a kind of bureaucratic oppressiveness about Scarborough at the time?

AA: I felt rather frustrated because I thought we were really rather good, and I felt most people seemed to acknowledge this except for Scarborough. There was a great apathetic feeling that we were the local rep, and one heard of people going through to York for a *really* good evening out. You can get a bit sour about things like that.

IW: It's one of the characteristics of Scarborians, isn't it, that they whinge a lot and cannot believe that anything within their midst can possibly be worth anything!

AA: 'If you're here, you can't be that good!'

IW: That's right: there's a constant tendency to talk down their own community.

AA: Yes, and it's very depressing. But I think between us – Ken, because he's a Scarborian, and I, because I came from a rather limp public school, where we were brought up to be very modest about what we did — we never really shouted quite loud enough about how good it was. But it's very hard.

IW: Did you take it amiss when, in the wake of *The Glory of the Garden* (the Arts Council's so-called 'strategy for a decade'), the Stephen Joseph Theatre in the Round, Scarborough, was one of the first regional theatres to have its main funding devolved to its regional arts association? Did that strike you as demotion?

AA: It struck me as being typical. The Arts Council will always put their money into buildings before they'll put it into people. And there is a point. Pick any theatre with a very large building, like the Sheffield Crucible (I'm not saying anything against it; I haven't been to Sheffield for a very long time): Sheffield will be closed down long after we are, simply because it's a bigger theatre, and therefore there would be much more scandal if it did close. Shutting down a disused school doesn't mean much. There would be a lot of people saying, 'Where's our theatre gone?' (I hope), but in the end it's the bricks and mortar that attract the money — the purpose-built bricks and mortar, that is. The Arts Council have always rather put their hands on their hips and said to me, 'You don't have to stay there, you know. You can go anywhere else.' To which I've said, 'I don't want to go anywhere else.' I have been offered other reps; it would be silly to say I haven't. But the fact is that Scarborough is the right size, and it also has an incredible history of doing the sort of plays that I believe in. To go and run a more conventional, perhaps more important, and a much larger operation would mean that I could no longer concentrate on other sides of my craft, such as writing. I'd be hamstrung by much more oppressive boards — with bigger sums of money — who would be constantly breathing down my neck. The great cry of artistic directors all over the country is that they have boards of management, trustees and boards of directors, who are forever putting their fingers into the artistic pudding and saying, 'Can we help?'

The marvellous thing about Scarborough over the years is that the very minimum of interference has gone on. Occasionally I wish that we'd had more support from our Trust, but you can't have both. What has been wonderful is the totally free hand we've had to run it. Having said that, it actually doubles the responsibility, because you've nobody to fall back on but yourself. When we've had a bad season, it's been entirely my fault. I don't think I could blame anybody else. I could say, 'Well, that was a bit of a duff performance' – but then, I cast the actor who gave the duff performance, so even there I'm still in the hot seat. But I'm a great believer that, in an ideal world, the funds should go where the particular flame is burning at a particular moment. You can trace the history of the English repertory movement. There's been excitement in Liverpool, then it's been reduced to a flicker; there's been a great burst in Nottingham, then it's gone quiet; Oldham had the most fantastic few years ... And I don't say that Scarborough should be financed for ever, but I do think that while it is doing the quality of work it's doing, they should not deny it.

IW: I don't think they ever have denied it, have they? The idea of devolution was always structural rather than financial. There was never any suggestion that they were trying to take money away from you.

AA: No, but there were certain emotive words in there, like 'centres of excellence', which got me a bit!

IW: This is the central nonsense, of course. 'Scarborough is primarily of regional, rather than national, importance.'

AA: Oh yes, because we don't do plays that are seen outside! We only do these strange little ethnic plays, of course, about Filey fishermen presumably! In fact, if you look at our output, our tentacles probably reach wider than any theatre in Britain.

IW: And this is a theatre that tours the world and that attracts people from all over the world to it.

AA: Well, I suppose in the end it was ludicrous. You know, when you see a list of the theatres that were *not* devolved! ...

IW: It's ultimately irrelevant. It doesn't actually matter where the money's being posted from.

AA: Not at all. I did write to Yorkshire Arts immediately I'd heard the devolution decision, and I said, 'We seem to be Yorkshire's National Theatre now: could we please have more money?' Didn't do much good.

IW: Except that they are, apparently, rather proud of the theatre.

AA: Yes, well we are, if you like, Yorkshire's premier theatre. The rest of them are blasted southern federal lackeys, aren't they?

IW: OK. We've strayed back to Scarborough when we were supposedly discussing your straying away from it. The word 'sabbatical' is nearly always written with inverted commas around it, as if: 'Ah, well, we all know what that means, don't we? That means he's buggering off.' There was a lot of speculation – and your mother was one of the first to fuel it – which said, 'If he goes, he'll never come back.' You always said that you would, but I have to admit that a lot of us did wonder at the time whether you were fully convinced. Were you?

AA: Let's put it this way. I thought I would, but I wanted to know how strong the tie was with Scarborough. I think I always intended to return, if only because everybody thought I wouldn't! And there is a slight state of bemusement down there at the National about the fact that I am back. The one single thing I really did want to achieve as a personal ambition was to establish a reputation as a director. It had always eluded me, because, somehow or other, an author directing his own plays goes completely unnoticed: he's a faceless man. People assume – I don't know why – that the play must have moved itself, because there's no obvious director in there, and although I think I've pulled off some quite complex and successful productions down there, they've barely been noticed. 'The author himself spiritedly directs,' is the most I've ever got. It was only by my standing behind two other people's plays and saying, 'Look, no hands: I haven't written a word of it!' that they've been able to judge them as productions. It is hard sometimes for critics to separate direction from writing and from acting. It's only when they have comparisons to make – and presumably, with *A View from the Bridge*, they had direct comparisons with several other productions – that they are able to see where it stands in their league. Most directors in this country make their reputation with established classics: 'a fine *Two Gentlemen of Verona*', or something like that. I tend to work mainly with new plays, so they can't really sus how good a production is – until they know the director very well, and then they give him *all* the credit, including the writer's credit!

I also had the ulterior motive, in going to the National to direct, that, when I came back here, I would have added perhaps a couple of inches to my status as a director, so that (1) I hoped people in Scarborough would wake up and come to see shows that weren't written by me, *because I'd directed them*; and (2) I hoped that actors would be that much more attracted to working with someone who obviously did have the clout to work in the National and in the West End. A lot of Scarborough, even today and even in the future, is good will: there is no way we're ever going to raise our salary levels to attract the type of actor – just in money terms – that I'd like to get. They've got to come because they want to work with the people and want to do the plays. So, with luck, I've coated myself in more honey, as they say!

IW: Your association with the National started with *Bedroom Farce*, which Peter Hall saw in Scarborough. Was that by chance?

AA: No, Peter asked me to write a play for him. I said, 'I don't write plays for people. I only write them for Scarborough, and people come and buy them. But if you like, you can have the next one.' I then went down to see the unfinished shell of the National Theatre, and he suggested the Lyttelton was the auditorium for new contemporary plays. It seemed to me – because it wasn't finished – to be even larger than it is: it was vast. I said, 'You'd have to write a play about a football team.' But I did, in the end, settle for *Bedroom Farce*, for which I just divided the stage into three. I said, 'I'll write for three small proscenium arches.' Cowardly!

IW: So, while you were writing for Scarborough, you knew that you were also writing for this great barn, did you?

AA: I knew they wanted it. I must say, Peter was very good, because he'd opened a theatre that was controversial anyway, and here he was, asking the most commercial of commercial writers (at that time) to write for him.

IW: Has he ever told you what it was that attracted him to your work? What had he been impressed by before *Bedroom Farce*?

AA: I'll tell you how I think he did it, but I might be wrong. He was a friend of Sheila Hancock's, who had worked for him, I think, as an actress and director; and she was in *Absurd Person Singular*, which she invited him to see. There's a great tendency in the theatre to slot people into pigeonholes, and then you don't have to go and see them. I don't think Peter had ever seen anything of mine – or anyway, he'd registered me as a *boulevardier*. But he went along to see this, and I think he was quite impressed: he found it quite dark, and more interesting than I think he suspected it would be. Then came a few other pieces: the *Normans*, *Absent Friends* and a few darker ones. I don't know how many of those he saw, but he did write and say he would like to include me among the modern dramatists – the Edward Bonds and people – that he was bringing in. It was, at the time, quite incongruous: it nearly caused Michael Codron heart failure. Obviously I spoke to Michael, who saw me as his property in the commercial marketplace of the West End. I said, 'Look, this is what is happening. It's not the end of a relationship, I hope, but just, for me, a chance to be seen somewhere else.'

IW: You wrote *Confusions* for Michael Codron at the same time, didn't you?

AA: Yes, I was trying to keep them both happy. I think I was sensible not to try and write a very serious play for the National: it would have been absolutely fatal suddenly to change my whole style. I wrote them a very jolly play: it had its moments, but it was jolly. Peter opted to direct it with me, which was probably wise for the first one, but in fact he left me very much to it, once he saw that I didn't cause actors to foam at the mouth. He'd cast it very well and done a lot of groundwork. The National was at one of its low ebbs – it had had a lot of technical problems and a lot of bad press, and people were asking, 'Why is all the national funding going to this?' I think what *Bedroom Farce* did at the time – which was really nice – was to provide the building, if not with its first, certainly with one of its earliest big hits. It certainly lifted the morale: it was during that terrible period of the strikes, and all that business with pickets. There had been a lot of very ugly feeling around.

IW: Was *Bedroom Farce* the first transfer from the South Bank?

AA: It must have been pretty nearly. It came out and went to the Prince of Wales for a long time, with about three casts. Then we put it together again and took it to America – through Canada, then Washington and into New York. It ran there, then came back and was made into a television film. It went on forever: some of those actors, like Stephen Moore, were so grateful to see the back of it. But it was certainly nice to have the Lyttelton ringing with laughter early on in its career.

IW: The success of that led Peter Hall to ask you for another one straight away?

AA: Yes, he did. We decided this was a relationship worth keeping on with. *Sisterly Feelings* was the next venture with the National. That was when I started to think, 'If the National wants me, I might as well use it to do plays that are less viable commercially, while at the same time trying not to make the terrible mistake of getting into very, very heavy plays. So I wrote *Sisterly*, which was just complex in its structure. It was the first of the 'alternate' plays, and it seemed to me that only a theatre with a repertoire system could run it. In fact, in the end, it was defeated, even given the National Theatre's box office. Peter always claimed it would have run for a lot longer, except that no one could understand the leaflet! It was terribly difficult: it was quite successful, but it would have been hell in the West End. People seemed to understand the structure of the *Normans*, but with this, you could see the same show twice if you weren't careful – unless you went to a 'fixed' performance.

IW: There were only a limited number of fixed ones, weren't there?

AA: What we suggested was to see a performance at random first. Then, once you'd found out what you'd seen, and if you wanted to see the alternative version, check the 'fixed' performance list and see the other half. But a lot of people didn't understand this: they'd go to a 'fixed' one and then couldn't understand why, when they went to a random one, they saw the same thing. The British public, I find, are very, very intelligent once they get into an auditorium, but they're as stupid as hell outside it: they can't understand anything. And it's not just the British public, either. I saw American tourists in despair, trying to work out what they'd seen and what they were seeing. Anyway, that was my first venture into the Olivier, which was interesting – though again I had a co-director, Christopher Morahan.

IW: Yes, they still hadn't quite got the confidence to let you direct your own.

AA: They didn't trust me, no. It was odd, really, because there were people elsewhere in the building – Edward Bond, to name but three! – who had a directing track record of zero, compared with mine. I mean, he really was quite new, and yet he was merrily directing *The Woman*, with scenery falling all over, and nobody seemed to mind. I, on the other hand, who had been directing plays since I was nineteen, was given a co-director! Not that I minded: it was fine. Christopher Morahan did all the donkey work and was very supportive: he was great. These days, I find co-directors rather irksome, but at the time I was quite happy to hide behind him.

IW: But you gave them cause to think twice about it, because they gave you *Way Upstream* to direct on your own next, and you nearly sailed the building down the river.

AA: My first solo. Yes, I did. Do you want the full story of that?

IW: Yes, I do. I'm intrigued by it.

AA: It was a very interesting case of under-estimating the size of a task. It had seemed rather an easy task, to move a boat, apparently on water, into the bank, and so on. We'd done it in Scarborough, for goodness' sake – and we'd made it rain! And we'd done it in a much bigger theatre – very similar to the Olivier – in Houston, Texas. Then we brought it into the Lyttelton. Alan Tagg designed a really very good set. He's not a mechanic; he's a designer. The National was going through a series of extraordinary economies at the time. They decided, therefore, not to bring in what should have been brought in – structural engineers – to design it, but asked for the metal workshop to build it and design it as they went. Now, the man there is an absolutely first-rate metal-worker, but he's not – for God's sake – a structural engineer. If he were, he wouldn't be working in the metal workshop. What happened was that the carpenters' shop got behind – Bill Bryden, I think, was doing *Don Quixote* at this time, and there was an awful lot of scenery being built and rejected, and they got tremendously behind. As a result, when the deadline came for them to start building my set, they weren't ready, so the metal workshop went ahead on its own and built it. The wood workshop then built it as well, and the result was that the thing turned out to be twice as heavy as it should have been. That was problem number one: the moving banks now weighed two tons as opposed to half a ton. The next problem was that whoever had done the sums with the tank (in which the boat was supposed to sit), had under-estimated the weight of water, and when they filled it, the tank split from one end to the other.

IW: With what result?

AA: It poured down into the sub-basement below the Lyttelton, to start with, into the switch rooms where all the main switchgear was for the theatres. Hundreds and thousands of gallons of water. The stage itself, which is built in a series of lifts, got very, very wet, warped, locked together, with the result that no play could be done on that stage for several days, let alone *Way Upstream*. There was about £125,000-worth of damage done to the stage – let alone what was going on with the rebuilding of my set. Meanwhile, the rehearsals themselves went very well. We had a boat in the rehearsal room, which was *the* boat, on wheels, as it was going to be inside the tank, operated by stage management. The boat – unlike in Scarborough, where it was operated from the shore – was operated from the boat itself, which meant that you had two winch-operators inside the boat. It's quite a small boat, and the two winch-operators, of course, were in the midst of all the actors; so you had two extra people in the boat, which doubled the weight. We also had stage managers down there to cue it – I mean, the boat was stuffed with people, so it was a much heavier object than we intended.

There were so many silly things. The boat was on a sort of pendulum action, operated from the shore, and it also tracked up and down the pendulum: the tracking up and down was operated within the boat. The result was, in theory, a most sophisticated series of movements. The boat could actually appear to do whole circles in the water – brilliant! In practice, the winches on the shore, when we came to do the first technical rehearsals, were not calibrated at all: there was no precise way of marking. What they marked them with, believe it or not, was pieces of coloured tape.

Now, the winch cables went through the water and scraped against the bank, so the coloured tape would end up about ten yards from its original place! So the boat would then smash into the bank, with the result that the already fragile, repaired tank would judder. One thing led to another: everything that could fail then began to fail. The lighting crew could not get at the lamps to light, because there were workmen strewn all over the bank trying to fix it. The moving bank couldn't move, because it was too heavy and kept jumping off its track. The boat couldn't move, because there were too many people on board and the winches weren't calibrated. For the sound, they decided to use radio control to send a signal to the boat, and that didn't work. So they had to redo that, putting the sounds on to the bank. The actors, in the middle of it all, were quietly going crazy, and I sent them home for several days while we tried to get it straight.

The National was a very strange building. I always say that it's extraordinary how many people take their holiday leave immediately there seems to be a problem! Peter was away – he was in Bayreuth doing some Wagnerian epic. There didn't seem to be any other directors in the building; for many, many days, the administrative side was completely missing, and the cry that I uttered at one technical conference was, 'Who the hell's in charge of this building?' There seemed to be no one. It's a fault I think the National recognized later and have remedied. There are now definite troubleshooters in the building. If I'd been anything other than a guest director, I'd have had a lot more knowledge of whom to turn to, but I was in fact just there for the show. Tempers started flying; people started to get very bitter, and the result was that a play that should have gone on and surprised people – and it was visually exciting when it worked – as something quite light and charming, became a *cause célèbre*. The press were determined to get in and were speculating. There's no business like disaster business.

IW: Once you start cancelling previews, rumours become very strong.

AA: The only way I could get any attention was to cancel the previews! Nobody seemed to take any notice. Eventually, Peter rang me to ask how it was going. I said, 'It isn't going: I've just cancelled it.' He said, 'It's Saturday night.' I said, 'I know.' And there was this tremendous pause on the international line, then he said, 'Put me through to my secretary. I'm coming back.' And he arrived back, because money was pouring out of that building like from a huge wound. I sat in there one night: the Olivier was in the throes of a technical rehearsal, the Cottesloe was the only theatre open, because I'd closed the Lyttelton, and the whole of that building on the South Bank was in darkness. It wasn't a very pleasing feeling, that I'd actually closed a theatre, but it was the only way. In the end, we opened, but it was obvious that the problems weren't going to get solved. Rather than laying the blame on any individual, one can say that it was underfunded and the size of the problem under-estimated. We made fatal economies at the wrong time, and maybe the National should in the end have said, 'We can't afford to do it.' If they'd come to me and said, 'Look, the water's great, but we actually cannot afford to do it', then I could have redesigned the production and we could have done it without the water. But we'd managed it twice with water, and it was terrific: there were images of light bouncing off water and visually it was very exciting. The nights when that big iron curtain opened on the Lyttelton stage and the boat came slowly into view, with the water lapping round it, it was just super.

IW: Was the play brought off prematurely?

AA: Yes, they couldn't keep it in repertoire. Although they eventually put it together once, every time it got dragged out . . . It was also by then a piece with a slight stigma to it. We had people coming again, for the wrong reasons, and critics turning up in gumboots for the first night.

IW: How does Peter Hall see that production in retrospect? Does he shudder at the memory, or is he quite proud that the National did it?

AA: He was very gracious about it. He's never fainted when it's been mentioned. I think he just felt it was one that got away.

IW: Did you sense any reluctance on his part to come back to you for more after that?

AA: No. I said I'd never go back there. I was angrier than most, because I felt that I'd lost a perfectly good play somewhere.

IW: And you blamed the National for this?

AA: Well, I blamed the fact that technically it was a cock-up. At the time, you stand there and scream at each other, don't you? But, in the end, it wasn't anyone's fault in particular. If the fault was anywhere, it was in the original underfunding. The National do take enormous risks because they don't have enough money. When they did *Guys and Dolls* – I remember somebody telling me at the time – it was a miracle that it came together: a miracle! There was so much short-cutting to get it on, and it was like a race. When it worked, it worked marvellously, and there was this huge sigh of relief that ran round. 'My God, we got away with it! That truck was only just ready and could have crashed; this could have happened, and that could have happened.' All the 'what-ifs'. With mine, it was the reverse: we missed by a whisker from getting it right. And then it was like a house of cards: everything fell down. And it all started, I suspect, from saying, 'Now, how can we do this cheaply? How can we keep this within the budget we've been given?' Instead of saying, 'We can do it, but we need more money.' It was a Lyttelton show that should have had an Olivier budget. There are all sorts of things that you live and learn. When I went in with *A Small Family Business*, I went upstairs and I said, 'Now look here, this is a show on two floors, and I want the two floors before I start rehearsing. Please. Sir.' And David Aukin, who is now there as a sort of hand-in-glove-with-the-artistic-director person, said, 'Fine!' And it was done. We thereby possibly avoided another problem.

IW: Before we come to that, Peter Hall came to you next for *A Chorus of Disapproval*.

AA: Yes, he let a discreet pause happen, and then he came back.

IW: Has he ever felt the need to defend himself against that attitude, which is epitomized, I suppose, by the second-string reviewer on the *Guardian*, whose notices of all your plays you could write before he ever sees them? It's always the same, and it goes something like: 'Why is this man sullying our National

Theatre? Why doesn't he stick to the commercial sector where he belongs?'

AA: Peter has said quite nice things, like: 'I think the National Theatre should be representative of *all* types of theatre.' He has a high opinion of my work and feels the National should do some of it.

IW: With respect, the National has done, and is continuing to do, rather a lot of it.

AA: Also, to be fair, the National needs to make money occasionally, and it does look to me a bit like Scarborough looks occasionally. One says, 'That would be nice, that would prop us up.' But when a play like *Way Upstream* comes along, which actually didn't make the money because it cost so much, it's quite a blow to the old box office. Yes, they have done rather a lot of them, but then . . .

IW: You've written rather a lot!

AA: That's true.

IW: So, *Chorus*: was that tailored for the National?

AA: Well, I wrote it with them in mind again. And I wrote it with a feeling that it could extend – which was another way of solving the problem.

IW: You mean it could get bigger for the National's stage?

AA: Yes, and it also meant, for once, that I could solve the understudy problem. I could employ every single member of that company on the stage, and they all felt part of it, which was very successful. It was a very happy group, but a very strange group. Although the whole lot, in the end, were hand-picked by Gillian Diamond and me, they were labelled as Peter Hall's Company – which was curious, as most of them had never met him! But we carried on, despite sailing under false colours.

IW: Was Michael Gambon not already working in the building?

AA: No. We sent him the script, secretly, and that clinched it. We rang up and said, 'We've got Gambon.' And they said, 'My God! How did you get him back here?' I think he and I have a special, loose working relationship which is rather affectionate. I try not to bombard him with too many plays, because he can almost play anything. He was in the *Norman*s, and he was in *Just Between Ourselves*, and he was in *Sisterly Feelings*, and he did the television version of *Absurd Person Singular*: we worked it out that he'd done nine of my plays altogether. He's quite a seasoned old campaigner, and he decided to do *Chorus*. We had a bit more problem finding who to play with him, and then I had the good, if somewhat belated, idea that Bob Peck – who had been up in Scarborough and indeed started life there as an ASM many years ago – was floating around the building, doing *Road to Mecca* and becoming a very old man on it. He was a happy second choice, and then a lot of nice things happened – like Imelda Staunton and Gemma Craven. It was a jolly company, and it ran and ran. Then it transferred, with the late, great Colin Blakely. I was very lucky: you don't often get a replacement that strong.

IW: And so you came into the National Theatre as a director. Presumably the deal was also that you would write them a play.

AA: The brief was simply: 'Come and form your own company' – not many strings to that. There is a sort of tacit agreement that all actors who come through the doors of the National Theatre are passed – or at least, their names are passed – under Peter's nose, just to make sure it's not someone he had a flaming row with three years ago. Also, he obviously had final say in the choice of plays, but he's quite tactful about never putting his boot down – he'll just suggest, tactfully, something else. In my case, he didn't really seem to mind. He wanted a play for each theatre, and he wanted the play in the Olivier to be one by me, as a sort of commercial wedge. So I sat down and thought about planning a season – getting the right play for the right auditorium, getting a balance of different flavours which would interest the actors and the public who followed the three plays, and getting a series of plays that would maximize the use of the actors.

IW: Did you have the entire, international history of theatre to choose from? If you'd wanted a new translation of some obscure Haitian epic, could you have done it?

AA: I suppose so, yes. I was restricted to a company of twenty, but I could probably have started with an eight-hander and built up to a forty-hander, if I'd decided to. In fact, I decided to try and form a hard core that would obviously mean some slight shifts. For instance, I brought the young lovers from *A View from the Bridge* in as understudies for *Tons of Money*, so that they were at least sitting there. They were both quite new and young, and so I thought it would be nice that they were already very familiar faces by the time we got to *Bridge*. By the time we did get there, we were purring. We started with the most difficult show. *Tons of Money* is the sort of team piece that demands a working knowledge of one another. But thanks particularly to Simon Cadell, Polly Adams and Michael Gambon, the company got going in a very generous and warm way quite early. The barriers came down and we were able to get a very good feeling going quite early.

IW: When you are given this great opportunity to direct just three plays in the British National Theatre – where you may never, ever, work again afterwards – to choose *Tons of Money* as one of them might, perhaps, be seen to be slightly perverse.

AA: Yes, it was a bit perverse. I wanted something very, very light. In the crudest terms, I wanted, at one end of the spectrum, to have something that seems to me a very valid part of the theatre, in which it would be very hard to find anything of any import at all, just fun. One does get a little bit fed up with oneself and other people in this constant search for messages. If you've had a good evening, you say, 'Ah yes, but it did say something very important about . . .'

IW: Well, you write the things!

AA: Well, yes, I do. But I thought, 'Secretly, the way to really enjoy yourself is to watch a Laurel and Hardy film. What this theatre needs is a bit of Laurel and Hardy, really.' I didn't want to do Travers, because I'd done the two of his that I wanted to do, and I wanted something a little bit different.

IW: You'd also done *Tons of Money*. In Scarborough.

AA: I'd also done *Tons of Money*. I needed to do that, actually, just to work through the script. It was in a terrible mess, partly, I suspect, because it never got written down properly. When Tom Walls and Ralph Lynn had finished bouncing about on it, there were huge holes in the logic which you could drive a lorry through. We slowly managed to get them right through rehearsals. It's now reasonably logical, and I'm glad to say they've brought it out as a new, revised Lyttelton text, which I hope has got some quite good jokes in. So it might have another life from what we've done. Anyway, that was the reason for *Tons*, and it was also essentially a proscenium-arch piece. It gave Michael Gambon a light way into the season, because he had only recently finished filming *The Singing Detective* for television, and it seemed to me that he was going to do – as, indeed, it turned out – one of the heaviest roles of his career. I know he'd done Lear, but Eddie Carbone is certainly . . . well, Michael was a wet wreck after every show! It was very good that he had Sprules, which was really a sort of Sunday School outing for him – a part he enjoyed, without having to put all his heavy acting boots on to do it. It finished up with a very successful run, and towards the end it went completely out of control: it became a wild, wild play.

IW: You mean the actors took over?

AA: They should do in the end, but they've got to have some quite firm basis to do it on. It's very tedious if the play has no life of its own. I used to go in occasionally and say, 'Don't forget the plot: it is important that they understand why you're doing this to this bloke.' But the audiences loved it, and we tried to re-create a flavour of what it might have been like. We got the tea-dance trio playing beforehand, and there was a lovely feeling in the auditorium on good nights of party-time. It was a sort of end-of-term romp which we did at the beginning!

IW: *A View from the Bridge* was a watershed in your career. It was the moment at which the London reviewers suddenly realized that they'd got a major director in their midst.

AA: It was a lot easier to do than *Tons of Money*, though.

IW: They didn't really notice your presence in *Tons of Money* very much.

AA: Not really. It's extraordinary: as anyone knows, directing a farce actually requires a very old head. Directing a play of the calibre of *A View from the Bridge* is a joy. I think, modestly, it was a good production, but a lot of it was that it's an excellent play. It was cast beautifully, and the cast all gelled in the right way. There were known talents: I knew that unless something dreadful happened, Gambon was going to be at least good – actually, he turned out to be extraordinary. And there were people like Liz Bell who, as it were, had a nice boost to her career, and new talents like Suzan Sylvester who really came on well and came back to do *'Tis Pity She's a Whore* with me. But having said that, what I think made it work better than, perhaps, it has done sometimes, was that we approached it in a slightly *Tons of Money*-ish way. We approached it saying, 'How can we legitimately get the laughter out of this show – early on, particularly?' (You can't start getting much laughter after the guy's tried to assault his own niece, but up to that point, how do you get the joy of that family, so that it's something you care about?) I've seen it done a bit solemnly and a bit po-facedly, telling the audience, 'You're in for a bad evening!' What our production did – and it was somewhat due to Mike Gambon's own ability to play tragedy and comedy quite easily – was to manage to balance it. It was moving because you liked the people, and you liked the people because you laughed with them.

IW: And after that, a sudden spate of directing offers?

AA: Well, no. I was asked to do another one at the National – and not 'Can you write another one for us?' but 'Can you direct any play?' They suggested it would be nice to do something different again – and it would be in the Olivier, because that was the space they had spare. Something had fallen through, and they thought of me – which was nice. Peter suggested *The Alchemist*, which I didn't want to do at all, partly because I didn't understand a word of it. It's so dense. It's not my sort of thing. I do know my limits. But I thought, 'No, I won't resist the challenge and do *A Doll's House* – which I know I can do – or a Chekhov – which I think I can do pretty well. I'll do something I'm not sure I can do, but I think I might. My knowledge of plays before about 1850 is practically zero: I know a few Restoration comedies, but as for the dark Jacobeans, I know *The Duchess of Malfi* and one or two others, but *The Revenger's Tragedy*, and those sorts of plays, are a complete mystery to me. Anyway, it was suggested I should have a look at *'Tis Pity She's a Whore*.

IW: You didn't know it?

AA: No, not at all. It's the sort of play I'd run a mile from normally. But I picked it up and read it, and I understood every word of it – which was the first good step. It also had a lot of the ingredients that, for me, are necessary in theatre. It had a good central relationship that I cared about, and it had quite a lot of laughter in it. It's quite cynical and it's terribly exciting and it's very violent – I find this terribly theatrical! And it seemed that it was something I might do OK. I was asked how I was going to approach it. I said, 'I'll approach it like Alfred Hitchcock, I think – make it very suspenseful, with a lot of his jokes in it.'

IW: *'Tis Pity* sees the end of your association with Sir Peter Hall's National Theatre. I wonder, do you ever get to talking with him about the structure of the National itself?

AA: Yes. We're both believers in much the same thing. I endorsed his decision to go for a company system, which he took a long time to reach. He, by his own admission, said, 'I've fumbled around with the National, trying to find a way round such a big building.' He tried a huge general company, which serviced all three theatres, but it was so big that the actors became rather lost and disorientated with no feeling of identity. He then tried companies attached to special theatres – the Olivier company, the Lyttelton company and the Cottesloe company – but that didn't make a lot of sense, because you again got a divided house and also a feeling that the actor wasn't getting a chance to play in all three auditoria – which, in a way, is one of the nice things about going to the National.

IW: Did that create any sort of hierarchy? Did the Cottesloe people feel they had to work their way 'up' to the Olivier?

AA: Well, yes. There was the very, very successful Bill Bryden mob that developed out of that, but who were completely separate. They worked in a different building, really. They did different stuff, and it was like those big companies that form Theatre in Education companies: they created their own reputation, and it might as well have been another theatre. Eventually, they tried to draw Bill's mob into the Olivier, but it was too late, really. The company was so Cottesloe-orientated and the shows they did in the Olivier were never as successful as they were in the Cottesloe. But also, it meant the other directors couldn't use the Cottesloe so much. One of the nice things about going in this last time has been the experience of working all three spaces, and I think for all the company that I had it's been very important. Certainly the last system that Peter brought in was the best, which was the idea of forming streams of actors, each with a so-called creative centre, someone they rallied around: it needn't necessarily have been a director, though it was normally, but equally it could have been two or three directors.

IW: With Ian McKellen and Ted Petherbridge, of course, it was a pair of actors.

AA: And I think they were even contemplating bringing in a sort of producer – someone who did nothing except bring people together.

IW: A fixer.

AA: Yes, a fixer. A sort of mini-Michael Codron could well have been another way of doing it. There seems to be no limit to it: I suppose it was even possible to have a designer as the central figure. Some of them chose to bring in other directors. I think it had two things going for it. It brought in a fresh angle every time. I brought in actors that I think the National Theatre would never have countenanced simply because they were not within the ken of a lot of people. A lot of Scarborough-based actors obviously got included and have enlivened the place no end. And it did mean that actors were able to have a certain continuity of similar work for a period. Not all, possibly, would want to work for me for the rest of their lives, but it's OK for a year.

IW: Is the short-term element an essential part of the theory?

AA: It shouldn't go on too long. A year is really best.

IW: I just got a feeling (and I could be totally mistaken) that McKellen and Petherbridge felt they were just beginning to mature into their work when they were thrown out again.

AA: They may have done. I think you can carry on, but you really need to replenish the stocks, otherwise you've got a rather incestuous little mob. A year is quite a nice time to get three plays in. The advantage of it also, as I found – and this is the best of a National company – is that you can bring in actors of a certain calibre to play lower calibre parts; so you have in-depth casting – you have Michael Gambon playing your butler, and you have Simon Cadell taking a much smaller role in my play than he would consider doing on the commercial stage. He'd say, 'I'm sorry, I'm above the title.' That helped it, and the danger is now that they're going back to the old system – which is inevitable when you bring in a new broom.

IW: This is Richard Eyre.

AA: Yes, and they're tending to sweep it all out and say, 'Let's have one big company again.' The danger is that people begin to find their level very much more. You're going to have the Tony Hopkins level; then you're going to have a middle level of good working actor, and then you're going to have the rather unrewarding level of understudy-and-that's-your-lot actor. The chances for interchange are going to be so much slenderer. It's always there. Lord Olivier's first ideal was that there would not be understudies as such – we would all cover each other. If you were playing Hamlet, you probably wouldn't be asked to cover for that particular show, but if you were playing Horatio, you probably would be – and the idea was that the understudies were the actors themselves, and therefore there was no second class and no first class.

IW: Did he ever go on as an understudy?

AA: He never got it off the ground. Most actors said, 'No, I finished doing that when I left the provinces.' Which is a shame. I can see why they don't, but what it does mean is you so easily get the 'B' team, who get to carry the odd spear and never do anything else.

IW: Peter Hall's multi-company system clearly brings into the building a number of very different identities: there's been Mike Alfreds's company, your company, Di Trevis's company, the McKellen–Petherbridge company, the Bill Bryden mob, Peter

Hall's own company, and so forth. Is there any sense in which cross-fertilization is possible? Do the companies feel they might like to tread across and try a bit of the work process of other groups?

AA: I think so. It's very difficult.

IW: Do you get furtive letters from members of Mike Alfreds's company, saying, 'Pssst! Do you want an actor?'

AA: One or two: he probably gets letters from mine. Yes, it does happen. It would be difficult, logically, to do – looking at the way they plan, to make sure that the same actor is not required in three different auditoria at the same time. It wouldn't be possible to hop backwards and forwards. And actually, the working methods . . . I don't know, possibly directors are the worst people to ask. We all, I suspect, work so differently.

IW: But that was what I saw as the attraction: that people might, just through osmosis, feel that a different way of working could stimulate them professionally.

AA: Oh yes, I think an actor can do that, but not all at the same time: it would be very confusing. Tony Haygarth came out of Bill Bryden's company to do *Way Upstream*, and his description of Bill's rehearsals is probably libellous. Tony's description was that they all sat around and had a good chat for about seven weeks, and then they got out on the last day and leapt into action! And it's possible. That was Tony's euphoric description of it, mainly brought on by the fact that I ran the play through on the first week, to see what it looked like. And he nearly had a collapse, because he said, 'I don't know what I'm doing!' I said, 'I just want to see what it runs like. I don't want any performances. I just want to put the whole thing together.' And he said, 'But we do this on the last day!' And it was a bit of a shock. And I think if you're jumping from Bill Bryden to me, to Mike Alfreds's trust exercises, it could be a bit of a shock. And you also bring in actors that you wouldn't get if they thought they would have to work in certain ways. I suspect Simon Cadell would probably not respond awfully well to long sessions of blindfolding and tactile exchanges. He'd prefer to be off having a glass of champers – or rehearsing: he works very hard. So the right actor would probably resist coming in at all.

IW: For the time being, you're finished with the National. While you've been away, you've been fairly swamped with honours of one sort and another. You've been granted the Freedom of the Borough of Scarborough, been dubbed a Companion of the Order of the British Empire and been given three honorary doctorates. How do you react to such honours?

AA: Not too seriously. It would be churlish to refuse them, because they are given in good spirit. I don't think they're going to change my life, any more than a good review would change my life. They're very nice, and all the doctorates were done with a great deal of style. They managed to get my name wrong at the Palace: the man reading out the names of the Companions called me 'Mr Alan Aitchbone'. I thought, 'Thank goodness, it's not a knight-hood, otherwise the Queen would have said, "Arise, Sir Alan Aitchbone," and I would have been kneeling there forever!'

IW: Except that she knew you anyway.

AA: Oh, she knew me. She said, 'How are the plays doing?'

IW: Is she a fan?

AA: She's been to some. I think I may have got a little bit dark for HM in recent years. Her equerries tend to pop along and vet them first, and I think they've thought they may be a bit strong stuff. Women in black corsets thumping around in thigh-length boots – it's maybe not quite what the Royal Family are supposed to be used to.

IW: You've returned to Scarborough now. Do you feel refreshed, with great new ambitions for the place?

AA: Quite a lot, yes. I'm looking forward to a season, which I haven't done for quite a while, and I'm ready for the fray again.

IW: Have you got ambitions for the building itself?

AA: I'd love it to be bigger. I'd love to take over the other two floors, above and below.

IW: Rather than build a new building?

AA: The space we would have with those two floors, if we could possibly find the finance to do quite an elaborate amount with them internally, would make us into an extraordinary theatre. I like the idea of remaining slightly temporary, because we can still do things that aren't architects' conceptions. We've gutted that auditorium about three times to do a show and we've even built grass hills over it. We don't feel any loyalty towards the auditorium, other than that it's nice the way it's laid out, and that we can play around with it. The things I'd like to do with it are not to alter it very much, but I'd love to get in another floor, and I have dreams of hydraulic lifts. We wouldn't use them in performance, but we could have workshops underneath and could lift the whole set up, saving hours of man time taking things in and bashing the auditorium about every time we want something. And I'd like to get in above the grid a little bit, so we could light shows from above. It would also be nice to enlarge the front-of-house space and have a much bigger restaurant area. And we could enlarge the second auditorium. And there are other activities the theatre has pursued successfully, but that I find obtrude into our work: the Sunday rock concerts, which are a bloody menace as far as I'm concerned because they leave the place looking horrible, are at the same time bringing people into the theatre. And not only are they spending money in there – which is nice – but they're also experiencing at least being in the building. It would be nice to have an area where we could say, 'They're safe to do that, down there in the Cavern Club' – or whatever. I've got other plans, too – like, if we move the workshops down below, that would possibly give us a little bit more green-room space, but we could also have what I've always wanted – a library, which is actually a quiet room for actors to sit and study. There's lots we could do, and it's rather fun. We could even, if we went up a little bit in the auditorium, put a cantilevered circle in above.

IW: How many seats would you want? You've got 307 at the moment.

AA: 450 would be nice. We've only got to put another back row in to go to 450.

IW: You're talking as if you intend to be around for all of this in the 1990s.

AA: Yes. I intend to be extremely clever and be in two places at once: that's my plan.

Appendix:
The Plays of Alan Ayckbourn

The Square Cat (1959)

Father, son and daughter are perturbed to discover that mother has developed an obsessive passion (from afar) for a teenage pop star, and even more concerned when they find she has invited him for a supposedly secret weekend *à deux* in the country. To save her from herself, they follow her and are as surprised as she is to find that Jerry Ross, the glittering star, is in fact a shy, bespectacled youth yearning for a quiet life. Penitent mum goes back to dad, while Jerry finds true love with daughter.
Not published and not available for production

Love After All (1959)

Set in Edwardian days, and based on *The Barber of Seville*, this farce tells the classic story of the mean father who wants to marry off his daughter to wealth, and who is foiled by the true-loving suitor who gets past him in a variety of disguises.
Not published and not available for production

Follow the Lover and Double Hitch

Two one-act plays, only ever presented in amateur productions in Scarborough.
Not published and not available for production

Dad's Tale (1960)

Written as a Christmas show to combine the companies of the Scarborough Theatre in the Round and the British Dance Drama Theatre, it was also intended to combine the writing talents of Alan Ayckbourn and David Campton. In fact, Campton wrote a synopsis based on *The Borrowers* which Ayckbourn was unable to

work to. The basis remained, but the show became 'the story of how my dad turned into a blackbird'.
Not published and not available for production

Standing Room Only (1961)

Described as 'a new traffic-jam comedy', the play envisages a world in the early twenty-first century in which all roads have been totally paralysed for more than twenty years. A London bus driver and his family live in the bus he was driving down Shaftesbury Avenue when the jam occurred. That was so long ago that his two grown-up daughters have never known any other home, and indeed he has come to think that the bus's destination board announces his name, Hammersmith, with the letters BRDWY after it being his recommendation from London Transport: 'Best Ruddy Driver We've 'ad Yet'. The engine has been replaced by a garden, and the play looks at the family's attempts to cope with, and circumvent, the bureaucracy of movement and population controls which have been thrown up by the immobilization of all traffic. Originally, the play ended with the traffic starting to roll again, but one of the revised versions, amended for the proposed West End showing which did not transpire, had the vehicles being removed vertically by helicopter cranes.
Not published and not available for production

Xmas v. Mastermind (1962)

A Christmas show for children, described as 'the most disastrous play I've ever done'. Father Christmas, an unpleasant old man, is faced with a strike by his gnomes. The chief gnome is incited to revolution by the Crimson Golliwog and his gang, who aspire to the takeover of Father Christmas.
Not published and not available for production

Mr Whatnot (1963)

Mint, a piano-tuner (played mute throughout), is summoned to the Grange in his professional capacity and becomes entangled in the life of the lord of the manor, his plummy family, his chinless prospective son-in-law and a visiting tweedy lady. Cast out once for ogling the daughter of the house and doing battle over the keyboard with her intended, he returns to play tennis, to have tea and – as this transforms into a fantasy rerun of trench warfare – to wheedle his way (by saving her ladyship from the grenades) into a hero's clinch with the daughter. Accepted now as a house guest, Mint continues to woo the girl through sustained farcical set-pieces; dinner, retirement to bed and, in the climax to the play, a mimed car chase and dash across the fields to a wedding in church. The wedding is not Mint's, though the girl finally is.

Meet My Father (1965), subsequently retitled *Relatively Speaking*

A pair of strange slippers under the bed strongly suggests to Greg that he is not entirely alone in receiving the favours of his girlfriend Ginny. He pursues her secretly to Bucks to request her father's permission to marry her. Unfortunately, he arrives before her, and Philip, to whom he addresses his request, is not Ginny's father at all, but her former boss and lover, whom she is due to visit to sign off their affair. Philip harbours suspicions about the fidelity of his own wife, Sheila, and immediately assumes that it is she whom Greg is seeking to marry. He refuses his consent, but is content for Greg and Sheila to go off and live together. Greg, however, is still talking about Ginny and understandably finds Philip's suggestion a strange paternal attitude. Ginny pitches in and is able to persuade Philip to play the role of Dad, and in that part he persuades Greg to allow him a last fling with Ginny on a Continental holiday. Sheila, however, has the measure of the situation and converts Philip's plot for an extended amorous ding-dong with Ginny on his own into a honeymoon for Ginny and Greg. She further manipulates the situation to taunt Philip with his own suspicions of her.
Published in French's Acting Editions (Samuel French)

The Sparrow (1967)

Drenched by the storm, Ed, an unassuming bus conductor, arrives back at his chaotic flat with Evie, the mini-skirted, rather plain girl he has met at the dance hall. As they dry out, Ed convinces Evie that the weather and the time of night have somewhat scuppered the chances of getting her home, and she reluctantly agrees to stay the night in Ed's bed – while he bunks down on the settee. Ed's flatmate, Tony, a cold, flash character, has other ideas, however: Evie spends the night in the bath. In Ed's absence next morning, Tony, through a mixture of bullying and flattery, takes on Evie as his secretary in his 'wholesale business' – an arrangement looked on with scepticism by Julia, Tony's estranged wife who wanders in and who is clearly at least as tough as he is, and with incredulity by Ed, who is less than pleased when 'business' gets in the way of his struggling social relationship with Evie. Slowly, Evie learns the truth: Tony has no business and is employed as a car salesman, and Julia left home after an aberrant roll on the bed with Ed, following one of her frequent rows with Tony. Evie is clearly the tool Tony is using to get back at both Julia and Ed. Julia and Tony return to the flat, obviously in harness once again, and begin a mammoth row in the kitchen. Ed and Evie, pawns no more, steal out to the pub, vowing never to marry.

Not published and not available for production

How the Other Half Loves (1969)

When Bob Phillips's liaison with his boss's wife, Fiona Foster, is in danger of being discovered by their respective spouses, each attempts to wriggle out of suspicion by projecting their own infidelity on to a third – totally innocent and socially retarded – couple, William and Mary Featherstone. The respective spouses, Theresa Phillips and Frank Foster, independently determine to try and help the hapless Featherstones in their supposed problem. Inevitably, their benevolent interference in the life of the Featherstones backfires disastrously and leads to a wild-eyed William descending upon the Phillips household bearing a monkey-wrench and seeking revenge on Bob for his supposed seduction of Mary. In the *dénouement*, the Featherstones are reconciled; Bob and Fiona are reduced to admitting the truth of their liaison with impunity, and Theresa Phillips and Frank Foster, as a result of another set of misunderstandings, find themselves making a telephone assignation with each other without realizing who the other is. Much of

the farcical comedy of this plot is in its stagescape, a living/dining room which manages simultaneously to be that of the Phillipses and the Fosters, with the two menages co-existing in the same stage space even when the times do not coincide: thus dinner at the Fosters on Thursday is played simultaneously with dinner at the Phillipses on Friday, with constant dovetailing and crosscutting.
Published in French's Acting Editions (Samuel French)

Ernie's Incredible Illucinations (1969)

Ernie's imaginings have an embarrassing habit of involving those around him. His parents are on the receiving end of a Gestapo house raid (Ernie saves them by machine-gunning the intruders); his auntie knocks out a heavyweight champion, and his father heroically undertakes a difficult mountain rescue in the public library. The doctor, to whom his parents take Ernie to have his illucinations cured, dismisses it all as mass hysteria and finds himself the drum major of a brass band composed of the patients in his waiting room.
A one-act play for children. Published in French's Acting Editions (Samuel French), and by Hutchinson (in Playbill One, *ed. Alan Durband)*

Countdown (1969)

A very brief dialogue, originally part of *Mixed Doubles*, 'an entertainment on marriage' by various authors. The desultory post-prandial conversation of a middle-aged couple is counterpointed by the mutual hostility revealed in the silent (but here voiced) thoughts of each.
Published (in Mixed Doubles*) in French's Acting Editions (Samuel French), and by Methuen*

The Story So Far (1970), subsequently revised (1972) as Me Times Me Times Me and retitled (1978) Family Circles

Polly, Jenny and Deirdre come down to their parents' home for the weekend to help them celebrate their anniversary. Polly and Jenny

have their husbands in tow and Deirdre her current man. Looming over the weekend is a persistent rumour that, despite all appearances to the contrary, something is going seriously wrong between Mum and Dad – indeed, that he is trying to do away with her – and right to the end there are little pieces of circumstantial evidence that may be interpreted as hinting at the truth of the rumour. The scenes of the play cover the arrival of the girls and their men: preparing to leave for the celebration dinner; returning from the dinner, and the following morning. By a theatrical conceit (for it is not intended naturalistically as a wife-swapping exercise), the author has each girl paired with a different man in each of the first three scenes, and in the final scene all nine permutations are intermingled, which makes for a hectic *dénouement*. It is difficult to resist Ayckbourn's own assessment of the play when he says, 'It is probably not vintage, but it's got a few good laughs in it, the premiss of the play being that, depending upon whom you marry, you become slightly different. And it's quite fun to watch.'
Not published and not available for production

Time and Time Again (1971)

Returning from a family funeral, Graham and Anna Baker, together with Anna's brother Leonard, are joined for tea by Peter, an employee of Graham's, with his delicious fiancée, Joan – at whom Graham makes a lecherous lunge. This pass is observed by Leonard, the family maverick, as he sits outside in the garden, where he normally repairs to quote poetry and discuss life with the garden gnome, and to reflect upon the rituals of football and cricket which are enacted on the recreation ground just beyond the garden. Peter, a sports fanatic, inveigles the reluctant and frankly useless Leonard into these rituals, while Leonard concentrates rather on wooing Joan, at which he is manifestly more adept. By the onset of the football season, Joan is all set to marry Leonard, but he has quite neglected to inform Peter, the lady's hopeless fiancé, that he has been supplanted in her affections. Recalling Graham's earlier advances towards Joan, however, Peter misreads the situation and launches into a violent attack upon Graham. Leonard witnesses this, but is little motivated to intervene as

Graham has dismissed him from the family home. Joan decides that Leonard's conduct has little to do with love for her, and walks out, leaving Peter and Leonard to console each other after the match at having 'mislaid the trophy', but also to agree that 'there's more to life than winning trophies'.
Published in French's Acting Editions (Samuel French)

Absurd Person Singular (1972)

Over three consecutive Christmas Eves, three couples come together to celebrate in one another's homes. We view the parties from the kitchens. First, we visit Sidney and Jane. He is an incurably hearty and pushy man who dominates his obsessively houseproud and accident-prone wife, and who is seeking a bank loan to develop his interests from the general stores they run. The guests are his bank manager Ronald and his wife Marion, a lady apparently secure in her supercilious patronage, and Geoffrey and Eva, whose marriage is already clearly in trouble because of his womanizing. Geoffrey is an architect angling for the job of designing a new shopping complex – a job towards which Ronald might be able to help him. In Act II, we move to Geoffrey's and Eva's high-rise flat, where Eva is clearly set on suicide. In absolute silence, she makes several attempts at this, while Geoffrey seeks a doctor and the guests busy themselves with domestic chores and repairs all around her. Marion retreats further into drink amid disasters on all sides. Finally, we move to Ronald's and Marion's house another year later. Marion has sunk deeper into alcoholic isolation, and Geoffrey's design for the shopping centre has collapsed. He is now dependent on Eva to rebuild his career. Meanwhile, Sidney's and Jane's property development scheme has come up trumps. Ronald finds he must woo them for their continued business for the bank, and Geoffrey's future as an architect could hang on their patronage. Fortunes are completely reversed from the position in Act I. The party games beloved of Sidney, previously disdained by the other couples, are played: Sidney calls the tune.
Published in French's Acting Editions (Samuel French); by Chatto and Windus, and by Penguin (in Three Plays)

The Norman Conquests (1973)

Three self-contained plays, featuring the same people at the same house over the same weekend. Each play stands as a complete entity and can be performed independently of the other two, although in practice, all three are usually played on consecutive nights, to be seen in any order. *Table Manners* covers events around meal times in the dining room; *Living Together* takes place in the living room; and *Round and Round the Garden* takes up the action as it occurs in the garden. Sarah and Reg arrive to relieve Annie, housebound with her and Reg's bedridden mother, for the weekend. Sarah, whose obsession with order and propriety borders on – and at time tips over into – the hysterical, quickly discovers to her horror that Annie is proposing to spend her weekend away in an East Grinstead hotel with Norman, the assistant librarian husband of her sister Ruth, who believes him to be away at a conference. The idea is quickly squashed with Sarah's intervention, as she tries both to send Norman back home to his wife, and to turn Annie instead towards Tom, the dim local vet, who is a regular visitor to the house but who has never initiated any amorous approach towards her. Norman declines to go home and self-pitifully gets drunk instead. When Ruth is summoned to take charge of her husband, the explosive tensions within the family are released and drag in the hapless Tom, who manages to grasp the wrong end of every proffered stick. Norman bounces from one woman to another, claiming in each case that his only desire is to make them happy. Finally, all three women turn their backs on Norman.

Published in French's Acting Editions (Samuel French); by Chatto and Windus, and by Penguin

Absent Friends (1974)

Colin's fiancée has recently drowned and Diana, wife of one of his former friends, Paul, has organized a tea party. The object is that they, along with John and Gordon – also old friends of his – should be reunited in an attempt to help Colin to forget his grief. Gordon can't make it, since, as is his wont, he is ill in bed, but his wife Marge turns up. Both Paul and John (whose bored wife

Evelyn turns out to have been briefly laid in the back of a car by Paul – an incident over which John bites his lip, being dependent on Paul for business) are less than enthusiastic. Diana, meanwhile, is profoundly unhappy in her marriage with Paul and suspects him of having a *grande affaire* with Evelyn, while Marge is constantly on the phone to Gordon, who has disaster after disaster through being left on his own in his illness. When Colin arrives, their attempts to take his mind off his tragedy are aborted by his determination to talk of his lost love, and by his wrong-headed attempts to sort out their problems. He is in fact blissfully happy in his sentimental memories, while they suffer the effects of love grown cold.

Published in French's Acting Editions (Samuel French); by Chatto and Windus and by Penguin (in Three Plays)

Confusions (1974)

Five interlinked one-act plays. *Mother Figure*: prompted by a telephone call from their next door neighbour Harry, who is away from home in a hotel in Middlesbrough, Rosemary and Terry pop round to see if his wife and kids are all right. Lucy's life is totally absorbed in her children, and Rosemary and Terry find themselves treated, and spoken to, as children by her. Under this influence, they begin to behave as children, too. Meanwhile, husband Harry turns up in *Drinking Companion* in a hotel bar, where he tries to lure two salesgirls into his bedroom, but succeeds only in getting himself drunk. *Between Mouthfuls* shows two couples, the Pearces and Polly and Martin, at dinner separately in the same restaurant. Martin works for Mr Pearce, who has just returned from three illicit weeks in Rome with Polly. Mrs Pearce, discovering this, is furious at her husband's deception and storms out. Polly is furious that, when she tells Martin, his only concern is that it will ruin his promotion prospects. She too storms out. Pearce and Martin retire to the bar for a brandy, in animated conversation. Gordon Gosforth, village publican, has secured the services of his local councillor, Mrs Pearce, to open the village fête he has supposedly organized, in *Gosforth's Fête*. Sadly, it is hopelessly disorganized. The ailing PA system returns to life at the wrong moment to broadcast to the assembled multitude the village teacher's

announcement to Gordon that she is pregnant by him – and this drives her cubmaster fiancé to drink. Other disasters include a jammed tea urn which causes the amplifier to blow up, electrocuting Mrs Pearce, and scaffolding that collapses under the weight of rampaging cub scouts. Finally, *A Talk in the Park* is a round of monologues by five characters on park benches, each trying to make contact with the next, while ignoring the plight of the last.
Published in French's Acting Editions (Samuel French)

Service Not Included (1974)

Ayckbourn's only television play transmitted as part of BBC2's *Masquerade* series. At the fancy-dress dance to mark the ending of a company conference, the camera follows Jace, the bar waiter, as he serves the delegates and their wives. As he moves from group to group, the desperate undertow of the social occasion – including adultery, alcoholism, boot-licking ambition and the remote and cavalier insensitivity of management – is revealed to him bit by bit, while he remains professionally impervious to it all.
Not published

Jeeves (1975)

Adaptation of the P.G. Wodehouse stories with book and lyrics by Ayckbourn and score by Andrew Lloyd Webber.
Not published; original cast recording issued by MCA (MCF 2726)

Bedroom Farce (1975)

Ernest and Delia go out to celebrate their anniversary, while their intensely incoherent son Trevor and his neurotic wife Susannah (who are immersed in severe compatibility problems) attend a house-warming party at Malcolm's and Kate's. The party is also attended by Jan, who once came close to marrying Trevor, and whose husband Nick is prevented from attending with her by a bad back which confines him to bed. The play is constantly cross-cut among the bedrooms of Ernest and Delia, Malcolm and Kate, and Nick and Jan, as they are invaded during the course of a long night

by Trevor and Susannah and their marital mess. In the process, the relationships between the natural inhabitants of the three bedrooms are inevitably stretched and infected.
Published in French's Acting Editions (Samuel French); by Chatto and Windus and by Penguin (in Three Plays*)*

Just Between Ourselves (1976)

Dennis is a hearty blusterer, immersed in chaotic do-it-yourselfery in his garage and wholly insensitive to the needs of his wife, Vera, whose personality is being systematically undermined in their home by the poisonous influence of his mother, who lives with them. Into this situation walks the feeble, mildly hypochondriac Neil, seeking to buy Dennis's old Morris Minor as a birthday present for his wife, Pam. It is clear, however, that Pam's needs are more basic and that she regards the car, which declines to work anyway, as a poor substitute. As we meet the characters on three separate birthdays during the course of a year, Pam becomes increasingly sour in her relationship with Neil, who leans on Dennis for support and is given ill-informed and disastrous investment advice as a result. Vera is finally driven into catatonia, but even this fails to shake Dennis into the vaguest awareness of the responsibility he has for her condition.
Published in French's Acting Editions (Samuel French), and by Chatto and Windus (in Joking Apart and Other Plays*)*

Ten Times Table (1977)

Using the local hotel ballroom as a committee room, a group of socially more-or-less dispossessed members of the community are brought together by Ray, a local shopkeeper, and his wife Helen (apparently as an extension to her activities with the Tory Ladies), to organize a town pageant. The would-be actors include a couple whose marriage is in the process of breaking up; a bureaucratically sound but otherwise ineffective local councillor, saddled with an ancient and deaf mother constantly in need of tasks to keep her occupied; a Marxist schoolteacher, with one common-law wife in tow, and seeking both a platform for his views and more female adulation (which he gets from a lady dog-breeder). The subject for the pageant is to be a hitherto unknown episode in the town's history, when the Earl of Dorset led the militia into the square to trounce a bunch of rebellious workers: the Massacre of the Pendon Twelve. The ideological polarities of the original event are rapidly adopted by different factions on the committee, and as the leftist faction increasingly comes to refer to the pageant as a rally, the lady dog-breeder's gun-toting fascist brother is recruited to master-mind the right-wing response, and, as it transpires, to provoke a bloody confrontation all decked out in motley. With the pageant farcically over, the committee becomes once again the bunch of individuals it originally was, their personal problems still intact. *Published in French's Acting Editions (Samuel French), and by Chatto and Windus (in* Joking Apart and Other Plays)

Joking Apart (1978)

The old vicarage is occupied by Richard and Anthea, an unmarried couple with her children by her earlier marriage. Meanwhile, the vicar and his wife, Hugh and Louise, live with their son in a small cottage at the bottom of the garden. Richard is a partner in business with Sven, an infinitely pedantic and preening work-fanatic, whose apparently boundless self-respect, fed by his doting wife Olive, is largely based in the fact that he was once Finnish junior tennis champion. They employ Brian, who innocently gave Anthea and her children sanctuary when her marriage broke up and who has nursed an obsessive passion for her ever since. This he unenthusiastically attempts to sublimate in a constant stream of inappropriate girlfriends. Over a twelve-year span, these people meet for social occasions in the garden of Richard and Anthea – an easy-going, endlessly generous, sensitive and successful couple, to whom everything comes easily, and who seek to give of their good fortune to the others through their hospitality. Louise is unable from the outset to manage her son, and his refusal to have any communication with his parents combines with the loss of her husband's love (Hugh conceives and declares a ludicrous passion for Anthea), to drive her into manic depression and drugged retreat. The fiercely competitive Sven is made increasingly aware that he is losing ground in business to Richard, despite his obsessive hard work (contrasted with Richard's casual flair) and, even at tennis, his narrow victory over Richard is revealed to be only because Richard played left-handed. ('I thought he needed to win,' says Richard.) Sven suffers a heart attack and descends into profound bitterness at the injustice of life. Debbie, Anthea's daughter, declines, as she comes of age, to continue the family's style of patronage by refusing to become another in Brian's list of Anthea-substitutes.

Published in French's Acting Editions (Samuel French), and by Chatto and Windus (in Joking Apart and Other Plays*)*

Men on Women on Men (1978)

A late-night revue. In sketch and song (the music is by Paul Todd), the revue worries, with little mercy or optimism, but with perception, poignancy and wit, at a variety of facets of the relationship between men and women, and at the self-deceit in their perceptions of each other and themselves.

Not published; live performance recording issued on cassette TSJTITR 001 *by the Stephen Joseph Theatre in the Round, Scarborough*

Sisterly Feelings (1979)

What the audience sees may be any one of four possible versions of *Sisterly Feelings*, depending upon the toss of a coin at the end of the first scene and the decision of one of two actresses at the end of the second scene. Scenes 1 and 4 remain constant, but there are two versions each of Scenes 2 and 3. Following the funeral of his wife, Ralph brings his family to a favourite spot on Pendon Common. With him are his two daughters, Abigail and Dorcas – trailing businessman husband Patrick and radical poet boyfriend Stafford respectively; his student son, Melvyn – with his fiancée Brenda and her brother Simon, and his brother-in-law, Detective Inspector Len, with his wife Rita. Both Abigail and Dorcas are attracted to the bronzed and athletic Simon. When Patrick has to leave prematurely to attend a business meeting, the rest are left with insufficient cars to get them all home. Either Abigail or Dorcas will have to walk home with Simon. They toss a coin and the loser goes home by car. Scene 2 is a picnic four months later. Responsible for the arrangements of the picnic is whichever daughter lost the toss in Scene 1. The other daughter arrives at the picnic by bicycle, accompanied by Simon, and the proceedings are disturbed by the unexpected presence at the picnic of the husband/boyfriend whom Simon is currently displacing. The picnic is curtailed by a rainstorm, at which point the daughter accompanying Simon has to decide whether to remain with him – and face a soaking bike ride – or to return to her original partner. On her decision rests the choice of a third scene: either a proposed romantic night under canvas with Simon and Abigail (which goes badly awry, thanks to vigilante patrolling by policeman Len), or the annual cross-country derby (which equally goes badly awry), in which Simon challenges the police champion. Meanwhile, Melvyn has failed his exams to become a doctor and has made Brenda pregnant. By the beginning of Scene 4, depending on which version of the work has been played, Simon has enjoyed the favours of either Abigail or Dorcas, or of both in either order. Scene 4 follows Melvyn's wedding to Brenda, as the family again gathers on the common to humour Ralph, who came here with his bride on his wedding day. Abigail and Dorcas are back with the partners they started with in Scene 1, aware, perhaps of the arbitrariness of the decisions they have taken to change the course of their lives. Simon is an embarrassed best man.

Published in French's Acting Editions (Samuel French), and by Chatto and Windus

Taking Steps (1979)

As in *How the Other Half Loves*, the set is a leading character in this farce. Here, the attic, master bedroom and living room of the Pines, along with two staircases, are flattened into a single stage space, and action is frequently concurrent in all parts of the house. Elizabeth, a pop dancer, is about to leave her bucket manufacturer husband Roland, after three and a half months of marriage. She has summoned her brother Mark to comfort Roland when, on his return from work, he will read her farewell note. Mark, however, has other preoccupations: his fiancée Kitty abandoned him at the altar to run off with a waiter, and she is just now being returned to

him by the police after being picked up on suspicion of soliciting on Haverstock Hill. While Mark takes Elizabeth to the station, and establishes the depressed Kitty in the spare bed in the attic, Tristram Watson, the befuddled junior partner of Roland's solicitor, arrives to complete the documentation for the sale of the Pines to Roland by Bainbridge, a local builder, whom Roland also wishes to retain to do repairs and alterations to the building – which in earlier days was a high-class brothel, and which is rumoured to be haunted still by one of the whores who formerly inhabited it. She, the story goes, seduces current occupants during the night and kills them at daybreak. On reading Elizabeth's note, Roland, believing himself alone in the house with Watson and Bainbridge – and already much the worse for drink – breaks down and prevails on Watson to stay the night at the house to keep him company, postponing all talk of completion to the morrow. Unable to face sleeping in the master bedroom, he installs Watson in there, while he retires to the spare bed in the attic. Hearing him approach, Kitty abandons the suicide note she had been writing and hides in a cupboard – where she becomes trapped as Roland shifts the bed across the door. Meanwhile, Elizabeth has had a change of heart and returns in the dark, crawling into bed with Watson and proceeding to pleasure him in the belief that he is Roland. Ever susceptible, Watson accepts the advances of those of the putative ghostly whore. So ends Act I. Act II plays out the farcical logic of this situation, with Mark discovering Kitty's suicide note, which they assume to have been written by Roland. Confusion piles upon confusion, Watson and Kitty discover each other (and leave), and Elizabeth decides once more to leave Roland – or does she?
Published in French's Acting Editions (Samuel French), and by Chatto and Windus

Suburban Strains (1980)

Ayckbourn's collaborator in this musical play was composer Paul Todd. Caroline, a teacher, throws out her layabout actor husband, after finding him in bed with one of her pupils, and takes as lover a doctor, whose main concern appears to be to demolish her and reconstruct her to his own prescription. Her two relationships are

presented in filmic counterpoint, while parents, professional col-
leagues and even her lover's wife observe from the periphery,
offering advice and sermons. She ends up back with husband
Kevin, now without illusions, as together they proclaim, 'Why not
settle for today, and cuddle up tonight?'
Published in French's Acting Editions (Samuel French)

First Course (1980)

A lunchtime musical revue, written in collaboration with Paul
Todd: ten songs charting impressions of the decades from the
1890s to the 1980s.

Second Helping (1980)

A lunchtime musical revue, written in collaboration with Paul
Todd: ten songs about aspects of love.

Season's Greetings (1980)

Belinda and Neville have gathered family and friends around them
for a traditional family Christmas. Among them are Harvey, a
retired security guard, who, when not immersed in old films on
television, sees himself as a one-man vigilante patrol defending
Civilized Standards; Belinda's thirty-eight-year-old unmarried
sister, Rachel, who has invited along a writer friend, Clive, and
Neville's brother-in-law, Bernard, a failed doctor whose ritual
Christmas puppet show annually bores the children as much as it
fills the adults with foreboding. Harvey immediately takes a dislike
to Clive and proceeds to build fantasies about him as a homosexual
looter. Clive and Belinda, however, fall for each other in a big way
and disastrously attempt midnight consummation beneath the
Christmas tree, following a declaration by Rachel that she is not
really interested in sex and that what she wants from Clive is
friendship. It is convenient, on Boxing Day, to pass off the previous
night's fracas as a drunken romp, but Clive knows it wasn't and, to
save further embarrassment, arranges to leave by the first train the

following morning. He duly leaves – though not by train – after Harvey's hate fantasy goes horribly over the top, and Bernard tragically confirms his medical incompetence.
Published in French's Acting Editions (Samuel French)

Me, Myself and I (1981)

A triptych of lunchtime musical shows, written in collaboration with Paul Todd and touching on ways in which personality is defined by context.

Way Upstream (1981)

Keith and his business partner Alistair are taking their holiday together, along with their respective wives, June and Emma, aboard a cabin cruiser going up the River Orb to Armageddon Bridge. Behind them, at work, they leave fermenting union problems, about which (it transpires) the office secretary, Mrs Hatfield, is to report to Keith each day at pre-arranged rendezvous. While Keith goes off to attend to business problems (about which Alistair maintains a pretty steadfast apathy), Alistair grounds the boat and they have to call on Vince, who happens to be passing, to refloat them and to pilot them to the next lock. It is quickly clear that June is besotted with Vince. She invites him for a drink and he stays aboard, gradually taking over the running of the cruiser. Back at the factory, a strike finally takes Keith right away from the boat, but Alistair, feeling he has nothing to offer the situation, declines to go with him. Vince takes advantage of Keith's absence to bring on board his lady friend, Fleur, and booze for a party. In the middle of the party, Keith returns (having been locked out of his own factory) and attempts to throw Vince and Fleur off the boat – only to find himself, thanks to the levels of alcohol in the others, deposed as skipper and replaced in that role by Vince. He leaves. Vince and Fleur decide to maroon Alistair on an island in midstream and, after an orgiastic night with June, to make Emma walk the plank for attempting to smuggle food to her exiled husband. Taking his first decision in years, Alistair steps in to save Emma and subsequently fights, and – by judicious wielding of a

bean can – beats, Vince. Alone now, Alistair and Emma sail off to Armageddon Bridge, losing behind them the voice of unreason.
Published in French's Acting Editions (Samuel French)

Making Tracks (1981)

A musical written in collaboration with Paul Todd. In the cold reality of a sober Sunday morning in his Saracen Recording Studios, Stan realizes that Sandy Beige (real name Susan Brown), winner of the Cascade Ballroom's talent contest, is an uncharismatic mousy individual with a sickly awful song. He had booked her in the alcohol-induced belief that, with her, he could produce the hit record with which he could repay the £8,500 borrowed from Wolfie to establish the studios. Wolfie turns up at the recording session with his new girlfriend, Lace (who, unbeknown to him, is Stan's ex-wife and co-songwriter). The musicians fail to make anything of Sandy or her song, and she retires gracefully, but as Wolfie becomes physically threatening, Lace is prevailed upon to revert to her former partnership.

Intimate Exchanges (1982–3)

Ayckbourn's version of the two-hander. One actress and one actor each play three main characters and one or two minor roles, in a play that has, technically, sixteen possible versions (of which eight are major variants). The whole project is the equivalent of five or six full-length plays, the object being to examine the possible repercussions on the same group of individuals of different decisions taken by one or more of them. The setting is, for the most part, in and around Bilbury Lodge Preparatory School, with its headmaster, Toby; his wife, Celia; the Chairman of the Governors, Miles, and his very physical wife, Rowena; the home-help, Sylvie, and the gardener, Lionel. Depending on whether she chooses to light a cigarette or not, Celia meets up, in the opening moment of the play, with either Miles or Lionel. Each of those encounters can go one of two ways, so that there are four possible scenes leading into the interval. Each of those four scenes, in turn, can lead into one of two major scenes at the start of the second half: *Affairs in a*

Tent, Events on a Hotel Terrace, A Garden Fête, A Cricket Match, A Game of Golf, A One-man Protest, A Pageant or *Love in the Mist*. Finally there are a possible sixteen brief epilogues in the churchyard.

Published in French's Acting Editions (Samuel French)

A Cut in the Rates (1983)

A one-act play, little more than a sketch, written for schools' television and designed to be played on the set of Michael Cashman's play, *Before Your Very Eyes* (which was receiving its première at Scarborough at the time the television crew wished to film). With the help of the sawing-a-woman-in-half equipment, the professional illusionist and his wife devise an original, if ghostly, means not to pay rates, gas and electricity bills.

Incidental Music (1983)

A late-night musical revue, written in collaboration with Paul Todd: includes a musical whodunnit, the first singing agony column and the cautionary operetta *Petra and the Wolves* (which later resurfaces, under the guise of *Hope*, in *The Seven Deadly Virtues*).

It Could Be Any One of Us (1983)

Set, appropriately, in the Gothic environment of the Chalkes' stone-built Victorian family home, this is Ayckbourn's long-heralded (and now withdrawn) shot at a whodunit. The family comprises an autocratic composer, his painter brother, his writer sister and her daughter. Also resident is the writer's live-in lover, a private detective who has signally failed ever to solve anything. The bone of contention is that the house has been left solely to the composer, Mortimer, by the parents and, since he has total contempt for the rest of them, he is intending to bequeath it to a former music student of his, rendering the rest of the family homeless and destitute. The former student, who wants to move in with her family and breed spaniels, arrives to give the place the once-over, and at once finds herself near the receiving end of a series of unpleasant 'accidents'. The private detective is excited into the belief that a murder is imminent. Murder there is not, but Mortimer does get a nasty – and ill-intended – biff on the head. Norris sets about uncovering the culprit. It could be the writer sister, her daughter or the painter brother, and, depending on the specific clues dropped in any given performance, Ayckbourn allows his audience to be its own detective. There are, in short, three possible *dénouements* – and Norris pointedly misses all of them.

A Trip to Scarborough (1983)

Described as 'variations on the original play by R.B. Sheridan' (itself a Bowdlerized version of Vanbrugh's *The Relapse*), *A Trip to Scarborough* takes one 1800 plot-line direct from Sheridan and runs two more of Ayckbourn's own – a 1942 wartime story and a plot from today – in parallel. The foyer of Scarborough's Royal Hotel, with its ever-present hall porter, Gander, and its young under-manager, Nigel Pestle, sees the arrival, in 1800, of the penniless Tom Fashion, who has come to try to wheedle money from his elder and incomparably richer brother, Lord Foppington. Failing in this, he impersonates Lord Foppington himself and woos and marries Miss Hoyden, daughter of the wealthy Sir Tunbelly Clumsy. Meanwhile, in 1942, Flight Lieutenant Faversham and his fighter-ace cronies drink to forget their funk, while Gander and Pestle fantasize about what happened to Major Loveless's wife (who seemed to be replaced by another lady during a visit to the Opera House), and while Mrs Holland awaits news of her husband, missing at war. And, woven into all this, the present-day Holly Tunberry arrives with her parents, Sir George and Lady Muriel, and the manuscript of R. B. Sheridan's play, *A Trip to Scarborough*, out of which Lance Foppington – a dealer from down south – proceeds to try to con her. Holly, however, is a little more fly than he bargains for, firmly underscoring the play's *Leitmotiv*:

Through all the drama — whether damned or not —
Love gilds the scene, and women guide the plot.

The Seven Deadly Virtues (1984)

Described, during its only outing in January 1984, as 'a new musical entertainment by Alan Ayckbourn and Paul Todd', this is probably more accurately classified as music-theatre — six narrative pieces, part spoken and part sung (plus a bleak little epilogue song), which aim to illustrate *The Natural Virtues* (*Fortitude, Prudence, Justice* and *Temperance*) and *The Supernatural Virtues* (*Faith, Hope* and *Charity*).

A Chorus of Disapproval (1984)

Welcomed into the Pendon Amateur Light Opera Society (PALOS) following the death of his wife, Guy Jones is immediately cast as Crook-Finger'd Jack, a one-line role, in the forthcoming production of *The Beggar's Opera*. Not that he retains the part for long, as he is rapidly promoted through the cast, in recognition of a variety of services rendered or assumed to be promised. The fact is he's just a Guy who can't say no: to Hannah, neglected wife of the producer Dafydd ap Llewellyn, who wants his love; to Fay, spouse-swapping wife of Ian, who is happy enough to encourage her in the bedding of Guy, in return for minor industrial espionage; or to Rebecca, wife of Councillor Jarvis Huntley-Pike, who has a vested interest in laying a false scent for the would-be industrial spies. In a plot skilfully counterpointed with the songs and characters from John Gay's *The Beggar's Opera*, Guy is finally seen in the role of Macheath as, centre stage, he stands 'like a Turk, with his doxies around'.
Published in French's Acting Editions (Samuel French), and by Faber and Faber Limited

The Westwoods (1984)

A matching pair of lunchtime musical revues, built around standard popular songs from the last three decades. *His Side* and *Her Side* take the male and female respectively through their teens, twenties, thirties and forties, pointing to the cyclical patterns of love and lust.

Woman in Mind (1985)

As she slowly regains consciousness in her garden after a bang on the head from the rake, Susan has some difficulty recognizing the doctor, Bill Windsor, who has been called to tend to her injury. While he goes off indoors to organize a cup of tea for her, she spends time with her delightful, happy and deeply loving fantasy family – ever-solicitous, ever-appreciative husband Andy, sporty and cheerful brother Tony, and brilliantly talented daughter Lucy – who bring her champagne and joy. When Bill returns, he has summoned her real family – Gerald, the parson absorbed in himself and his history of the parish, with whom she drifted out of love years ago, and his bitch of a sister, Muriel, who lives with them but never lifts a finger in practical help. Susan's son, Rick, the only other member of the family, belongs to some Trappist-like sect in Hemel Hempstead and has not spoken to the family for years. He is due to visit them, to collect his remaining belongings (which, to Susan's dismay, he wishes to sell). As he arrives, Susan is strongly lobbied by her fantasy family to take lunch al fresco with them, rather than to go in to lunch with reality. But when Rick himself comes out to collect her, he speaks, and she collapses. When she comes round again, Rick explains that he has now left the sect, got married and is about to depart to live in Thailand. He reveals, too, that he is protecting his new wife by not allowing her to meet his family before they leave. Susan passes on this news to Gerald, whose immediate reaction is to blame her. From this point, her real family and her fantasy family fight for possession of her mind, with the doctor, Bill Windsor, creating a bridge between the two by declaring his attraction to her. Fantasy takes over and becomes deranged, as fantasy daughter Lucy's wedding becomes a Lewis Carroll-like race meeting in which both existences inter-mingle grotesquely – until Susan is finally abandoned by them all and left with just the flashing blue light of the ambulance which has come to take her away.

Published in French's Acting Editions (Samuel French) and by Faber and Faber Limited

Boy Meets Girl/Girl Meets Boy (1985)

A pair of lunchtime musical revues, written in collaboration with Paul Todd, charting aspects of 'this age-old chemistry that happens' when the two sexes, under whatever different circumstances, come face to face.

Mere Soup Songs (1986)

A lunchtime music-theatre piece, casting a glance at truth and untruth in husband-and-wife relationships, written in collaboration with Paul Todd.

A Small Family Business (1987)

At the age of forty-five, Jack McCracken is leaving his job with a frozen-foods firm, to take over the running of the family furniture business, Ayres and Graces, started by his father-in-law, Ken. At the surprise family party to celebrate the move, he makes an inspiring speech about the need for absolute honesty in business and exhorts everyone to eradicate even the nicking of paper clips. The party is broken up by the arrival of a private detective, Hough, who has caught Jack's teenage daughter, Samantha, shoplifting goods to the value of £1.87. Hough lets it be known (a) that he is prepared not to proceed to a prosecution, and (b) that he would like a security job at Ayres and Graces. True to his principles, Jack shows him the door and is not prepared for the scorn and anger of his wife, Poppy, and other daughter, Tina, for abandoning Samantha over such a minor infringement: both confess to having committed similar minor dishonesties. Since Ken confides to Jack that all the family firm's furniture lines are being pirated by Italians, and that this must result from the activities of an industrial spy within the company, Jack rethinks his hasty dismissal of Hough and brings him in to investigate. Hough identifies an Italian firm called Rivetti as being on the receiving end of the information, and Jack recognizes the name as being a business contact of his brother Cliff. In fact there are five brothers Rivetti, and Cliff's wife

Anita is in the process of bedding number two when Jack arrives to confront Cliff. Anita and Cliff, it transpires, have been buying furniture 'legitimately' from Ayres and Graces and reselling to the Italians. So who has been underselling A. & G.? Ken's son, Desmond, it appears, who is busy investing in a restaurant and villa in Minorca, to which he intends to disappear to escape his wife, Harriet. It is clear that Hough now knows too much and is a danger to the family unity, but his assessment of his value is very much higher than the family is initially prepared to pay him off with. Again he uses blackmail, but as the family rushes round from house to house trying to raise the extra money, he begins to fear for his life and decides to take the originally proffered sum. This he attempts to wrest from Poppy and her two daughters who have been left at home, but in a scuffle that ensues, he cracks his head in the bath and is killed. At the family birthday party for his father-in-law, Jack learns that the Rivettis' price for disposing of the cadaver is that the company's furniture-distribution network be made available for the Rivetti drug ring.

Published in French's Acting Editions (Samuel French) and by Faber and Faber Limited

Henceforward . . . (1987)

It is the near future in a North London suburb. Outside, 'justice' is in the distinctly belligerent hands of the Daughters of Darkness, a roaming band of young female vigilantes apparently modelled on Hell's Angels (but not as nice). Inside, behind steel shutters and with video surveillance over his front door, Jerome, a composer of electronic music, tries to overcome the creative block that has blighted him ever since his wife left him, taking their daughter with her. His only companion is a robotic children's nanny, which he has tinkered about with to give it the image of his wife. In an attempt to regain access to his daughter, Jerome hires an actress, records her every sound to use as samples in his composing, makes love to her and reprogrammes the robot in her image. The robot is then introduced to ex-wife, social worker and daughter as his new fiancée, to present an impression of domestic stability. It is daughter, Geain, who, delightedly, discovers the truth, but the final family reconciliation is foiled at the last moment by Jerome's

breaking through his composer's block to create his 'Love' Concerto, using his wife's impassioned tones as his sample.
Published by Faber and Faber Limited

Man of the Moment (1988)

Having served his nine years for armed bank robbery, Vic Parks reckons he has paid his debt to society. He has written his autobiography (and had a second, sanitized version ghosted), is now host of two highly successful television programmes – one for kids and a late-night show, has re-married, fathered two children and bought his holiday villa, complete with swimming pool, on the Spanish Mediterranean. To this villa comes Jill Rillington, television programme-maker, with camera crew, to film an edition of *Their Paths Crossed*, in which she intends to bring Vic face to face, after seventeen years, with Douglas Beechey, the former bank clerk who 'had a go' at him during the bank raid – an escapade which resulted in the maiming of the girl Douglas loved (and subsequently married), and with his being briefly lionized as a hero in the tabloid press. Jill wishes her programme to underline the irony that the villain of the robbery has turned the experience into conspicuous success, fortune and media 'hero-worship', whilst the actual hero of the event has, along with its victim, been effectively ruined for life by it. She fails, however, to find in Douglas any of the signs of bitterness or envy she expected him to evince on being faced with the opulence of Vic's lifestyle: he is, to all appearances, a man who has accepted totally what life has thrown at him – loss of his career, a sexless and childless marriage to a woman whose beauty has been blasted by shot and whose nerves have made her virtually a recluse – while wishing only that his reign as the have-a-go hero had lasted a little more than a year. It is clear, on the other hand, that becoming a TV hero has in no way altered the callousness and vicious cruelty which enabled Vic, seventeen years ago, to enter a bank with a loaded shotgun and fire it: he routinely abuses and mistreats his wife, his Spanish servants and his children's nanny. This latter, utterly infatuated by him, is finally driven by his persecution of her to attempt suicide. He goads her on, his wife tries to intervene and gets into a struggle with him. Re-enter, seventeen years on, Douglas on metaphorical white charger. Vic ends up drowned at the bottom of the swimming pool, appropriately with the nanny standing on top of him. Jill fails to recognize that she has very nearly the story she came for – though rather better, since it is now a murder story – and instead concocts another sanitized media fiction about the tragic accident that 'marked not only the end of a life but the end of a living legend'.